DIVINE HEALING HANDS

Other Books in the Soul Power Series

Tao Song and Tao Dance

Tao II

Divine Transformation

Tao I

Divine Soul Mind Body Healing and Transmission System

Divine Soul Songs

The Power of Soul

Soul Communication

Soul Wisdom

DIVINE
HEALING
HANDS

Experience Divine Power to Heal You,
Animals, and Nature, and to
Transform All Life

Dr. and Master
Zhi Gang Sha

ATRIA BOOKS

New York   London   Toronto   Sydney   New Delhi

Heaven's Library
Toronto

ATRIA BOOKS
A Division of Simon & Schuster, Inc.
1230 Avenue of the Americas
New York, NY 10020

Toronto, ON

First Atria Books hardcover edition September 2012

ATRIA BOOKS and colophon are trademarks of Simon & Schuster, Inc.

Heaven's Library and Soul Power Series are trademarks of Heaven's Library Publication Corp.

For information about special discounts for bulk purchases, please contact Simon & Schuster Special Sales at 1-866-506-1949 or business@simonandschuster.com.

The Simon & Schuster Speakers Bureau can bring authors to your live event. For more information or to book an event contact the Simon & Schuster Speakers Bureau at 1-866-248-3049 or visit our website at www.simonspeakers.com.

Manufactured in the United States of America

10   9   8   7   6   5   4   3   2

Library of Congress Cataloging-in-Publication Data is available.

ISBN 978-1-4767-1442-4
ISBN 978-1-4767-1444-8 (ebook)

Contents

Soul Power Series   xi

How to Receive the Divine and Tao Soul Downloads
    Offered in the Books of the Soul Power Series   xxvii

    • What to Expect After You Receive Divine and
      Tao Soul Downloads   xxx

Foreword to the Soul Power Series by Dr. Michael
    Bernard Beckwith   xxxiii

How to Receive Maximum Benefits from My Books   xxxv

List of Divine Soul Downloads   xxxix

List of Figures   xli

Introduction   xliii

1: *Divine Healing Hands: What, Why, and How*   *1*

    • What Are Divine Healing Hands?   3

    • Why Do Divine Healing Hands Work?   4

    • The Divine Releases His Soul Hands to Humanity
      for the First Time   9

• Why Is the Divine Releasing His Soul Hands?   12
• How to Apply Divine Healing Hands for Healing,
  Blessing, and Life Transformation   15
  ○   For How Long Can a Divine Healing Hands
      Blessing Be Offered?   18
• How to Use Divine Healing Hands Properly   19

2: *Experience the Power of Divine Healing Hands*   25
• The Power and Significance of Divine Healing
  Hands   25
• The Divine Downloads His Soul Healing Hands
  to This Book   29
• Apply Divine Healing Hands for Healing   39

3: *Apply Divine Healing Hands to Boost Energy,*
   Stamina, Vitality, and Immunity, and for
   Rejuvenation and Longevity   55
• Develop the Kundalini   56
  ○   Apply Divine Healing Hands to Develop the
      Kundalini   61
• Develop the Lower Dan Tian   63
  ○   Apply Divine Healing Hands to Develop the
      Lower Dan Tian   67
• Divine Sacred Circle for Healing All Sicknesses   69
  ○   Apply Divine Healing Hands to Develop
      the Seven Soul Houses, Wai Jiao, and Divine
      Inner Yin Yang Circle   75

- Divine Sacred Circle for Rejuvenation and
  Longevity   77
  - o Apply Divine Healing Hands to Develop the
    Divine Sacred Circle for Rejuvenation
    and Longevity   79

4: *Apply Divine Healing Hands to Heal Human
   Beings*   **85**
- Spiritual Body   86
  - o Apply Divine Healing Hands to Heal the
    Spiritual Body   93
- Mental Body   100
  - o Apply Divine Healing Hands to Heal the
    Mental Body   101
- Emotional Body   105
  - o Anger   107
  - o Depression and Anxiety   109
  - o Worry   112
  - o Grief and Sadness   113
  - o Fear   115
  - o Other Emotional Imbalances   117
  - o Apply Divine Purple Light Ball and Purple
    Liquid Spring of Divine Love to Heal
    Emotional Imbalances   119
  - o Apply Divine Healing Hands to Heal the
    Emotional Body   121
- Physical Body   124
  - o Apply Divine Healing Hands to Heal the
    Physical Body   131

5: *Apply Divine Healing Hands for Life*
   Transformation   *139*

- Relationships   139
  - Relationships Between People   143
  - Relationships Between Organizations   147
  - Apply Divine Healing Hands to Transform
    Relationships   149
- Finances   152
  - Apply Divine Healing Hands to Transform
    Finances   154
- Increasing Intelligence   155
  - Mind Intelligence   156
    - Apply Divine Healing Hands to Increase
      Mind Intelligence   160
  - Heart Intelligence   161
    - Apply Divine Healing Hands to Increase
      Heart Intelligence   163
  - Soul Intelligence   165
    - Apply Divine Healing Hands to Increase
      Soul Intelligence   169
  - Apply Divine Healing Hands to Increase
    Children's Intelligence   171
  - Apply Divine Healing Hands to Increase
    Students' Intelligence   173
  - Apply Divine Healing Hands to Increase
    Adults' and Seniors' Intelligence   175

6: *Apply Divine Healing Hands to Heal Animals and Nature* **181**
- Healing Animals 181
  - o Apply Divine Healing Hands to Heal Animals 184
- Healing Nature 188
  - o Apply Divine Healing Hands to Heal Nature 194

7: *Apply Divine Healing Hands to Open Your Spiritual Channels* **199**
- Open Your Soul Language Channel 201
  - o Apply Soul Language for Healing and Rejuvenation 208
  - o Apply Soul Language with Forgiveness Practice in Order to Self-clear Bad Karma 210
  - o Apply Soul Language to Purify Your Soul, Heart, Mind, and Body in Order to Uplift Your Soul Standing in Heaven 213
  - o Apply Soul Language to Transform Relationships 223
  - o Apply Soul Language to Transform Finances 227
- Translate Your Soul Language 232
- Open Your Direct Soul Communication Channel 237
- Open Your Third Eye Channel 241
- Open Your Direct Knowing Channel 253
  - o Apply Divine Healing Hands to Open All Four of Your Spiritual Channels 261

Conclusion	269
Acknowledgments	273
A Special Gift	279
Other Books of the Soul Power Series	281

Soul Power Series

THE PURPOSE OF life is to serve. I have committed my life to this purpose. Service is my life mission.

My total life mission is to transform the consciousness of humanity and all souls in all universes, and enlighten them, in order to create love, peace, and harmony for humanity, Mother Earth, and all universes. This mission includes three empowerments.

My first empowerment is to teach *universal service* to empower people to be unconditional universal servants. The message of universal service is:

> *I serve humanity and all universes unconditionally.*
> *You serve humanity and all universes unconditionally.*
> *Together we serve humanity and all souls in all universes unconditionally.*

My second empowerment is to teach *healing* to empower people to heal themselves and heal others. The message of healing is:

I have the power to heal myself.
You have the power to heal yourself.
Together we have the power to heal the world.

My third empowerment is to teach *the power of soul,* which includes soul secrets, wisdom, knowledge, and practical techniques, and to transmit Divine Soul Power to empower people to transform every aspect of their lives and enlighten their souls, hearts, minds, and bodies.

The message of Soul Power is:

> *I have the Soul Power to transform my consciousness*
> *and every aspect of my life and enlighten my soul,*
> *heart, mind, and body.*
> *You have the Soul Power to transform your conscious-*
> *ness and every aspect of your life and enlighten your*
> *soul, heart, mind, and body.*
> *Together we have the Soul Power to transform con-*
> *sciousness and every aspect of all life and enlighten*
> *humanity and all souls.*

To teach the power of soul is my most important empowerment. It is the key for my total life mission. The power of soul is the key for transforming physical life and spiritual life. It is the key for transforming and enlightening humanity and every soul in all universes.

The beginning of the twenty-first century is the transition period into a new era for humanity, Mother Earth, and all universes. This era is named the Soul Light Era. The Soul Light Era began on August 8, 2003. It will last fifteen thousand years. Natural disasters—including tsunamis, hurricanes, cyclones, earthquakes,

floods, tornados, hail, blizzards, fires, drought, extreme temperatures, famine, and disease—political, religious, and ethnic wars,
terrorism, proliferation of nuclear weapons, economic challenges,
pollution, vanishing plant and animal species, and other such up-
heavals are part of this transition. In addition, millions of people
are suffering from depression, anxiety, fear, anger, and worry. They
suffer from pain, chronic conditions, and life-threatening illnesses.
Humanity needs help. The consciousness of humanity needs to be
transformed. The suffering of humanity needs to be removed.

The books of the Soul Power Series are brought to you by
Heaven's Library and Atria Books. They reveal soul secrets and
teach soul wisdom, soul knowledge, and practical soul techniques
for your daily life. The power of soul can heal, prevent illness,
rejuvenate, prolong life, and transform consciousness and every
aspect of life, including relationships and finances. The power of
soul is vital to serving humanity and Mother Earth during this
transition period. The power of soul will awaken and transform
the consciousness of humanity and all souls.

In the twentieth century and for centuries before, *mind over
matter* played a vital role in healing, rejuvenation, and life transformation. In the Soul Light Era, *soul over matter*—Soul Power—
will play *the* vital role to heal, rejuvenate, and transform all life.

There are countless souls on Mother Earth—souls of human
beings, souls of animals, souls of other living things, and souls of
inanimate things. *Everyone and everything has a soul.*

Every soul has its own frequency and power. Jesus had miraculous healing power. We have heard many heart-touching
stories of lives saved by Guan Yin's[1] compassion. Mother Mary's

---

1. Guan Yin is known as the Bodhisattva of Compassion and, in the West, as the Goddess of
Mercy.

love has created many heart-moving stories. All of these great souls were given Divine Soul Power to serve humanity. In all of the world's great religions and spiritual traditions, including Buddhism, Taoism, Christianity, Judaism, Hinduism, Islam, and more, there are similar accounts of great spiritual healing and blessing power.

I honor every religion and every spiritual tradition. However, I am not teaching religion. I am teaching Soul Power, which includes soul secrets, soul wisdom, soul knowledge, and practical soul techniques. Your soul has the power to heal, rejuvenate, and transform life. An animal's soul has the power to heal, rejuvenate, and transform life. The souls of the sun, the moon, an ocean, a tree, and a mountain have the power to heal, rejuvenate, and transform life. The souls of healing angels, ascended masters, holy saints, Taoist saints, Hindu saints, buddhas, and other high-level spiritual beings have great Soul Power to heal, rejuvenate, and transform life.

Every soul has its own standing. Spiritual standing, or soul standing, has countless layers. Soul Power also has layers. Not every soul can perform miracles like Jesus, Guan Yin, and Mother Mary. Soul Power depends on the soul's spiritual standing in Heaven. The higher a soul stands in Heaven, the more Soul Power that soul is given by the Divine. Jesus, Guan Yin, and Mother Mary all have a very high spiritual standing.

Who determines a soul's spiritual standing? Who gives the appropriate Soul Power to a soul? Who decides the direction for humanity, Mother Earth, and all universes? The top leader of the spiritual world is the decision maker. This top leader is the Divine. The Divine is the creator and manifester of all universes.

In the Soul Light Era, all souls will join as one and align their consciousnesses with divine consciousness. At this historic time, the Divine has decided to transmit divine soul treasures to humanity and all souls to help humanity and all souls go through Mother Earth's transition.

Let me share two personal stories with you to explain how I reached this understanding.

First, in April 2003, I held a Power Healing workshop for about one hundred people at Land of Medicine Buddha, a retreat center in Soquel, California. As I was teaching, the Divine appeared. I told the students, "The Divine is here. Could you give me a moment?" I knelt and bowed down to the floor to honor the Divine. (At age six, I was taught to bow down to my tai chi masters. At age ten, I bowed down to my qi gong masters. At age twelve, I bowed down to my kung fu masters. Being Chinese, I learned this courtesy throughout my childhood.) I explained to the students, "Please understand that this is the way I honor the Divine, my spiritual fathers, and my spiritual mothers. Now I will have a conversation with the Divine."

I began by saying silently, "Dear Divine, I am very honored you are here."

The Divine, who was in front of me above my head, replied, "Zhi Gang, I come today to pass a spiritual law to you."

I said, "I am honored to receive this spiritual law."

The Divine continued, "This spiritual law is named the Universal Law of Universal Service. It is one of the highest spiritual laws in the universe. It applies to the spiritual world and the physical world."

The Divine pointed to the Divine. "I am a universal servant." The Divine pointed to me. "You are a universal servant." The Divine swept a hand in front of the Divine. "Everyone and everything is a universal servant. A universal servant offers universal service unconditionally. Universal service includes universal love, forgiveness, peace, healing, blessing, harmony, and enlightenment. *If one offers a little service, one receives a little blessing from the universe and from me. If one offers more service, one receives more blessing. If one offers unconditional service, one receives unlimited blessing.*"

The Divine paused for a moment before continuing. "There is another kind of service, which is unpleasant service. Unpleasant service includes killing, harming, taking advantage of others, cheating, stealing, complaining, and more. If one offers a little unpleasant service, one learns little lessons from the universe and from me. If one offers more unpleasant service, one learns more lessons. If one offers huge unpleasant service, one learns huge lessons."

I asked, "What kinds of lessons could one learn?"

The Divine replied, "The lessons include sickness, accidents, injuries, financial challenges, broken relationships, emotional imbalances, mental confusion, and any kind of disorder in one's life." The Divine emphasized, "This is how the universe operates. This is one of my most important spiritual laws for all souls in the universe to follow."

After the Divine delivered this universal law, I immediately made a silent vow to the Divine:

Dear Divine,

I am extremely honored to receive your Law of Universal Service. I make a vow to you, to all humanity, and to all souls in all universes that I will be an unconditional universal servant. I will give my total GOLD [gratitude, obedience, loyalty, devotion] to you and to serving you. I am honored to be your servant and a servant of all humanity and all souls.

Hearing this, the Divine smiled and left.

My second story happened three months later, in July 2003, while I was holding a Soul Study workshop near Toronto. The Divine came again. I again explained to my students that the Divine had appeared, and asked them to wait a moment while I bowed down 108 times and listened to the Divine's message. On this occasion, the Divine told me, "Zhi Gang, I come today to choose you as my direct servant, vehicle, and channel."

I was deeply moved and said to the Divine, "I am honored. What does it mean to be your direct servant, vehicle, and channel?"

The Divine replied, "When you offer healing and blessing to others, call me. I will come instantly to offer my healing and blessing to them."

I was deeply touched and replied, "Thank you so much for choosing me as your direct servant."

The Divine continued, "I can offer my healing and blessing by transmitting my permanent healing and blessing treasures."

I asked, "How do you do this?"

The Divine answered, "Select a person and I will give you a demonstration."

I asked for a volunteer with serious health challenges. A man named Walter raised his hand. He stood up and explained that he had liver cancer, with a two-by-three-centimeter malignant tumor that had just been diagnosed from a biopsy.

Then I asked the Divine, "Please bless Walter. Please show me how you transmit your permanent treasures." Immediately,

I saw the Divine send a beam of light from the Divine's heart to Walter's liver. The beam shot into his liver, where it turned into a golden light ball that instantly started spinning. Walter's entire liver shone with beautiful golden light.

The Divine asked me, "Do you understand what software is?"

I was surprised by this question but replied, "I do not understand much about computers. I just know that software is a computer program. I have heard about accounting software, office software, and graphic design software."

"Yes," the Divine said. "Software is a program. Because you asked me to, I transmitted, or downloaded, my Soul Software for Liver to Walter. It is one of my permanent healing and blessing treasures. You asked me. I did the job. This is what it means for you to be my chosen direct servant, vehicle, and channel."

I was astonished. Excited, inspired, and humbled, I said to the Divine, "I am so honored to be your direct servant. How blessed I am to be chosen." Almost speechless, I asked the Divine, "Why did you choose me?"

"I chose you," said the Divine, "because you have served humanity for more than one thousand lifetimes. You have been very committed to serving my mission through all of your lifetimes. I am choosing you in this life to be my direct servant. You will transmit countless permanent healing and blessing treasures from me to humanity and all souls. This is the honor I give to you now."

I was moved to tears. I immediately bowed down 108 times again and made a silent vow:

Dear Divine,

I cannot bow down to you enough for the honor you have given to me. No words can express my greatest grati-

tude. How blessed I am to be your direct servant to download your permanent healing and blessing treasures to humanity and all souls! Humanity and all souls will receive your huge blessings through my service as your direct servant. I give my total life to you and to humanity. I will accomplish your tasks. I will be a pure servant to humanity and all souls.

I bowed again. Then I asked the Divine, "How should Walter use his Soul Software?"

"Walter must spend time to practice with my Soul Software," said the Divine. "Tell him that simply to receive my Soul Software does not mean he will recover. He must practice with this treasure every day to restore his health, step by step."

I asked, "How should he practice?"

The Divine gave me this guidance: "Tell Walter to chant repeatedly: *Divine Liver Soul Software heals me. Divine Liver Soul Software heals me. Divine Liver Soul Software heals me. Divine Liver Soul Software heals me.*"

I asked, "For how long should Walter chant?"

The Divine answered, "At least two hours a day. The longer he practices, the better. If Walter does this, he could recover in three to six months."

I shared this information with Walter, who was excited and deeply moved. Walter said, "I will practice two hours or more each day."

Finally I asked the Divine, "How does the Soul Software work?"

The Divine replied, "My Soul Software is a golden healing ball that rotates and clears energy and spiritual blockages in Walter's liver."

I again bowed to the Divine 108 times. Then I stood up and offered three Soul Softwares to every participant in the workshop as divine gifts. Upon seeing this, the Divine smiled and left.

Walter immediately began to practice as directed for at least two hours every day. Two and a half months later, a CT scan and MRI showed that his liver cancer had completely disappeared. At the end of 2006 I met Walter again at a signing in Toronto for my book *Soul Mind Body Medicine*.[2] In May 2008 Walter attended one of my events at the Unity Church of Truth in Toronto. On both occasions Walter told me that there was still no sign of cancer in his liver. For nearly five years his Divine Soul Download healed his liver cancer. He was very grateful to the Divine.

This major event of being chosen as a direct divine servant happened in July 2003. As I mentioned, a new era for Mother Earth and all universes, the Soul Light Era, began on August 8, 2003. The timing may look like a coincidence but I believe there could be an underlying spiritual reason. Since July 2003 I have offered divine transmissions to humanity almost every day. I have offered more than ten divine transmissions to all souls in all universes.

I share this story with you to introduce the power of divine transmissions or Divine Soul Downloads. Now let me share the commitment that I made in *Soul Wisdom*,[3] the first book of my

---

2. *Soul Mind Body Medicine: A Complete Soul Healing System for Optimum Health and Vitality* (Novato, California: New World Library, 2006).
3. *Soul Wisdom: Practical Soul Treasures to Transform Your Life* (Toronto/New York: Heaven's Library/Atria Books, 2008).

Soul Power Series, and that I have renewed in every one of my books since:

From now on, I will offer Divine Soul Downloads in every book I write.

Divine Soul Downloads are permanent divine healing and blessing treasures for transforming your life. There is an ancient saying: *If you want to know if a pear is sweet, taste it.* If you want to know the power of Divine Soul Downloads, experience it.

Divine Soul Downloads carry divine frequency with divine love, forgiveness, compassion, and light. Divine frequency transforms the frequency of all life. Divine love melts all blockages, including soul, mind, and body blockages, and transforms all life. Divine forgiveness brings inner peace and inner joy. Divine compassion boosts energy, stamina, vitality, and immunity. Divine light heals, prevents sickness, rejuvenates, and prolongs life.

A Divine Soul Download is a new soul created from the heart of the Divine. The Divine Soul Download transmitted to Walter was a Soul Software. Since then, I have transmitted several other types of Divine Soul Downloads, including Divine Soul Herbs, Divine Soul Acupuncture, Divine Soul Massage, Divine Soul Operation, and Divine Soul Mind Body Transplants.

A Divine Soul Transplant is a new divine soul of an organ, a part of the body, a bodily system, cells, cell units, DNA, RNA, the tiny matter in cells, or the spaces between cells. When it is transmitted, it replaces the recipient's original soul of the organ, part of the body, system, cells, cell units, DNA, RNA, tiny matter in cells, or spaces between cells. A new divine soul can also replace the soul of a home or a business. A new divine soul can be transmitted to a pet, a mountain, a city, or a country to replace their original souls. A new divine soul can even replace the soul of Mother Earth.

A Divine Mind Transplant is also a light being created by the Divine. It carries divine consciousness to replace the original consciousness of the recipient's system, organ, part of the body, cells, cell units, DNA, RNA, tiny matter, or spaces.

A Divine Body Transplant is another light being created by the Divine. This light being carries divine energy and divine tiny matter to replace the original energy and tiny matter of the recipient's system, organ, part of the body, cells, cell units, DNA, RNA, tiny matter, or spaces.

Everyone and everything has a soul. The Divine can download any soul you can conceive of. These Divine Soul Downloads are permanent divine healing, blessing, and life transformation treasures. They can transform the lives of anyone and anything. Because the Divine created these divine soul treasures, they carry Divine Soul Power, which is the greatest Soul Power among all souls. All souls in the highest layers of Heaven will support and assist Divine Soul Downloads. Divine Soul Downloads are the crown jewel of Soul Power.

Divine Soul Downloads are divine presence. The more Divine Soul Downloads you receive, the faster your soul, heart, mind, and body will be transformed. The more Divine Soul Downloads your home or business receives and the more Divine Soul Downloads a city or country receives, the faster their souls, hearts, minds, and bodies will be transformed.

In the Soul Light Era, the evolution of humanity will be created by Divine Soul Power. Soul Power will transform humanity. Soul Power will transform animals. Soul Power will transform nature and the environment. Soul Power will assume the leading role in every field of human endeavor. Humanity will deeply understand that *the soul is the boss*.

Soul Power, including soul secrets, soul wisdom, soul knowledge, and practical soul techniques, will transform every aspect of human life. Soul Power will transform every aspect of organizations and societies. Soul Power will transform cities, countries, Mother Earth, all planets, stars, galaxies, and all universes. Divine Soul Power, including Divine Soul Downloads, will lead this transformation.

I am honored to have been chosen as a divine servant to offer Divine Soul Downloads to humanity, to relationships, to homes, to businesses, to pets, to cities, to countries, and more. In the last few years I have already transmitted countless divine souls to humanity and to all universes. I repeat to you now: *I will offer Divine Soul Downloads within each and every book of the Soul Power Series.* Clear instructions on how to receive these Divine Soul Downloads and, since 2010, Tao Soul Downloads[4] will be provided in the next section, "How to Receive the Divine and Tao Soul Downloads Offered in the Books of the Soul Power Series," as well as on the appropriate pages of each book.

I am a servant of humanity. I am a servant of the universe. I am a servant of the Divine. I am a servant of Tao. I am extremely honored to be a servant of all souls. I commit my total life and being as an unconditional universal servant.

I will continue to offer Divine and Tao Soul Downloads for my entire life. I will offer more and more Divine and Tao Soul

---

4. Tao Soul Downloads are offered in the sixth, eighth, and ninth books of the Soul Power Series, *Tao I: The Way of All Life; Tao II: The Way of Healing, Rejuvenation, Longevity, and Immortality;* and *Tao Song and Tao Dance: Sacred Sound, Movement, and Power from the Source for Healing, Rejuvenation, Longevity, and Transformation of All Life.*

Downloads to every soul. I will offer Divine and Tao Soul Downloads for every aspect of life for every soul.

I am honored to be a servant of Divine and Tao Soul Downloads.

Human beings, organizations, cities, and countries will receive more and more Divine and Tao Soul Downloads, which can transform every aspect of their lives and enlighten their souls, hearts, minds, and bodies. The Soul Light Era will shine Soul Power. The books in the Soul Power Series will spread Divine and Tao Soul Downloads, together with Soul Power—soul secrets, soul wisdom, soul knowledge, and practical soul techniques—to serve humanity, Mother Earth, and all universes. The Soul Power Series is a pure servant for humanity and all souls. The Soul Power Series is honored to be a Total GOLD[5] servant of the Divine, Tao, humanity, and all souls.

The final goal of the Soul Light Era is to join every soul as one in love, peace, and harmony. This means that the consciousness of every soul will be totally aligned with divine consciousness. There will be difficulties and challenges on the path to this final goal. Together we will overcome them. We call all souls of humanity and all souls in all universes to offer unconditional universal service, including universal love, forgiveness, peace, healing, blessing, harmony, and enlightenment. The more we offer unconditional universal service, the faster we will achieve this goal.

The Divine and Tao give their hearts to us. The Divine and Tao give their love to us. The Divine and Tao give Divine and Tao Soul Downloads to us. Our hearts meld with the Divine's

---

5. "Total GOLD" means total gratitude, total obedience, total loyalty, and total devotion to the Divine and Tao.

and Tao's hearts. Our souls meld with the Divine's and Tao's souls. Our consciousnesses align with the Divine's and Tao's consciousnesses. We will join hearts and souls together to create love, peace, and harmony for humanity, Mother Earth, and all universes.

> *I love my heart and soul*
> *I love all humanity*
> *Join hearts and souls together*
> *Love, peace and harmony*
> *Love, peace and harmony*

Love all humanity. Love all souls.
Thank all humanity. Thank all souls.
Thank you. Thank you. Thank you.

Zhi Gang Sha

How to Receive the Divine and Tao Soul Downloads Offered in the Books of the Soul Power Series

$\mathcal{T}$HE BOOKS OF the Soul Power Series are unique. For the first time in history, the Divine and Tao are downloading their soul treasures to readers as they read these books. Every book in the Soul Power Series will include Divine or Tao Soul Downloads that have been preprogrammed. When you read the appropriate paragraphs and pause for a minute, divine or Tao gifts will be transmitted to your soul.

In April 2005 the Divine told me to "leave Divine Soul Downloads to history." I thought, "A human being's life is limited. Even if I live a long, long life, I will go back to Heaven one day. How can I leave Divine Soul Downloads to history?"

In the beginning of 2008, as I was editing the paperback

edition of *Soul Wisdom*, the Divine suddenly told me: "Zhi Gang, offer my downloads within this book." The Divine said, "I will preprogram my downloads in the book. Any reader can receive them as he or she reads the special pages." At the moment the Divine gave me this direction, I understood how I could leave Divine Soul Downloads to history.

The Divine is the creator and spiritual father and mother of all souls.

Tao is the Source and creator of countless planets, stars, galaxies, and universes. Tao is The Way of all life. Tao is the universal principles and laws.

At the end of 2008 Tao chose me as a servant, vehicle, and channel to offer Tao Soul Downloads. I was extremely honored. I have offered countless Divine and Tao Soul Downloads to humanity and *wan ling* (all souls) in countless planets, stars, galaxies, and universes.

Preprogrammed Divine Soul Downloads are permanently stored within this book. Preprogrammed Divine or Tao Soul Downloads are permanently stored within every book in the Soul Power Series. If people read this book thousands of years from now, they will still receive the Divine Soul Downloads. As long as this book exists and is read, readers will receive the Divine Soul Downloads.

Allow me to explain further. The Divine has placed a permanent blessing within certain paragraphs in this book. These blessings allow you to receive Divine Soul Downloads as permanent gifts to your soul. Because these divine treasures reside with your soul, you can access them twenty-four hours a day—as often as you like, wherever you are—for healing, blessing, and life transformation.

It is very easy to receive the Divine and Tao Soul Downloads in the books of the Soul Power Series. After you read the special paragraphs where they are preprogrammed, close your eyes. Receive the special download. It is also easy to apply these divine and Tao treasures. After you receive a Divine or Tao Soul Download, I will immediately show you how to apply it for healing, blessing, and life transformation.

You have free will. If you are not ready to receive a Divine or Tao Soul Download, simply say *I am not ready to receive this gift.* You can then continue to read the special download paragraphs, but you will not receive the gifts they contain. The Divine and Tao do not offer Divine and Tao Soul Downloads to those who are not ready or not willing to receive the Divine's and Tao's treasures. However, the moment you are ready, you can simply go back to the relevant paragraphs and tell the Divine and Tao *I am ready.* You will then receive the stored special download when you reread the paragraphs.

The Divine and Tao have agreed to offer specific Divine and Tao Soul Downloads in these books to all readers who are willing to receive them. The Divine and Tao have unlimited treasures. However, you can receive only the ones designated in these pages. Please do not ask for different or additional gifts. It will not work.

After receiving and practicing with the Divine and Tao Soul Downloads in these books, you could experience remarkable healing results in your spiritual, mental, emotional, and physical bodies. You could receive incredible blessings for your love relationships and other relationships. You could receive financial blessings and all kinds of other blessings.

Divine and Tao Soul Downloads are unlimited. There can be a Divine or Tao Soul Download for anything that exists in the physical world. The reason for this is very simple. *Everything has a soul, mind, and body.* A house has a soul, mind, and body. The Divine and Tao can download a soul to your house that can transform its energy. The Divine and Tao can download a soul to your business that can transform your business. If you are wearing a ring, that ring has a soul. If the Divine downloads a new divine soul to your ring, you can ask the divine soul in your ring to offer divine healing and blessing.

I am honored to have been chosen as a servant of humanity, the Divine, and Tao to offer Divine and Tao Soul Downloads. For the rest of my life, I will continue to offer Divine and Tao Soul Downloads. I will offer more and more of them. I will offer Divine and Tao Soul Downloads for every aspect of every life.

I am honored to be a servant of Divine and Tao Soul Downloads.

What to Expect After You Receive
Divine and Tao Soul Downloads

Divine and Tao Soul Downloads are new souls created from the heart of the Divine or the heart of Tao. When these souls are transmitted, you may feel a strong vibration. For example, you could feel warm or excited. Your body could shake a little. If you are not sensitive, you may not feel anything. Advanced spiritual beings with an open Third Eye can actually see a huge golden, rainbow, purple, or crystal light soul enter your body.

These divine and Tao souls are your yin companions[1] for life. They will stay with your soul forever. Even after your physical life ends, these divine and Tao treasures will continue to accom-

---

1. A yang companion is a physical being, such as a family member, friend, or pet. A yin companion is a soul companion without a physical form, such as your spiritual fathers and mothers in Heaven.

pany your soul into your next life and all of your future lives. In these books, I will teach you how to invoke these divine and Tao souls anytime, anywhere to give you divine and Tao healing or blessing in this life. You also can invoke these souls to radiate out to offer divine and Tao healing or blessing to others. These divine and Tao souls have extraordinary abilities to heal, bless, and transform. If you develop advanced spiritual abilities in your next life, you will discover that you have these divine or Tao souls with you. Then you will be able to invoke these souls in the same way in your future lifetimes to heal, bless, and transform every aspect of your life.

It is a great honor to have a divine or Tao soul downloaded to your own soul. The divine or Tao soul is a pure soul without bad karma. The divine or Tao soul carries divine and Tao healing and blessing abilities. The download does not have any side effects. You are given love and light with divine and Tao frequency. You are given divine and Tao abilities to serve yourself and others. Therefore, humanity is extremely honored that the Divine and Tao are offering Divine and Tao Soul Downloads. I am extremely honored to be a servant of the Divine, of Tao, of you, of all humanity, and of all souls to offer Divine and Tao Soul Downloads. I cannot thank the Divine and Tao enough. I cannot thank you, all humanity, and all souls enough for the opportunity to serve.

Thank you. Thank you. Thank you.

Foreword to the Soul Power Series

I HAVE ADMIRED DR. Zhi Gang Sha's work for some years now. In fact, I clearly remember the first time I heard him describe his soul healing system, Soul Mind Body Medicine. I knew immediately that I wanted to support this gifted healer and his mission, so I introduced him to my spiritual community at Agape. Ever since, it has been my joy to witness how those who apply his teachings and techniques experience increased energy, joy, harmony, and peace in their lives.

Dr. Sha's techniques awaken the healing power already present in all of us, empowering us to put our overall well-being in our own hands. His explanation of energy and message, and how they link consciousness, mind, body, and spirit, forms a dynamic information network in language that is easy to understand and, more important, to apply.

Dr. Sha's time-tested results have proven to thousands of students and readers that healing energies and messages exist within specific sounds, movements, and affirmative perceptions. Weaving in his own personal experiences, Dr. Sha's theories and practices of working directly with the life-force energy and spirit are practical, holistic, and profound. His recognition that Soul Power is most important for every aspect of life is vital to meeting the challenges of twenty-first-century living.

The worldwide representative of his renowned teacher, Dr. Zhi Chen Guo, one of the greatest qi gong masters and healers in the world, Dr. Sha is himself a master of ancient disciplines such as tai chi, qi gong, kung fu, the *I Ching*, and feng shui. He has blended the soul of his culture's natural healing methods with his training as a Western physician, and generously offers his wisdom to us through the books in his Soul Power Series. His contribution to those in the healing professions is undeniable, and the way in which he empowers his readers to understand themselves, their feelings, and the connection between their bodies, minds, and spirits is his gift to the world.

Through his Soul Power Series, Dr. Sha guides the reader into a consciousness of healing not only of body, mind, and spirit, but also of the heart. I consider his healing path to be a universal spiritual practice, a journey into genuine transformation. His professional integrity and compassionate heart are at the root of his being a servant of humankind, and my heartfelt wish for his readers is that they accept his invitation to awaken the power of the soul and realize the natural beauty of their existence.

Dr. Michael Bernard Beckwith
Founder, Agape International Spiritual Center

How to Receive Maximum Benefits from My Books

*L*IKE MANY PEOPLE worldwide, you may have read my books before. You may be reading my books for the first time. When you start to read my books, you may realize quickly that they include many practices for healing, rejuvenation, and longevity, as well as for transforming relationships and finances. I teach the Four Power Techniques to transform all life. I will summarize each of my Four Power Techniques in one sentence:

Body Power: Where you put your hands is where you receive benefits for healing and rejuvenation.

Soul Power: Apply Say Hello Healing and Blessing to invoke the Divine, Tao, Heaven, Mother Earth, and countless planets, stars, galaxies, and universes, as well as all kinds of spiritual fathers and mothers on Mother Earth and in all layers of Heaven, to request their help for your heal-

ing, rejuvenation, and transformation of relationships and finances.

Mind Power: Where you put your mind, using creative visualization, is where you receive benefits for healing, rejuvenation, and transformation of relationships and finances.

Sound Power: What you chant is what you become.

My books are unique. Each one includes many practices with chanting (Sound Power). I repeat some chants again and again in the books. The most important issue for you, dear reader, is to avoid thinking *I already know this*, and then quickly read through the text without doing the practices. That would be a big mistake. You will miss some of the most important parts of my teaching: the practices.

Imagine you are in a workshop. When the teacher leads you to meditate or chant, you have to do it. Otherwise, you will not receive the benefits from the meditation and chanting. People are familiar with the ancient Chinese martial art and teaching of kung fu. A kung fu master spends an entire lifetime to develop power. In one sentence:

Time is kung fu and kung fu is time.

You have to spend time to chant and meditate. Remember the one-sentence secret for Sound Power: *What you chant is what you become.* Therefore, when you read the practices where I am leading you to chant, please do it. Do not pass it by. The practices are the jewel of my teaching. Practice is necessary to transform and bring success to any aspect of your life, including health, relationships, finances, intelligence, and more.

There is a renowned spiritual teaching in Buddhism. Millions of people throughout history have chanted *Na Mo A Mi Tuo Fo*. They chant only this one mantra. They could chant *Na Mo A Mi Tuo Fo* for hours a day for their entire life. It is a great practice. If you are upset, chant *Na Mo A Mi Tuo Fo* (pronounced *nah maw ah mee twaw faw*). If you are sick, chant *Na Mo A Mi Tuo Fo*. If you are weak, chant *Na Mo A Mi Tuo Fo*. If you are emotional, chant *Na Mo A Mi Tuo Fo*. If you have relationship challenges, chant *Na Mo A Mi Tuo Fo*. If you have financial challenges, chant *Na Mo A Mi Tuo Fo*. To transform life takes time. You must understand this spiritual wisdom so that you will practice chanting and meditation more and more. The more you practice, the more healing and life transformation you could receive.

For success in any profession, one must study and practice again and again to gain mastery. My teaching is soul healing and soul transformation of every aspect of life. One must apply the Four Power Techniques again and again to receive the maximum benefits of soul healing and soul transformation for every aspect of your life.

If you go into the condition of *what you chant is what you become*, a wonderful healing result may come suddenly, and transformation of relationships and finances may follow. "Aha!" moments may come. "Wow!" moments may come.

I bring my workshop or retreat to you in every book. Take time to practice seriously. Chant and meditate using the Four Power Techniques.

My books have another unique aspect: the Divine and Tao offer Soul Mind Body Transplants as you read. Divine and Tao

Soul Mind Body Transplants are permanent healing and blessing treasures from the Divine and Tao.

These treasures carry Divine and Tao frequency and vibration, which can transform the frequency and vibration of your health, relationships, finances, intelligence, and more.

These treasures also carry Divine and Tao love, which melts all blockages and transforms all life.

These treasures carry Divine and Tao forgiveness, which brings inner joy and inner peace.

These treasures carry Divine and Tao compassion, which boosts energy, stamina, vitality, and immunity.

These treasures carry Divine and Tao light, which heals, prevents sickness, purifies and rejuvenates soul, heart, mind, and body, and transforms relationships, finances, and every aspect of life.

I summarize and emphasize the two absolutely unique aspects of my books: First, I bring my workshops and retreats to you in my books. Please practice seriously, just as though you were in a workshop with me in person. Second, as you read, you can receive permanent treasures (Soul Mind Body Transplants) from the Divine and Tao to transform your health, relationships, finances, and more.

Pay great attention to these two unique aspects in order to receive maximum benefits from this book and any of my books.

I wish you will receive maximum benefits from this book to transform every aspect of your life.

Practice. Practice. Practice.

Transform. Transform. Transform.

Enlighten. Enlighten. Enlighten.

Success. Success. Success.

List of Divine Soul Downloads

1. Divine Golden Light Ball and Golden Liquid Spring of Divine Forgiveness Soul Mind Body Transplants, liv
2. Divine Healing Hands Soul Mind Body Transplants (to this book), 33
3. Divine Purple Light Ball and Purple Liquid Spring of Divine Lower Dan Tian Soul Mind Body Transplants, 65
4. Divine Purple Light Ball and Purple Liquid Spring of Divine Forgiveness Soul Mind Body Transplants, 94
5. Divine Purple Light Ball and Purple Liquid Spring of Divine Clarity of Mind Soul Mind Body Transplants, 101
6. Divine Purple Light Ball and Purple Liquid Spring of Divine Love Soul Mind Body Transplants, 119

7. Divine Purple Light Ball and Purple Liquid Spring of Divine Light Soul Mind Body Transplants, 152

8. Divine Purple Light Ball and Purple Liquid Spring of Divine Compassion for Brain, Heart, and Soul Soul Mind Body Transplants, 175

9. Divine Purple Light Ball and Purple Liquid Spring of Divine Balance of Soul, Heart, Mind, and Body Soul Mind Body Transplants, 182

10. Divine Purple Light Ball and Purple Liquid Spring of Divine Nourishment and Balance Soul Mind Body Transplants, 189

11. Divine Purple Light Ball and Purple Liquid Spring of Divine Soul Language Soul Mind Body Transplants, 208

12. Divine Purple Light Ball and Purple Liquid Spring of Divine Purification Soul Mind Body Transplants, 220

13. Divine Purple Light Ball and Purple Liquid Spring of Divine Message Center Soul Mind Body Transplants, 238

14. Divine Purple Light Ball and Purple Liquid Spring of Divine Kundalini Soul Mind Body Transplants, 247

List of Figures

1. Body Power for forgiveness from the heart, xlviii
2. Soul Light Era Prayer Position, 16
3. Location of kundalini/Ming Men area, 58
4. Ying Yang Palm Hand Position, 64
5. Divine Inner Yin Yang Circle, 71
6. Outer Yin Yang Circle, 72
7. Body Power to develop the Divine Inner Yin Yang Circle, 73
8. Five Elements Hand Position, 117
9. Location of Zhong, 129
10. Sacred number code to develop the entire brain, 157
11. The divine sacred code 3396815, 166
12. Soul Language Channel, 202
13. Nine layers of Heaven (Jiu Tian), 214

Introduction

E VERY TIME I speak about Divine Healing Hands:

I always think how blessed I am to be a servant of humanity, Mother Earth, all souls, and the Divine.

I always think how blessed I am to be given the divine honor and authority to transmit Divine Healing Hands to the chosen ones.

I always think that the Divine has given me so much that I can never repay the Divine, no matter how much service I offer.

I always think that I will serve humanity, Mother Earth, and all souls forever as an unconditional universal servant.

I always think of billions of people who are suffering in any aspect of life, including health, relationships, finances, and more.

I always think of spreading Divine Healing Hands in order to bring love, peace, and harmony to humanity, Mother Earth, and all universes.

I am always moved to tears and touched in my heart and soul when I think about the Divine's generosity to give his soul healing hands to the chosen ones.

I cannot bow down enough to the Divine.

I am speechless.

On August 8, 2003, the Divine held a meeting in Heaven and announced that the last universal era was ending and a new era, the Soul Light Era, would begin on that day. A universal era lasts fifteen thousand years.

Human beings reincarnate. You may not realize that time also reincarnates. There are three eras on Mother Earth that reincarnate:

- Xia Gu—下古 (pronounced *shya goo*) means *near ancient*. It is the era that began fifteen thousand years before August 8, 2003, and ended on that day.
- Zhong Gu—中古 (pronounced *jawng goo*) means *middle ancient*. It is the era that started approximately thirty thousand years ago and ended approximately fifteen thousand years ago.
- Shang Gu—上古 (pronounced *shahng goo*) means *far ancient*. It is the era that lasted from about forty-five thousand years ago to about thirty thousand years ago.

On August 8, 2003, the Xia Gu era ended and the Shang Gu era returned. The current Shang Gu era will also last fifteen thousand years and then the Zhong Gu era will return. The next Zhong Gu era will also last fifteen thousand years. Then the next Xia Gu era will return.

In summary, Shang Gu, Zhong Gu, and Xia Gu eras rotate, one after another. This is time reincarnation. This is sacred wisdom.

Since August 8, 2003, when the current Shang Gu era started, Mother Earth's transition has accelerated. What is Mother Earth's transition? Mother Earth's transition is the transition from the Xia Gu era that ended on August 8, 2003, to the Shang Gu era that began on that day.

You and humanity can very clearly see more and greater challenges happening on Mother Earth, including natural and man-made disasters, war, climate change, disease, economic challenges, and more. Why are these challenges happening? They are due to bad karma.

For centuries and millennia, humanity has created huge bad karma by harming each other and Mother Earth. In one of my authority books, *The Power of Soul: The Way to Heal, Rejuvenate, Transform, and Enlighten All Life,*[1] I shared a teaching that I received from the Divine. It is the one-sentence secret of karma:

**Karma is the root cause of success and failure
in every aspect of life.**

Karma is the record of services. Karma is also named "deed," "virtue," or "de" (Chinese, pronounced *duh*) in different spiritual teachings. Karma can be divided into good karma and bad karma. Good karma is the record of one's good services in all lifetimes, present and past. Good karma includes offering unconditional love, forgiveness, care, compassion, sincerity, honesty, generosity, kindness, purity, and all other kinds of good service to humanity and all souls. Bad karma is the record of one's unpleasant services in all lifetimes to humanity and all souls, such as

---

1. Toronto/New York: Heaven's Library/Atria Books, 2009.

killing, harming, taking advantage of others, cheating, stealing, lying, complaining, and all other kinds of unpleasant service.

Karma is a universal law. According to karmic law:

Good karma can bring one rewards in every aspect of life, including health, relationships, finances, intelligence, parents, and children.
Bad karma can bring one lessons in every aspect of life, including health, relationships, finances, intelligence, parents, and children.

For centuries and millennia, humanity has accumulated a huge amount of bad karma from:

- killing in multinational and civil political, religious, and ethnic wars
- testing and using nuclear weapons
- causing all kinds of harm to humanity, animals, and nature
- depleting and wasting natural resources
- greed
- cheating
- stealing
- and much more

Karma is cause and effect. The examples above are part of the root cause of the natural disasters, economic stresses, and other challenges on Mother Earth now.

Billions of people are concerned about Mother Earth's transition. How can we transform Mother Earth's transition? How can we reduce the natural disasters and other challenges for humanity and Mother Earth?

Because karma is the root cause of Mother Earth's transition, the solution is to clear bad karma. If millions and billions of people knew how to clear bad karma, Mother Earth's transition would be softened beyond comprehension.

How does one self-clear bad karma? The most important and powerful technique is a regular forgiveness practice. Apply the Four Power Techniques that I have taught in all my previous books[2] to self-clear bad karma.

The Four Power Techniques are Body Power, Sound Power, Mind Power, and Soul Power.

Body Power is to use special hand and body positions for healing, rejuvenation, longevity, and life transformation.

Sound Power is to chant sacred mantras, Divine Soul Songs, Tao Songs, or special vibratory sounds for healing and rejuvenation.

Mind Power is creative visualization.

Soul Power is to say *hello*. It is to invoke the Divine, Tao, Heaven, Mother Earth, and countless planets, stars, galaxies, and universes, as well as all kinds of spiritual fathers and mothers on Mother Earth and in all layers of Heaven, to request their help for healing, rejuvenation, and transformation of relationships and finances.

We will apply the Four Power Techniques now to self-clear bad karma:

---

2. For example, see my book *Power Healing: The Four Keys to Energizing Your Body, Mind, and Spirit* (San Francisco: HarperSanFrancisco, 2002).

Body Power. Sit up straight with your feet flat on the floor and your back free and clear. You may also stand up straight but relaxed, with your knees slightly bent. Put one palm on your lower abdomen below the navel. Put your other palm over your heart. Forgiveness must be from the heart. Five thousand years ago, traditional Chinese medicine shared the wisdom that the heart houses the mind and the soul. Be sure to ask for and offer forgiveness from the heart.

Figure 1. Body Power for forgiveness from the heart

There are many great teachings for the spiritual journey from different religions and all kinds of spiritual groups on Mother Earth. I do not teach religion, but I respect all great teachings. I believe true spiritual teaching always teaches people how to purify the heart.

Soul Power. Say *hello:*

> *Dear my beloved heart,*
> *I love you.*
> *I am honored to do a forgiveness practice.*
> *Thank you.*

Forgiveness practice is a practice to self-clear our bad karma. We do not need to clear our good karma. We want to keep our good karma in order to receive blessings in health, relationships, finances, and more. To clear karma is to clear bad karma that was created by the mistakes we made in past lifetimes and in this lifetime. Mistakes create a spiritual debt. We owe the people and souls we have hurt or harmed. To clear bad karma is to have our spiritual debt forgiven.

Continue the forgiveness practice by applying more Soul Power:

> *Dear all the souls who were harmed by any of the*
>   *mistakes I have made in this lifetime and all my*
>   *previous lifetimes,*
> *Dear all the souls, including human beings, ani-*
>   *mals, the environment, and Mother Earth, who*
>   *were harmed by any of the mistakes my ancestors*
>   *have made in all of their lifetimes,*
> *I love you.*
> *I sincerely apologize to all the souls we have*
>   *harmed.*
> *Please forgive my ancestors and me.*
> *In order to receive your total forgiveness, I will*
>   *serve unconditionally.*
> *Thank you.*

If millions and billions of people truly understood the significance of the forgiveness practice, knew how to do the forgiveness practice, and actually *did* the forgiveness practice every day, humanity's karma would be transformed. Mother Earth's transition would be softened.

When doing a forgiveness practice, it is important to say the words sincerely and humbly from the heart. Do not expect to simply say the words and be forgiven easily. It may not be easy at all to receive forgiveness from some of the souls you and your ancestors have harmed. Your mistakes could have been huge; the harm could have been very cruel.

Continue from the bottom of your heart:

> *I will serve humanity.*
> *I will serve animals.*
> *I will serve society.*
> *I will serve Mother Earth in order to receive forgiveness.*
> *Thank you for your forgiveness.*

This is how to ask for forgiveness for your mistakes. You must include your ancestors because each of us carries part of our ancestors' karma, both good and bad. This is called ancestral karma. Think of it as your genetic or inherited karma. It includes not only your ancestors in this lifetime, but also your ancestors in all of your past lifetimes. This could include millions of souls.

Forgiveness practice has two parts. In one part you ask for forgiveness for all of the mistakes that you and your ancestors have made in all of your previous lifetimes and in this lifetime. In the other part you and your ancestors offer forgiveness to all souls who have hurt, harmed, or taken advantage of you or your ancestors in all lifetimes. These two sides of forgiveness are vital to bring love, peace, and harmony to you, your loved ones, your community, your city, your society, your country, and Mother Earth.

Now let us do the second part of the forgiveness practice where you and your ancestors offer forgiveness to others:

> *Dear all people and all souls who have harmed me*
>   *and my ancestors in any of our lifetimes,*
> *We love you.*
> *We forgive you totally.*
> *We are honored to offer you our forgiveness.*
> *Thank you.*

Mind Power. Visualize the golden light of forgiveness embracing you, your ancestors, and all the souls you have invoked.

Sound Power. Chant for a few minutes silently or aloud, but always from your heart:

> *Forgiveness*
> *Forgiveness*
> *Forgiveness*
> *Forgiveness*
> *Forgiveness*
> *Forgiveness*
> *Forgiveness . . .*

Do it now for three minutes.
Then chant or sing silently or aloud:

I forgive you.
You forgive me.
Bring love, peace, and harmony.
Bring love, peace, and harmony.

I forgive you.
You forgive me.
Bring love, peace, and harmony.
Bring love, peace, and harmony.

I forgive you.
You forgive me.
Bring love, peace, and harmony.
Bring love, peace, and harmony.

I forgive you.
You forgive me.
Bring love, peace, and harmony.
Bring love, peace, and harmony.

Hao! Hao! Hao!

Thank you. Thank you. Thank you.

Gong Song. Gong Song. Gong Song. Pronounced *gohng sohng*, this is Chinese for *respectfully return*. This is to return the countless souls who came for the forgiveness practice.

In July 2003 the Divine chose me to be a servant of humanity, all souls, and the Divine. The Divine has given me the honor and authority to offer Divine Soul Mind Body Transplants to humanity.

What is a Divine Soul Transplant? The Divine creates a light being in his heart and transmits it through a Divine Channel (one of my Worldwide Representatives or me) to the recipient. It is a new karma-free divine soul that replaces the original soul of the requested organ, system, or part of the body with a divine soul.

What is a Divine Mind Transplant? The Divine creates a divine consciousness, which is another light being created in his heart, and transmits it through a Divine Channel to the recipient, replacing the consciousness of the requested organ, system, or part of the body with divine consciousness.

What is a Divine Body Transplant? The Divine creates divine energy and divine tiny matter, which is another light being created in his heart, and transmits it through a Divine Channel to the recipient, replacing the energy and tiny matter of the requested organ, system, or part of the body with divine energy and divine tiny matter.

When my Worldwide Representatives or I offer Divine Soul Mind Body Transplants, we are offering these three light beings together. In 2008 I offered Divine Soul Mind Body Transplants in the first book of my Soul Power Series, *Soul Wisdom: Practical Soul Treasures to Transform Your Life*.[3] This was the first time I offered these permanent divine treasures within one of my books. Since then I have offered Divine Soul Mind Body Transplants or Tao Soul Mind Body Transplants in every book of my Soul Power Series. For first-time readers of my books, I offer an introduction to Soul Mind Body Transplants in the "How to Receive the Divine and Tao Soul Downloads Offered in the Books of the Soul Power Series" section at the beginning of this book.

---

3. Toronto/New York: Heaven's Library/Atria Books, 2008.

Divine Soul Mind Body Transplants carry divine frequency and vibration with divine love, forgiveness, compassion, and light, which can remove soul mind body blockages from every aspect of life, including health, relationships, finances, business, intelligence, children, and more.

Now I am offering the first Divine Soul Mind Body Transplants in this book:

Divine Golden Light Ball and Golden Liquid Spring of Divine Forgiveness Soul Mind Body Transplants

Prepare. Sit up straight. Close your eyes. Totally relax. Put both palms on your lower abdomen.

Divine Order: Divine Golden Light Ball and Golden Liquid Spring of Divine Forgiveness Soul Mind Body Transplants

Transmission!

Congratulations! You are extremely blessed.

Thank you, Divine, for your generosity to offer these priceless permanent divine treasures as a gift to every reader.

The Divine Forgiveness Soul Transplant is the soul of Divine Forgiveness.

The Divine Forgiveness Mind Transplant is the consciousness of Divine Forgiveness.

The Divine Forgiveness Body Transplant is the energy and tiny matter of Divine Forgiveness.

Each one is a huge golden light being from the heart of the Divine.

Now I will lead you to apply your Divine Forgiveness Soul Mind Body Transplants to self-clear your bad karma.

Body Power. Put one palm on your lower abdomen below the navel. Put the other palm over your Message Center (heart chakra) in the middle of your chest.[4]

Soul Power. Say *hello:*

> *Dear all the souls my ancestors or I have hurt or*
>   *harmed in any way in any of our lifetimes,*
> *I love you.*
> *I sincerely apologize to all the souls we have harmed.*
> *Please forgive my ancestors and me.*
> *In order to receive your total forgiveness, I will serve*
>   *unconditionally.*
> *Thank you.*
> *Dear all people and all souls who have harmed me*
>   *and my ancestors in any of our lifetimes,*
> *We love you.*
> *We forgive you totally.*
> *We are honored to offer you our forgiveness.*
> *Thank you.*
> *Dear my Divine Forgiveness Soul Mind Body*
>   *Transplants,*
> *I love you.*

---

4. The Message Center, also known as the heart chakra, is a fist-sized energy center located in the center of your chest, behind the sternum. The Message Center is very important for healing and for developing soul communication abilities. It is also the love center, forgiveness center, karma center, emotion center, life transformation center, soul enlightenment center, and more. Clearing blockages from and developing your Message Center are keys for developing your healing power and your ability to communicate with your own soul and other souls.

Please turn on to bless this forgiveness practice.
Thank you.

Mind Power. Visualize golden light embracing you, your ancestors, and all the souls you have invoked.

Sound Power. Chant or sing silently or aloud:

> *Divine Forgiveness*
> *Divine Forgiveness*
> *Divine Forgiveness*
> *Divine Forgiveness*
> *Divine Forgiveness*
> *Divine Forgiveness*
> *Divine Forgiveness . . .*

Put the book down and chant or sing for five minutes now.

Do this forgiveness practice and apply your Divine Forgiveness Soul Mind Body Transplants every day. Every aspect of your life could transform beyond comprehension.

Practice more.

Receive great benefits from the Divine Forgiveness Practice.

The Divine Forgiveness Practice is a daily practice. There is no time limit. Learn it. Remember it. Just do it—the more, the better. For chronic blockages, including issues with health, relationships, finances, and more, practice for two hours or more per day. You can add up all of your practice time to total two hours.

To self-clear bad karma is to help not only yourself; it is also to help with humanity's transition. The more people on Mother Earth do the Divine Forgiveness Practice, the more bad karma could be cleared, and the more Mother Earth's disasters and challenges could be reduced.

If one has heavy bad karma created by making huge mistakes in some lifetimes, it could take one years or even lifetimes to self-clear bad karma, even with the Divine Forgiveness Practice. This book is to teach you and humanity about Divine Healing Hands. Divine Healing Hands are sacred treasures to further help ease Mother Earth's transition and to heal humanity, animals, and nature.

Divine Healing Hands carry divine frequency and vibration with divine love, forgiveness, compassion, and light, which can remove all kinds of soul mind body blockages in every aspect of life.

I was given the honor and authority to offer Divine Healing Hands to humanity in 2005. My Worldwide Representatives also received the honor and authority to offer Divine Healing Hands in 2011.

As of August 2012 my Worldwide Representatives and I have offered Divine Healing Hands to more than 3,500 chosen ones. Everyone who wants to receive Divine Healing Hands must apply to receive this honor. One applies to the Divine through a Divine Channel. The Divine has to approve the readiness of the applicant to receive this sacred treasure and become a Divine Healing Hands Soul Healer. Every Divine Healing Hands Soul Healer must understand that to receive this treasure is to help humanity pass through this difficult time.

In the last few years Divine Healing Hands Soul Healers have created thousands of heart-touching and moving healing stories.

Divine Healing Hands carry divine power to heal.

Words are not enough.

Thoughts are not enough.

Imagination is not enough.

Comprehension is not enough to understand the power of Divine Healing Hands. Humanity is extremely blessed to have the opportunity to receive Divine Healing Hands.

In chapter 2 I will ask the Divine to download his Divine Healing Hands to this book. If you want to know if a pear is sweet, taste it. If you want to know the power of Divine Healing Hands, experience it. This book becomes a carrier of Divine Healing Hands. However, the Divine told me very clearly that every reader can ask for a soul healing blessing only twenty times from the Divine Healing Hands downloaded to this book. (If you ask for soul healing blessings more than twenty times, it will not work.) You will be able to experience the power of Divine Healing Hands twenty times from this book. You are extremely blessed.

To continue to receive healing blessings from Divine Healing Hands, you will need to connect with a Divine Healing Hands Soul Healer. You also have the opportunity to receive Divine Healing Hands yourself and become a Divine Healing Hands Soul Healer through the Divine Healing Hands Soul Healer Training Program offered by my Worldwide Representatives and me worldwide.

Divine Healing Hands are divine sacred treasures to bless and heal you, your loved ones, humanity, and Mother Earth.

Divine Healing Hands are divine sacred treasures to bless and transform relationships.

Divine Healing Hands are divine sacred treasures to bless and transform finances.

Divine Healing Hands are divine sacred treasures to bless and transform your children.

Divine Healing Hands are divine sacred treasures to bless and transform animals.

Divine Healing Hands are divine sacred treasures to bless and transform nature.

Divine Healing Hands are divine sacred treasures to bless and increase intelligence.

Divine Healing Hands are divine sacred treasures to bless and transform every aspect of life.

Divine Healing Hands are divine sacred treasures to bring love, peace, and harmony to you, your family, your loved ones, societies, cities, countries, Mother Earth, and all universes.

Thank you so much, Divine, for your generosity and willingness to give your soul light healing hands to the chosen ones. Your chosen ones are the recipients who want to serve and remove the suffering of humanity, animals, nature, and all souls, as well as help humanity pass through this difficult time.

> *Divine Healing Hands heal and bless me.*
> *Divine Healing Hands heal and bless my loved ones.*
> *Divine Healing Hands heal and bless humanity.*
> *Divine Healing Hands heal and bless all souls.*
> *Divine Healing Hands heal and bless Mother Earth.*
> *Divine Healing Hands heal and bless all universes.*

> *I love my heart and soul*
> *I love all humanity*
> *Join hearts and souls together*
> *Love, peace and harmony*
> *Love, peace and harmony*

Divine Healing Hands: What, Why, and How

W HEN YOU READ any of my books you could realize that in every book, in every chapter, and in every teaching I always explain *what*, *why*, and *how*.

What? "What" is the concept. The concept must be clear and precise. Science, academics, business, and every part of life should have a clear and precise concept. Otherwise, readers and students will not grasp the meaning. To write a book is to share teachings and practices with readers. To give readers a very clear concept is the direction for all the teachings, secrets, wisdom, knowledge, and practical techniques I have shared in all of my books.

Why? "Why" means *why do people need to learn this or practice this*? It includes the power and significance of what I am teaching. This is service oriented. If I share a secret or some special wisdom, knowledge, or practical technique, or if I offer any kind of service, you must understand why I am doing it. Does this service benefit you? If there is no benefit, why do I need to share it? Why do you need to do it? Therefore, *why* is very important in all of my writings and teachings.

How? "How" refers to the method or technique to accomplish a goal. If I teach or offer any service, how do you do it? How can you carry out the methods and strategies? In my Soul Power Series the *how* includes practical techniques for healing, rejuvenation, and transformation of relationships and finances, as well as of every aspect of life. Techniques are very important. The Divine Forgiveness Practice is an example.

To teach or achieve anything in your life there are two parts: theory and practice. Theory and practice are yin and yang. Yin and yang are opposites but united. They complement one another. To accomplish anything you must include both yin and yang. You cannot accomplish your task or goal by using only yin or only yang.

I am extremely blessed that the Divine has chosen me as a servant, vehicle, and channel for humanity and the Divine. The Divine has given me the authority to offer permanent divine treasures to humanity. Divine treasures carry divine power to heal and transform all life, but recipients must practice in order to receive the benefits. This belongs to the *how.*

In summary, my teaching is based on *what, why,* and *how.* I teach *da Tao zhi jian* (pronounced *dah dow jr jyen*), which means *the Big Way is extremely simple.* The simplest wisdom and techniques are the best. Simple is powerful. I am the servant of humanity. I love simplicity.

Billions of people need healing.

Billions of people need transformation of relationships.

Billions of people need transformation of finances.

Billions of people need rejuvenation.

Billions of people need to purify their souls, hearts, minds, and bodies.

Billions of people need to increase their intelligence.

Billions of people need to open their hearts and souls.

Billions of people need to apply love, forgiveness, compassion, and light to transform themselves, humanity, Mother Earth, and all souls.

Billions of people need to join hearts and souls together to transform Mother Earth's transition and to bring love, peace, and harmony to humanity, Mother Earth, and all universes.

Complexity cannot serve billions of people and all souls. Simplicity is the way to serve billions of people and all souls.

I am a servant of humanity and countless souls. Ever since I wrote my first book the Divine has guided me that simplicity is the key to service. *What, why*, and *how* is the way to write, teach, and serve every aspect of my life. *What, why*, and *how* is the way to serve every aspect of your life.

What Are Divine Healing Hands?

Divine Healing Hands are God's soul hands. God creates his new soul hands and transmits them to the chosen ones through the service of a Divine Channel (one of my Worldwide Representatives or me). *Chosen one* means a person who has gone through the process of applying for, receiving approval by Divine Guidance, and registering to receive Divine Healing Hands.

The Divine chose me as a servant of humanity and the Divine in July 2003 and gave me the honor and authority to download or transmit permanent divine treasures to humanity. In 2011 about twenty of my Worldwide Representatives, who are also Divine Channels, received the honor and authority to download

Divine Healing Hands. If you are not a Divine Channel, you cannot download Divine Healing Hands to others. To download Divine Healing Hands is an honor beyond words, comprehension, and imagination. Divine Channels are divine presence on Mother Earth. They are divine servants to represent the Divine to serve humanity, Mother Earth, and all souls.

The Divine Healing Hands treasure created by the Divine is hundreds of feet high and hundreds of feet wide. Once the Divine Healing Hands treasure is downloaded to a chosen one, it takes two or three days for the divine treasure to shrink to a condensed size, which is two or three times the size of the recipient's hand.

After one receives Divine Healing Hands, the recipient receives proper training from a Divine Channel to become certified as a Divine Healing Hands Soul Healer.

When a Divine Healing Hands Soul Healer offers a soul healing blessing, the Divine Healing Hands treasure will come out from the Divine Healing Hands Soul Healer to serve the recipient. Divine Healing Hands Soul Healers can offer soul healing blessings in person and remotely. They can offer healing blessings one on one or to a group of people. There is no limit to the number of people who can receive soul healing blessings from Divine Healing Hands.

Why Do Divine Healing Hands Work?

Why does a person become sick? Sickness is due to soul mind body blockages.

Soul blockages are bad karma. Karma is the record of services from one's previous lifetimes and this lifetime. Karma is divided into good karma and bad karma. Good karma is accumulated from one's good service offered in all lifetimes, including love, care, compassion, sincerity, honesty, generosity, kindness, integrity, purity, and more.

Bad karma is accumulated from the mistakes one has made in all lifetimes, including killing, harming, taking advantage of others, cheating, stealing, lying, and more.

As I noted in the introduction, there is a karmic law in Heaven:

Good service brings rewards.
Bad service brings lessons.

This law applies to all souls in all universes. There is an ancient saying: *Heaven is most fair.* No good deed goes unnoticed. No bad deed goes unnoticed.

The Divine chose me as a servant of humanity and the Divine in July 2003. The Divine gave me the honor and authority to offer Divine Karma Cleansing and Divine Soul Mind Body Transplants to humanity.

What is Divine Karma Cleansing? Divine Karma Cleansing means the Divine offers divine forgiveness by paying one's spiritual debt and clearing one's bad karma.

When one has bad karma, one could learn lessons in any aspect of life, including health, relationships, finances, business, children, and more. There is only one way to self-clear bad karma: serve others unconditionally. To serve others is to make others happier and healthier. To serve unconditionally is to serve without asking for or expecting anything in return.

If one has heavy bad karma it could take thirty to fifty years of unconditional universal service in one lifetime to remove the bad karma and to be forgiven. It could take many lifetimes of unconditional universal service to remove one's heavy bad karma.

Bad karma is spiritual debt. It must be paid. How is it paid? Normally it is paid by learning one's karmic lessons—blockages in one's health, relationships, finances, business, and any aspect of life. Divine Karma Cleansing means the Divine gives his virtue, which is spiritual currency, to pay one's spiritual debt. This is divine generosity. If one has bad karma, there are dark blockages inside the body. When the Divine offers virtue, the darkness will leave the body. The darkness is the root cause of sickness, broken relationships, financial challenges, and more.

I and my more than twenty Worldwide Representatives, who, like me, are also divine servants, vehicles, and channels, have offered tens of thousands of Divine Karma Cleansings for humanity. We have received thousands of heart-touching and moving soul healing stories and soul healing miracles from Divine Karma Cleansing. In the last three years, nearly one thousand heart-touching and moving stories have been video recorded and posted on my YouTube channel, YouTube.com/zhigangsha. I encourage you to view some of them. In addition, you will read stories related to Divine Healing Hands throughout this book. Divine Healing Hands blessings can remove bad karma little by little.

In one sentence:

**To clear soul blockages is to remove
the darkness inside the body.**

The second cause of sickness is mind blockages, which include negative mind-sets, negative beliefs, negative attitudes, ego, attachments, and more. Millions of people have all types of mind blockages.

The third cause of sickness is body blockages, which are energy and matter blockages.

In ancient spiritual teaching a human being has three internal treasures: jing qi shen. Jing is *matter*. Qi (pronounced *chee*) is *vital energy or life force*. Shen is *soul*.

Jing qi shen is soul, mind, and body. To remove soul mind body blockages is to remove blockages in jing qi shen. Soul mind body and jing qi shen are different ways to express the same thing. "Jing qi shen" is the ancient term. "Soul mind body" is the new term for the Soul Light Era.

Why do Divine Healing Hands work? In one sentence:

Divine Healing Hands remove soul mind body blockages, which are blockages in the jing qi shen of the body, for healing and rejuvenation, and remove soul mind body blockages in relationships, finances, children, intelligence, and more in order to transform every aspect of life.

Divine Healing Hands carry divine power, which includes:

- divine frequency and vibration, which can transform the frequency and vibration of all life, including health, relationships, finances, business, children, and every aspect of life
- divine love, which melts all blockages and transforms all life
- divine forgiveness, which brings inner joy and inner peace to all life
- divine compassion, which boosts energy, stamina, vitality, and immunity of all life
- divine light, which heals, prevents sickness, purifies

and rejuvenates soul, heart, mind, and body, and transforms health, relationships, finances, intelligence, and every aspect of life

Words are not enough to express the power of Divine Healing Hands.

Thoughts are not enough to express the significance of Divine Healing Hands.

Imagination is not enough to express the honor of receiving Divine Healing Hands.

How blessed we are that the Divine is giving his soul hands to the chosen ones to empower them to serve as divine healers. Anyone who can receive Divine Healing Hands cannot express enough the honor, appreciation, and blessing of being a Divine Healing Hands Soul Healer.

I always teach: *If you want to know if a pear is sweet, taste it. If you want to know if Divine Healing Hands are powerful, experience it.*

This story is a taste of the pear:

> *I am an acupuncturist in Honolulu, Hawaii, specializing in treating infertility and the prevention of miscarriage. Recently one of my patients who was thirteen weeks pregnant with twins (after more than five years of trying to conceive) began bleeding heavily upon awakening one morning. Her obstetrician told her that there was nothing they could do and that she should just stay home and rest.*
>
> *She called me immediately after speaking with her doctor. At that time I was unable to go to her house, so I offered her a remote Divine Healing Hands blessing with guided self-healing for about thirty minutes. Two hours*

later, she got up and the bleeding had slowed considerably. Five hours later I called her and we went through another session of Divine Healing Hands blessing along with guided self-healing by applying the Four Power Techniques and a forgiveness practice.

I asked her to remain lying down until the next morning when she would have an ultrasound. By the time she went to bed that evening, the bleeding appeared to have stopped. Indeed, there was no more bleeding after that and the ultrasound the next day showed that both fetuses were in good health!

She continues to do a daily forgiveness practice and comes to see me once a week. She is now in her twentieth week of pregnancy, and just had an ultrasound that revealed she is carrying two healthy baby boys!

Thank you, Divine, Tao, and Master Sha. Thank you for the power of Divine Healing Hands and other divine treasures. I am extremely grateful.

Thank you. Thank you. Thank you.

Love you. Love you. Love you.

Gina Musetti, L.Ac.
Honolulu, Hawaii

The Divine Releases His Soul Hands to Humanity for the First Time

The Divine chose me as a divine servant in July 2003. He teaches me every day. The Divine communicates with me through soul communication. He appears above my head and we have a conversation through soul communication daily. At this moment I am doing soul communication. I will ask questions of the Divine and receive the Divine's answers. Then I will share this conversation with you and humanity in this book.

This book is the tenth book in my Soul Power Series. The second book, *Soul Communication: Opening Your Spiritual Channels for Success and Fulfillment*,[1] teaches how to open one's four spiritual channels, which are:

- **Soul Language Channel**—Open this channel to use Soul Language to communicate with the Soul World, including your own soul, all kinds of spiritual fathers and mothers, nature, and the Divine.
- **Direct Soul Communication Channel**—Open this channel to converse directly with the Divine and all souls.
- **Third Eye Channel**—Open this channel to receive guidance and teachings through spiritual images.
- **Direct Knowing Channel**—Open this channel to have direct knowing through instant soul communication with the Divine and all souls.

In chapter 7 of this book I will teach you how to apply Divine Healing Hands to open your spiritual channels. I will have a conversation with the Divine now.

I asked the Divine at this moment:

> *Dear Divine, beloved father,*
> *In history, how many people have you given your Divine Healing Hands to?*

---

1. Toronto/New York: Heaven's Library/Atria Books, 2008.

The Divine replied:

Dear my son,
    I have given my Divine Healing Hands in total to seven people in all of history.

I then asked:

Could you give me a few of their names that I know of in history?

The Divine then replied:

I have offered my soul healing hands to the following buddhas and saints whose names you recognize:

- *Shi Jia Mo Ni Fo, who is also known as Shakyamuni, Siddhartha Gautama, and the Buddha*
- *Guan Yin, Bodhisattva of Compassion and Goddess of Mercy*
- *Jesus*
- *Mother Mary*

Dear my son, Zhi Gang, you do not know the names of the other three who have received my divine soul hands.

I continued to ask the Divine:

Have you ever given your soul healing hands to the masses?

The Divine answered:

> *No, my son. The time was not ready for me to give my divine soul healing hands to the masses.*

I bowed down 108 times in appreciation.

Why Is the Divine Releasing His Soul Hands?

I continued to ask the Divine questions:

> *Dear Divine,*
> *You downloaded Divine Healing Hands to me in 2005. Then you gave me the honor and authority to offer Divine Healing Hands to the chosen ones. Up to now, my Worldwide Representatives and I have transmitted your soul healing hands to more than 3,500 recipients all over the world.*
> *Why are you releasing your Divine Healing Hands to so many people now?*

The Divine replied:

> *Dear my son,*
> *The time is ready for me to offer my divine soul hands to many chosen ones. This is due to Mother Earth's transition. In the last eight years you have witnessed more and more natural disasters and other challenges happening on Mother Earth. In the next eleven years Mother Earth could go through a more serious transition. This means Mother*

Earth will go through more serious natural disasters and greater challenges in every aspect of life.

You are my chosen servant, vehicle, and channel. You have created more than twenty divine servants, vehicles, and channels for me. My chosen Divine Channels are also given the authority and honor to offer my Divine Healing Hands to the chosen ones all over the world.

The Divine continued:

Everyone who would like to receive my Divine Healing Hands must apply. I have to personally approve them through my Divine Channels. Then the recipients must complete the proper training to be certified as a Divine Healing Hands Soul Healer. I give my Divine Healing Hands to help humanity pass through this difficult time and to save people's lives.

Those who receive Divine Healing Hands are chosen ones because they have responded to my calling to receive Divine Healing Hands to remove the suffering of humanity and to bless every aspect of life for humanity, Mother Earth, and all souls in this historic period and beyond.

I replied:

Thank you, my beloved father. I am extremely honored and all Divine Channels are extremely honored to offer your Divine Healing Hands, which are priceless treasures.

The Divine continued:

> *Everyone who has received my Divine Healing Hands has a special light line that connects with me. When they offer Divine Healing Hands soul healing, I will be aware right away and bless their healing.*

I said:

> *Thank you. Thank you. Thank you.*

I bowed another 108 times. Finally I said:

> *I cannot bow down enough.*

I deeply appreciated the Divine for directly answering my questions. I am very honored to be given the authority to offer Divine Healing Hands to humanity at this time.

Mother Earth is going through a serious transition. The Divine said that this transition could last eleven more years and could intensify tremendously. I feel in my heart and soul that Divine Healing Hands are urgently needed at this time because divine healing power is being given through Divine Healing Hands. It is no coincidence that this powerful divine healing treasure is being offered to the masses at this time in history.

The Divine said that when Divine Healing Hands Soul Healers offer healing blessings, he will be aware of this right away and offer his blessings. This means that the Divine is personally involved in every healing blessing offered by Divine Healing Hands Soul Healers. We are so blessed. Humanity is so blessed.

The power and significance of Divine Healing Hands will be explained further in the next chapter. You can also experience the power of Divine Healing Hands very soon. I will download Divine Healing Hands to this physical book. You will then be able to invoke the Divine Healing Hands and directly experience their power.

I emphasize again that you are given only twenty opportunities to experience the power of the Divine Healing Hands downloaded to this book. If you are moved and touched by the power of Divine Healing Hands after experiencing it twenty times, you can apply to become a Divine Healing Hands Soul Healer through www.drsha.com. If you are approved by Divine Guidance, you will then need to join a three-day workshop led by one of my Worldwide Representatives or me to receive training. After you are certified as a Divine Healing Hands Soul Healer you can offer Divine Healing Hands soul healing blessings to transform health, relationships, finances, children, intelligence, and every aspect of life.

How to Apply Divine Healing Hands for Healing, Blessing, and Life Transformation

To apply Divine Healing Hands for healing, blessing, and life transformation, the Divine guided me to instruct all Divine Healing Hands Soul Healers to always remember to apply the Four Power Techniques:

Body Power. Divine Healing Hands Soul Healers use the Soul Light Era Prayer Position by placing the left palm over the Message Center and the right hand in the traditional prayer position. (See figure 2.) Shake the right hand.

Figure 2. Soul Light Era Prayer Position

Soul Power. Say *hello*:

> *Dear Divine Healing Hands,*
> *I love you, honor you, and appreciate you.*
> *Please offer healing, blessing, and life transformation*
>   *as appropriate for* _____ (state the request).
> *I am very grateful.*
> *Thank you.*

Mind Power. Visualize golden, rainbow, purple, or crystal light vibrating in the sickness area for healing and rejuvenation. If the blessing is for relationships or finances, the Divine Healing Hands Soul Healer's mind must be on the soul of the relationship or finances.

Sound Power. Chant silently:

> *Divine Healing Hands, please heal, rejuvenate, and*
> *transform* _____ (name the healing, blessing,
> and life transformation offered).
> *Thank you.*

Another option is to chant Soul Language[2] while offering the healing, blessing, or life transformation with Divine Healing Hands. In this case, the Divine Healing Hands Soul Healer would say:

> *Dear my Divine Healing Hands,*
> *Please continue to heal, bless, and transform* _____
> *as appropriate.*
> *I will speak Soul Language to assist.*
> *Thank you.*

If you do not know how to speak Soul Language, simply chant:

> *Divine Healing Hands, please heal, rejuvenate, and*
> *transform. Thank you.*

Repeat this silently again and again.

---

2. Soul Language is the language of your soul. It is your own soul's voice. Learn more about Soul Language, including how to bring out your Soul Language, in chapters 5 and 7 of this book. See also the first book of my Soul Power Series, *Soul Wisdom: Practical Soul Treasures to Transform Your Life* (Toronto/New York: Heaven's Library/Atria Books, 2008).

For How Long Can a Divine Healing Hands Blessing Be Offered?

I suggest spending ten minutes when offering a one-time blessing session with Divine Healing Hands. A Divine Healing Hands Soul Healer can offer blessings as many as three or four times a day to a recipient for one condition or issue.

For chronic and life-threatening conditions I suggest offering thirty-minute sessions.

If someone has an emergency situation such as a heart attack, stroke, bleeding, difficulty breathing, a car accident, or other serious situations, the Divine Healing Hands Soul Healer must immediately seek emergency medical assistance. Divine Healing Hands Soul Healers must understand this important principle. Emergency cases must receive immediate medical attention or be transported to a hospital. Of course, you can also offer Divine Healing Hands soul healing blessings.

In an emergency situation the Divine Healing Hands Soul Healer can send a subdivided Divine Healing Hands treasure to the person and ask the Divine Healing Hands to stay with the person for a few days to continue to offer soul healing blessings *as appropriate*. Make sure you continue to chant silently as much as you can.

Before you send your subdivided Divine Healing Hands treasures out for an emergency condition, instruct the Divine Healing Hands as to when they are to return. For example:

Dear my Divine Healing Hands, please offer three days of continuous healing as appropriate and then return to me. Thank you.

Divine Healing Hands Soul Healers will receive important training in the certification workshop to learn how to determine how many days the Divine Healing Hands should stay to offer healing in an emergency situation.

How to Use
Divine Healing Hands Properly

To become a Divine Healing Hands Soul Healer is a tremendous honor. To receive the Divine's healing hands is to be a chosen servant of the Divine. To receive the Divine's healing hands is to be a better servant of humanity, animals, nature, Mother Earth, and beyond.

If you are a Divine Healing Hands Soul Healer, you must follow some very important guiding principles when offering Divine Healing Hands soul healing blessings.

You must honor and respect Divine Healing Hands from your soul, heart, mind, and body. The moment that you apply Divine Healing Hands to offer a blessing, show honor and respect. Silently tell your Divine Healing Hands:

> *Dear my Divine Healing Hands,*
> *I am extremely honored to have received you from the*
>   *Divine.*
> *I am so honored to be a servant and to ask you to offer*
>   *healing, blessing, and life transformation.*
> *Thank you.*

When offering a Divine Healing Hands blessing, quiet your heart and mind right away. Place your left hand over your

Message Center and your right hand in the traditional prayer position. This is called the Soul Light Era Prayer Position (figure 2, page 16). To put your hands in this position is to show your honor and respect, as well as your commitment to serve in the Soul Light Era.

With your hands in the Soul Light Era Prayer Position, say *hello* as follows:

> *Dear Divine Healing Hands,*
> *I love you, honor you, and respect you.*
> *I cannot honor you enough.*
> *You have the power to remove soul mind body block-*
>   *ages for healing, blessing, and life transformation.*
> *I thank you from the bottom of my heart for your*
>   *blessings.*

Always remember to ask the Divine Healing Hands to offer the appropriate blessing:

> *Please offer healing, blessing, and life transformation*
>   *as appropriate.*

This is a very important teaching. Many people suffer from chronic and life-threatening conditions. They could have very heavy soul mind body blockages.

Soul blockages are bad karma. There are many types of bad karma, including personal karma, ancestral karma, relationship karma, curses, negative memories, mental body karma, emotional body karma, systems and organs karma, cells karma, and more.

Mind blockages include negative mind-sets, negative attitudes, negative beliefs, ego, attachments, and more.

Body blockages include energy and matter blockages.

Some people have extremely heavy bad karma. They carry a lot of darkness. Divine Healing Hands can remove bad karma little by little. Therefore, when invoking Divine Healing Hands, always say the following:

> *Dear Divine Healing Hands,*
> *Please offer healing, blessing, and life transformation*
>   *as appropriate.*

The words *as appropriate* are key. **Never demand or force healing** by saying *you must get well* or *you must recover right away.*

Even though Divine Healing Hands blessings can clear bad karma little by little, you as a Divine Healing Hands Soul Healer have not been given the authority to clear bad karma. To offer Divine Karma Cleansing service, one must be a Divine Channel who has been given the authority by the Divine.

If you demand or force healing, high-level darkness could become agitated and very upset and harm you as a Divine Healing Hands Soul Healer. This could be very dangerous. This point must be very clear for you and every Divine Healing Hands Soul Healer. Do not make this mistake.

As a Divine Healing Hands Soul Healer, you have received a Divine Protection Package.[3] You are safe if you do not demand

---

3. When one becomes a Divine Healing Hands Soul Healer, one receives a Divine Protection Package, which includes Divine Protection Soul Mind Body Transplants, Divine Light Wall Soul Mind Body Transplants, and Divine Prevention and Healing of Communicable Diseases Soul Mind Body Transplants that protect the divine healer from physical and spiritual harm.

healing or ask for bad karma to be cleansed. When any Divine Healing Hands Soul Healer offers healing blessings, the Divine is responsible. Do not force the healing. Let the Divine offer the appropriate healing. If you do this, you are completely safe. This teaching is to make sure that Divine Healing Hands Soul Healers include the words *as appropriate* with every Divine Healing Hands soul healing and transformation blessing offered.

The Divine Healing Hands Soul Healer does not need to force the healing, blessing, or life transformation. The Divine knows how much healing, blessing, and life transformation to give each recipient. It does take more than a one-time Divine Healing Hands blessing to heal chronic and life-threatening conditions. Some challenging cases could take weeks or months to receive complete healing. Some very challenging cases may not receive complete healing.

Therefore, always remember to say:

> *Divine Healing Hands, please offer healing, blessing,*
> *and life transformation as appropriate.*

In addition:

- Never promise any healing result. The Divine does not promise anything. The Divine blesses us.
- Do not touch recipients when offering healing blessings.
- It is not appropriate to ask Divine Healing Hands to heal all humanity, all animals, and all of nature.
- It is not appropriate to ask Divine Healing Hands to stop natural disasters, wars, economic challenges, or any other aspect of Mother Earth's transition.

- It is not appropriate to ask Divine Healing Hands for blessings for financial gain, including the stock market, investments, gambling, or lottery.
- It is not appropriate to ask Divine Healing Hands to clear bad karma of any kind.
- It is not appropriate to ask Divine Healing Hands to bless political outcomes.
- It is not appropriate to ask Divine Healing Hands to bless police investigations.
- It is not appropriate to ask Divine Healing Hands to benefit one person at another person's expense.

In summary, always remember to ask Divine Healing Hands to offer *appropriate* healing, blessing, and life transformation.

Experience the Power of Divine Healing Hands

J ALWAYS TEACH: *If you want to know if a pear is sweet, taste it. If you want to know if Divine Healing Hands are powerful, experience it.*

Divine Healing Hands are the Divine's soul hands, which carry the Divine's healing power.

We do not have enough words to express the power of the Divine's soul hands.

We do not have enough thoughts to comprehend the power of the Divine's soul hands.

We do not have enough imagination to contain the power of the Divine's soul hands.

The Power and Significance of Divine Healing Hands

Mother Earth is in a time of serious transition. Humanity is suffering. The Divine is offering his powerful treasures to the chosen ones because humanity needs help.

The power and significance of Divine Healing Hands are vast. Divine Healing Hands can be applied for:

- divine self-healing of the spiritual, mental, emotional, and physical bodies
- divine healing of the spiritual, mental, emotional, and physical bodies of others
- divine group healing of the spiritual, mental, emotional, and physical bodies
- divine remote healing of the spiritual, mental, emotional, and physical bodies
- divine transformation of relationships
- divine transformation of finances
- divine transformation of intelligence
- divine transformation of every aspect of life
- divine blessing to boost energy, stamina, vitality, and immunity
- divine blessing to purify and rejuvenate the soul, heart, mind, and body
- divine blessing to prolong life
- divine blessing to bring love, peace, and harmony to you, your loved ones, your family, society, organizations, cities, countries, Mother Earth, and countless planets, stars, galaxies, and universes
- divine blessing to help humanity and Mother Earth pass through this difficult time in history

In this book I will share many soul healing miracles and heart-touching and moving stories created by Divine Healing Hands.

As of August 2012 the Divine Channels who are my World-wide Representatives and I have downloaded Divine Healing

Hands to more than 3,500 chosen ones throughout the world. The chosen ones are those who want to remove the suffering of humanity and help humanity pass through this historic period on Mother Earth.

I received a message from Heaven that Mother Earth's transition could last for another eleven years, into 2023. There could be extremely severe natural disasters. There could be major financial collapses. There could be a widespread war. There could be a very serious new communicable disease. There could be many more challenges in every aspect of life.

Divine Healing Hands are divine sacred treasures to help humanity deal with these disasters and challenges. Divine Healing Hands carry the Divine's healing and blessing power. The chosen ones are the ones who want to serve. They are honored and delighted to help humanity pass through this difficult time with all its potential disasters and challenges.

I will now share a story about Divine Healing Hands that brought blessings for a jet plane that had an electrical failure, as well as blessings for two fellow workers with shoulder pain.

One evening in December 2011 in Sydney, Australia, I offered a Divine Healing Hands blessing to our Boeing 767 aircraft, which was having an electrical failure.

As the International In-Flight Purser, I was called to the cockpit to receive the bad news. The flight would be cancelled if we were not off the blocks of the gate by 10:59 p.m. It was 9:30 p.m. What was a mild mechanical problem escalated to a serious one, because the electrical problem could not be identified. A full plane load of two hundred forty-one passengers would be disembarked, hotels would need to be found for these passengers, and the flight would be cancelled. This situation would cost our company thousands of dollars and it would create unhappy passengers.

The mechanics worked for an hour trying to solve the electrical issue. I saw that their faces reflected a doom and gloom look, which mirrored the look of our captain.

As I had recently finished my Divine Healing Hands Soul Healer certification, I gave the aircraft's electrical system a blessing, and then asked our captain to start the engines. I also asked Master Sha, the Divine, and Tao to help. In the seconds after the blessing, the crew started the engines and, to our amazement, the aircraft started and all the panels in the cockpit lit up. Two other crew members looked at me and asked what I had done. I replied that it was not me doing the healing of the electrical system, but the Divine working through me. They had a look of awe on their faces. I knew we had all witnessed a true miracle!

I also gave blessings to two fellow workers, both with rotator cuff pain. One pilot was experiencing such extreme pain that he could not lift his arms to start the engines. After giving him a Divine Healing Hands blessing, he called me an hour later and said that his pain was reduced tremendously. The other friend asked me to please help him with his rotator cuff pain, and made sure that I knew he generally didn't let anyone touch him. As I am also a licensed massage therapist, I massaged his shoulders and gave him a blessing. He understood about dark souls causing the pain. I asked that he do a forgiveness practice to reduce the pain, to which he said he was not ready to forgive this person who hurt him.

The following day, his wife sent me an email expressing her gratitude for healing her husband's shoulder. He had had this condition for months and had tried everything, including doctor visits, medication, and chiropractic services, none of which helped. She said his shoulder pain was greatly reduced, and they knew that having me in their lives was indeed a blessing!

Cherilyn Moloney
Kapolei, Hawaii

THE DIVINE DOWNLOADS HIS SOUL HEALING HANDS
TO THIS BOOK

At this moment I just asked the Divine:

Is it time for me to download Divine Healing Hands to this book?

The Divine answers:

Yes, but I want to say something first. After transmitting my divine soul hands to this book, every reader can ask for healing and blessing only twenty times. After twenty times, if one feels the power and honor of my Divine Healing Hands, then these individuals need to apply to receive Divine Healing Hands.

To become a Divine Healing Hands Soul Healer is to answer a divine calling. Experience the power of Divine Healing Hands first. Then you are called to be one of the chosen ones to receive Divine Healing Hands.

The Divine will approve your readiness to receive Divine Healing Hands at the soul, heart, mind, and body levels. If approved, you may join an upcoming training with me or one of my Worldwide Representatives to become a certified Divine Healing Hands Soul Healer.

At this moment it is 7:07 PM EDT on March 16, 2012, in Toronto, Ontario, Canada. I connected via an Internet video call with Master Peter Hudoba and Master G. K. Khoe, two of my Worldwide Representatives, in Vancouver, British Columbia, Canada. These two Masters are teaching an Opening Spiritual Channels workshop at this moment.

I am saying "hello" to everyone. The whole group responds "hello." We are able to see each other. This is the beauty of technology. Master Cynthia Marie Deveraux is typing my flow at this moment.

I am asking all of the participants in the Vancouver workshop to prepare for Divine Healing Hands to be downloaded into this book. They are applying the Four Power Techniques that I have shared in every book in my Soul Power Series, including in the introduction to this book. I will offer a little more teaching about the Four Power Techniques.

The first power technique is Body Power. Body Power means special hand and body positions for healing, rejuvenation, prolonging life, and transforming every aspect of life, including relationships and finances.

Body Power can be summarized in one sentence:

Body Power means where you put your hands is where you receive the blessing, which can include healing,

rejuvenation, prolonging life, and transformation of every aspect of life, including relationships and finances.

The second power technique is Soul Power. Soul Power is to invoke inner souls and outer souls for healing, rejuvenation, prolonging life, and transforming every aspect of life, including relationships and finances.

Inner souls include the souls of your systems, organs, cells, cell units, DNA, RNA, spaces between the cells and organs, and tiny matter inside the cells. Outer souls include the souls of the Divine, Tao, Heaven, Mother Earth, and countless planets, stars, galaxies, and universes, as well as countless healing angels, archangels, Ascended Masters, lamas, gurus, buddhas, bodhisattvas, kahunas, holy saints, and all kinds of spiritual fathers and mothers in Heaven and on Mother Earth. Soul Power is extremely special because you do not need to move one step to find the Divine and other souls to request healing or blessing.

Soul Power can be summarized in one sentence:

Soul Power is Say Hello Healing and Say Hello Blessing by invoking inner and outer souls.

The third power technique is Mind Power. Mind means consciousness. Mind Power is to use and apply the power of consciousness of the soul, heart, mind, and body for healing and blessing.

Mind Power can be summarized in one sentence:

Mind Power is creative visualization for healing and blessing in every aspect of life.

The fourth power technique is Sound Power. Sound Power is to chant sacred mantras, vibrational healing sounds, Divine Soul Songs, or Tao Songs, which carry special frequencies and vibrations for healing and blessing. Sound Power can be summarized in one sentence:

What you chant is what you become.

Many healing modalities apply one power technique. To apply one power technique is powerful. To apply the Four Power Techniques together is extremely powerful.

Now I am ready to ask the Divine to download his Divine Healing Hands to this book. I ask the Vancouver workshop participants to apply the Four Power Techniques:

Body Power. Sit up straight and put both feet flat on the floor. Put the tip of your tongue gently against the roof of your mouth. Close your eyes.

Soul Power. Say *hello*:

> *Dear Divine,*
> *We are so honored to witness and experience your*
>   *Divine Healing Hands that will be downloaded to*
>   *this book.*
> *Thank you.*

Mind Power. Visualize Divine Healing Hands coming to this book. If your Third Eye is open you could see the Divine creating Divine Healing Hands and downloading it to this book.

Sound Power. After the Divine downloads his Divine Healing Hands to this book, we will chant.

I am ready to ask the Divine to download his soul healing hands to the book. We do not have a physical book yet. I am flowing the book at this moment. The Divine can download his soul healing hands to the book that is within Master Cynthia's computer. When the physical book is published, Divine Healing Hands will go automatically to every book that is printed. What we can conceive—and even what we cannot conceive—the Divine can do. This is the power of the Divine. This is what the Divine has told me at this time.

Prepare!

I will download Divine Healing Hands to the words in this computer first. I am asking Master Peter, Master G. K., and Master Cynthia, as well as every participant in the Opening Spiritual Channels workshop, to observe and experience the power of Divine Healing Hands. Master Cynthia and I are in Toronto. Master Peter, Master G. K., and their advanced students are in Vancouver. I am asking the Divine to download his Divine Healing Hands to this computer and in this book. Then I will ask every participant to connect with the Divine Healing Hands in this computer to receive a healing blessing. Finally they will share their personal experiences.

Divine Order: Divine Healing Hands Soul Mind Body Transplants to this book

Transmission!

I am asking Master Peter to share his Third Eye images and to do a direct soul communication with the Divine. I am asking

Master G. K. and Master Cynthia to share their experiences also. I will also ask some of the students in the Vancouver workshop to share their experiences.

Master Peter Hudoba shared his experience first:

> *We are very excited and very grateful for this amazing opportunity. This has never happened before that we can have Master Sha directly present in our workshop through the help of modern technology.*
>
> *I will share my Third Eye images.*
>
> *What I saw was the Divine holding an open book in his right hand in front of him. He was looking down on the pages and when Master Sha gave the order, from the heart of Divine came a very beautiful bright soul which entered the book. At that moment there was an explosion of light. I am extremely grateful and blessed to witness these beautiful images.*

I then asked Master Peter to do a direct soul communication with the Divine. Master Peter flowed the following:

> *My dearly beloved Zhi Gang Sha,*
>
> *We are very grateful to you for creating this opportunity to bring Divine Healing Hands to humanity. This is a very innovative approach that will serve the divine mission in a very magnificent way. It will bring Divine Healing Hands to tens of thousands of people in a very short time. Heaven is extremely happy. All souls are extremely happy. Humanity is extremely blessed.*
>
> *Your loving Divine.*

I then asked Master G. K. to share his experience:

Thank you, Master Sha, the Divine, and Tao, for the opportunity to serve. I first saw the image of Heaven opening up. The clouds parted and I saw Heaven and the Divine. I saw the Divine's heart in front of the book. I saw a strong bright light radiating from the Divine's heart to the book. All of Heaven has witnessed this. There was a great celebration in Heaven. Many holy beings and saints are having a procession with banners and musical instruments.

When the blessing started there was an explosion of light coming out from the book to all of us, engulfing each one totally in the intense light. It feels very good. It feels very pleasant. It gives us all the feeling of connectivity with the Divine. It is as though wan ling rong he *(all souls join as one) is instantly manifested with this blessing.*

I then asked Master G. K. to do a direct soul communication with the Divine.

My dear son Zhi Gang Sha,

Thank you for all of your great prayers. Thank you for all of your great compassion for humanity. Your prayers I will fulfill by giving you this present to serve humanity; to help them overcome Mother Earth's transition time and help them to be more aligned with Heaven and Mother Earth; to be aware of Soul Power; to be aware that they have to be total GOLD with me: gratitude, obedience, loyalty, and devotion. This is an important time and I am happy to reward you with the tools to do so.

You are blessed beyond any words.
Thank you. Thank you. Thank you.

I then asked Master Cynthia to share her experience with the download and blessing of Divine Healing Hands.
She shared:

As Master Sha started to download the Divine Healing Hands, I saw many levels of Heaven open up. All stood still for that moment. This moment has never been experienced on Mother Earth at any time, so the significance of this was such that even the souls in the Soul World were witnessing and experiencing.

The Divine was seated in a very special chair or throne. There came out to him the book Divine Healing Hands. *This book has been placed in a very special place in the Akashic Records. As Master Sha gave the Divine Order, I heard and saw all of Mother Earth and beyond shake.*

The frequency and vibration has changed for all souls at inner levels whether they realize it at a mental or conscious level or not. The love, light, and compassion that will be spread from this book will awaken the heart and soul like never before.

Once this book received the download, the Divine said the following:

My dear beloved Zhi Gang,
I thank you for being the leader and my special chosen servant to bring my divine soul healing hands to human-

ity. Many have walked upon Mother Earth with many abilities to heal, but this is the first time that my Divine Healing Hands have been given to the masses.

You have stepped on the path and have bravely taken the steps to bring my Divine Healing Hands to humanity through this book. The power and significance of this cannot be ignored or diminished. The power and significance of what humanity and the chosen ones will receive is far beyond their own comprehension. This is indeed needed for the transition that is happening with Mother Earth, but it is also needed for the transition that is taking place with every soul upon Mother Earth.

My Divine Healing Hands will awaken what has been asleep within the soul, heart, mind, and body.

My Divine Healing Hands will bring healing to the soul, heart, mind, and body of humanity, Mother Earth, and all universes.

My Divine Healing Hands will unite hearts and souls together.

I thank you, my dear son Zhi Gang, for taking a part of my essence, my hands, which are filled with love and light, to all who will read this book.

Today is a day of celebration not only here in Heaven and in the Soul World, but for all of humanity.

I thank you.

I love you.

I am your loving Divine.

Then I asked the participants in Vancouver who were in the Opening Spiritual Channels workshop with Master Peter

Hudoba and Master G. K. Khoe to share their experiences of the Divine Healing Hands being downloaded to this book.

A. V. shared:

> When the power was transmitted into the book I saw a tremendous amount of golden light coming upon a big book. The light that is in the book is in the form of a large sphere of golden light. That light has intelligence, wisdom, love, and compassion. The light that is in the book will always be in the book. It is meant to heal and ground people. It brings light to everyone. It was spectacular to witness.

The second participant to share was Marina Hubbard:

> I witnessed a brilliant golden light coming into the book. There was an explosion of light that was so beautiful. The light was already traveling to the book even though it has not been published yet. The light went in many directions. I saw the pages of the book and they had an immense amount of love and light. At that moment something touched my heart. It is the Divine's love and light that we have all been searching for.
>
> We are so blessed to have such a compassionate teacher as Master Sha and such a generous Divine who is always giving and loving. Moments later, I realized that the love and light extended beyond the book, and I saw joy coming from Heaven to all who will be touched by this book. I am grateful for the opportunity to share what I experienced.

I thanked Master Peter, Master G. K., Master Cynthia, A. V., and Marina for sharing their Third Eye images and direct soul communications from the Divine.

I transmitted the Divine Healing Hands to this book during a soul communication workshop. This was a great opportunity for everybody to communicate with the Divine and to share their Third Eye images and direct soul communications from the Divine.

APPLY DIVINE HEALING HANDS FOR HEALING

This is the first time for everyone in the Vancouver workshop and for you and every reader to apply the Divine Healing Hands downloaded to this book for healing and blessing.

I always teach you to apply the Four Power Techniques to do any self-healing and to offer soul healing to others.

Body Power. Dear reader, please sit up straight. This is the first time you are applying the Divine Healing Hands within this book to offer you a soul healing and blessing for your request. Close your eyes. Connect with the Divine Healing Hands in this book.

Soul Power. Say *hello*. You can ask for soul healing for your physical body, for example, back pain, knee pain, a stiff neck, or any part of the body that needs healing;

or

You can ask for soul healing for your emotional body. For example, you can ask for healing of depression, anxiety, fear, anger, worry, grief, guilt, or more;

or

You can ask for soul healing for your mental body, including mental confusion, poor memory, or even for mental disorders;

or

You can ask for soul healing of your heart and soul, including opening the heart and soul and blessing the heart and soul;

or

You can ask for soul healing for your relationships. Silently ask Divine Healing Hands to bless the relationship between you and another person (silently mention his or her name);

or

You can ask for a blessing for your business and finances;

or

You can ask for a blessing to find a new job or career;

or

You can ask for a blessing to increase your intelligence.

In one sentence:

**You can ask Divine Healing Hands
to bless any aspect of your life.**

Everyone could have a different request. Divine Healing Hands downloaded to this book will offer a soul healing blessing to serve your unique request.

Everyone silently request:

> *Dear Divine Healing Hands downloaded to this book,*
> *Please offer me a soul healing or blessing for* _____
>   (silently make your request).

The most important sentence to say silently to the Divine Healing Hands is:

Dear Divine Healing Hands, please give me the soul healing and blessing that is appropriate for me at this time.

Thank you.

Divine Healing Hands are the Divine's soul healing hands. When you say the above sentence, Divine Healing Hands hear. The Divine hears. Divine Healing Hands Soul Healers have a special line of light with the Divine. When you ask Divine Healing Hands to offer any soul healing and blessing, the Divine will be aware of it through this special light line connection.

Therefore, anyone who requests a soul healing from Divine Healing Hands, and every Divine Healing Hands Soul Healer, must say this sentence before receiving the soul healing or before offering the Divine Healing Hands soul healing blessing to others. Remember this wisdom.

Never force the soul healing or blessing by saying *you must heal* or *you must transform*. This is disrespectful. Divine Healing Hands and the Divine will offer the appropriate soul healing and blessing that is the best healing or blessing for the request. For chronic and life-threatening conditions, it does take time to restore health. Requesting the appropriate soul healing and blessing each time you request a Divine Healing Hands soul healing blessing, or each time you offer one to someone else, is a *must*.

There are a few possible responses to receiving a soul healing and blessing either from Divine Healing Hands in this book or from a Divine Healing Hands Soul Healer.

One could experience:

- instant heart-touching and moving results, including a soul healing miracle

- significant improvement
- little improvement
- no improvement

Irrespective of the results, always close the blessing by saying *Thank you. Thank you. Thank you.* This is showing proper spiritual courtesy to the Divine and Divine Healing Hands.

If you do not feel any improvement, it does not mean that nothing happened. According to my teaching of Soul Mind Body Medicine, the Soul Power Series, and the Divine Power Series, all sickness is due to soul mind body blockages.

Divine Healing Hands remove soul mind body blockages. For chronic conditions, life-threatening conditions, and serious challenges with relationships and finances, Divine Healing Hands could remove soul mind body blockages partially. It could take several more Divine Healing Hands blessings to see noticeable improvement. Therefore, if you did not feel any improvement, it does not mean there is no progress. There is an ancient saying:

病来如山倒; 病去如抽丝
Bing lai ru shan dao, bing qu ru chou si

"Bing" means *sickness*. "Lai" means *to come*. "Ru" means *just like*. "Shan" means *mountain*. "Dao" means *to fall*. "Qu" means *to leave*. "Chou si" means *spin silk*.

"Bing lai ru shan dao, bing qu ru chou si" (pronounced *bing lye roo shahn dow, bing chü roo cho sz*) means *sickness comes like a mountain falling; sickness leaves like spinning silk.* This tells us that sickness can come suddenly and could be very serious, just like a mountain falling. But to have sickness leave can be a slow process, just like spinning silk.

This teaches us to be patient when doing self-healing. When you receive soul healing from Divine Healing Hands, or when you offer a Divine Healing Hands soul healing to others, be patient. Do not expect anyone to be healed instantly. Chronic and life-threatening conditions can take time to heal, but miracle healings could happen right away.

It does not matter whether you are healed instantly or receive significant improvement, little improvement, or no perceptible change. It is always important to show gratitude from your heart to the Divine and Divine Healing Hands. Blockages could have been present for a very long time. They could be very strong. Healing could take time. Know that the Divine and Divine Healing Hands always heal and bless you unconditionally as appropriate.

Let us continue with the Divine Healing Hands blessing from the book.

Mind Power. Visualize golden light shining continuously in the area of your request.

Sound Power. Chant repeatedly, silently or aloud:

> *Divine Healing Hands heal and bless me. Thank you.*
> *Divine Healing Hands heal and bless me. Thank you.*
> *Divine Healing Hands heal and bless me. Thank you.*
> *Divine Healing Hands heal and bless me. Thank*
> *you . . .*

When you invoke the Divine Healing Hands and chant, Divine Healing Hands will come out from this book to you to serve your request for soul healing and blessing.

For the Vancouver workshop participants, Divine Healing Hands will now come out from the computer where this book is stored. This book is a carrier of Divine Healing Hands that will come to you to offer soul healing and blessing.

Everyone in the workshop, silently make your request and receive the blessing. We will spend ten minutes in silence to receive a major blessing from Divine Healing Hands. Then I will ask five participants to share their experiences. I will also ask the three Divine Channels, Master Peter, Master G. K., and Master Cynthia, to share their experiences. Everyone, start to receive the blessings now.

You can also make a request for Divine Healing Hands to open your spiritual channels. You can request this now.

We remained silent for ten minutes while the Divine Healing Hands in the book offered soul healing blessings to each workshop participant.

Hao! You are extremely blessed.

Now I would like to have the three Divine Channels and four students share their experience of this blessing.

Master Peter:

> *Thank you, Master Sha, Divine, and Divine Healing Hands. I asked for a soul healing blessing for the cough I have had for two days. I feel healthy, but am coughing. In front of me I saw an enormous soul and exquisite light came pouring into every cell of my body. I also saw light coming to every participant in the workshop. My body feels light and very pleasant. I do not know how it has affected my cough, but at the moment I feel great!*
>
> *I am extremely honored to have received this blessing. We are all very blessed.*

Sara Baker:

I asked for a blessing for my spiritual journey. I saw a brief image. It was symbolic. I was watching myself walking down a road. It represented my many lifetimes ahead. Suddenly I saw so many holy beings helping me and removing blocks to help me move forward in my journey. I felt so blessed and loved that this help will be with me always.

I am so very grateful. Thank you.

Master G. K.:

Thank you, Master Sha, Divine, and Divine Healing Hands. I cannot thank you enough.

I was almost knocked out. I asked for a blessing for my knees. I saw blinding light coming to every cell and DNA, and not only in my knees. I was expanded and engulfed with that bright light and it makes me feel transformed from head to toe, skin to bone. I am hot. I am vibrating. I almost did not know where I was when the blessing ended.

Thank you so much for this exquisite special blessing. We are really truly blessed beyond words. I cannot thank you enough, Master Sha.

Thank you, Divine and Divine Healing Hands.

Karen McGuire:

I saw tremendous light pouring from the heavens. It started before the blessing started. It was like snowflakes

*and little Divine Healing Hands, and went to every part
of my body. It went to my soul journey with many tablets,
like Moses's tablets ahead of my own soul journey.*

I melted into the journey.

Master Cynthia:

*Thank you, Master Sha, Divine, and Divine Healing
Hands.*

*I did not ask for anything specific, as I requested what-
ever I needed that was appropriate for my spiritual body,
mental body, emotional body, and physical body.*

*I then saw Divine Healing Hands that were huge.
The light was so blinding. I first felt something taking
place in my Message Center, and then heat was within my
whole spinal column going up to my head. The frequency
and vibration were so high that they totally knocked
me out.*

*I, as Master G. K. shared, felt like I was not even in
my body, that I was taken out, and then slowly brought
back into my body when Master Sha said, "Hao!"*

*I am very grateful for what has been received. I am
grateful and thankful to Master Sha, the Divine, and
Divine Healing Hands. Hao!*

Magdalena A. Blatchford:

*I am very, very honored and profoundly touched to the
bottom of my heart with deep appreciation.*

*I am left speechless for what I have experienced. Prior
to this experience we were connecting heart to heart and*

soul to soul. My body was stretching and growing. I was preparing for Divine Healing Hands to bless my soul, so that the heart of my soul would be open.

As I requested the blessing I saw a beautiful, beautiful light coming from the Divine Healing Hands. It was rainbow colored.

I am profoundly grateful to the Divine, to Divine Healing Hands, and to you, Master Sha, for bringing this to humanity. I commit myself to be an unconditional servant.

As I opened more and more and saw my soul's heart opening, I felt a deeper level of compassion. As I delved into the realm of that compassion I almost disappeared. I have no more words to express my experience of this blessing. Thank you from the bottom of my heart.

A. V.:

It was absolutely beautiful to connect with the power. I asked for a healing for my heart, because I have had some palpitations and discomfort with my heart. Once I connected with the power, right away a tremendous, powerful rain of light came upon my heart. It was powerful but not invasive.

There were many golden and white hands fixing my heart. The light was nourishing. The discomfort disappeared. It was comfortable, peaceful, and grounding.

Thank you so much.

Before the next student shared, I thought of two psychologists from Victoria, British Columbia. Almost immediately one of them appeared on my computer through the Internet video.

What I want to share with you and humanity is that in the spiritual journey what you think is what could happen. Everybody can gain these abilities. For the last few years, I have experienced many times that what I think is what happens. Now I have witnessed more and more that when I think about a healing, the healing happens. The result is beyond words, comprehension, and imagination.

What is the secret? I can summarize in one sentence:

To gain the abilities of "what you think is what happens" is to offer unconditional universal service to humanity; the more service you offer, the more abilities will appear.

I said, *Now, sir, could you introduce yourself and share your experience?*

Mark E. Jackman:

> *I am a master of psychology and my wife is a doctor of psychology. I have been doing this work for a very long time. I am often perceived as a doctor.*
>
> *I asked for Divine Healing Hands to remove my anxiety about work and financial responsibilities. My mind disappeared when the Divine Healing Hands came. The room was flooded with light and we are still all bathed in the light.*
>
> *The feeling of divine generosity—huge divine generosity—is all that I can say is flooding me and everyone here.*

I then said, *Can I ask your wife to share?*
Dr. Mary Louise Reilly:

> *Thank you, Divine Healing Hands, for such a powerful gift.*
>
> *I did not know what to begin to ask for. Then I asked for three things and then I turned it over to the Divine. Then Master Sha said you can request the Divine Healing Hands to open your spiritual channels and I asked for opening of the Message Center.*
>
> *I saw violet light coming into my eyes. I felt blockages and my body moving a lot, uncontrollably. It was jerking a lot. I felt blockages being removed. I felt filled with light and filled with love. I also had a sense of not being here, emptiness.*
>
> *There was so much love and gratitude. Thank you, Master Sha, Divine Healing Hands, and Divine.*

During the doctor's sharing, I heard that there were five souls in this group that said *I want to share something also.* If you had this thought, please come up and confirm.
Marina Hubbard:

> *A moment ago when we received the Divine Healing Hands blessing from the book, I left it up to the Divine to decide what was best for me. I felt a tornado moving through my hands and different parts of the body in positive, powerful, and unexpected ways.*
>
> *Master Sha mentioned that we could request a blessing to open our spiritual channels. I immediately thought it would be wonderful. I started to see images in my Third*

Eye. Not all of them were pleasant. There were images of my past coming forward. I felt nothing but love, safety, and forgiveness with this light, and I realized how important it is to remember the Divine in our actions, thoughts, and words. We can be impactful in how we can help others.

I am thankful for the healing and the learning that came through the healing. I am grateful that all souls will have a chance to connect with healing through the Divine Healing Hands *book.*

Master G. K.:

I feel my heart and whole being are being engulfed and transformed with the teaching and the blessing. I remembered suddenly the ancient proverb of Yin shui si yuan, *which means "Drink water, remember the source." This proverb teaches one to always be grateful to whoever delivers the profound teaching, wisdom, blessings, and nourishment. When I was young my father taught me the calligraphy and the teaching of that saying. Now I remembered it.*

I have so much gratitude for all of this. I cannot thank you enough, Master Sha, Divine, and Tao. Countless bowdowns.

Magdalena A. Blatchford:

I would like to ask for forgiveness from the bottom of my heart. There are so many times that I see beautiful images and part of me keeps quiet.

During the November 2011 Tao II Retreat in Niagara

Falls, Canada, my heart was pounding. I saw this amazing image of your physical body growing so big and huge, Master Sha. Out of your body this beautiful arm started growing and growing to the point that the arm was no longer a human arm or hand. It was embracing everyone and beyond the retreat and hotel. I felt so immensely blessed, cocooned, loved, and held. I felt in that moment that all of humanity would be held with your arms. I felt safe.

Today I wanted to express that long before the Divine Healing Hands blessing, everyone's hands in the room grew and came more and more together. Eventually everyone's hands became one huge hand and this hand came your way and into the book. Out of that came a rainbow light toward us.

What can I say? There are no words to describe the magnificent treasures from the Divine and Tao. It is beyond words and explanation that this magnificent gift of Divine Healing Hands is given to humanity. Thank you so much. Even the words thank you *are not enough. Infinite gratitude. I do feel safe. Thank you.*

Participant:

I was keeping my eyes closed the whole time because the light is so immense, beautiful, and filled with love. When we received the blessing, I asked for a blessing for a special person and a relationship. I had my eyes closed and this person's face showed up. Then members of my family showed up strong also.

It is because I am having difficulty at home—not me personally, but there is disharmony in the family. I sud-

denly went into divine forgiveness and I started to chant divine forgiveness. It was about blessing relationships and forgiveness.

Thank you very much.

Adrian V.:

I initially asked for a healing for my neck. My neck was very stiff and had a lot of pain. I think it was purification because it was very, very stiff. Even before Master Sha said "healing start," I felt the pain being released.

When Master Sha said that we could ask for a blessing to open our spiritual channels, I thought it was good but I did not want to cheat and ask for two blessings.

I saw a laser going into the middle of my spine and something was removed. It was like a surgery. Also blockages were being removed from my Third Eye. Then it came to my neck and performed the same operation.

Thank you.

I thank the three masters and all of the people who shared their experiences.

Now I am going to offer two minutes of Divine Healing Hands and Tao Song together to open your spiritual channels.

There are four spiritual channels. They are:

- Soul Language Channel
- Direct Soul Communication Channel
- Third Eye Channel
- Direct Knowing Channel

Silently request what you wish to open.

Dear every reader, when you read to this point, please stop reading. These two minutes of Divine Healing Hands and Tao Song blessings will be stored in this book. You can receive the blessings also.

Totally relax.

>*Dear everyone, I am offering Divine Healing Hands and Tao Song for opening your spiritual channels for two minutes. Start!*

(I sing a Soul Song to open everyone's spiritual channels.)
Master Peter translates my Tao Song:

Dear our beloved son, Zhi Gang Sha,

>*This blessing is the most extraordinary blessing. This blessing has opened the soul, heart, mind, and body of all participants in this workshop and every reader.*

>*You have received enormous amounts of virtue to open your spiritual channels, an amount of virtue beyond your comprehension. To share is to serve. Serve a little, receive a little blessing. Serve more, receive more blessing. Serve unconditionally, receive unlimited blessing.*

>*We are so grateful to our son, Zhi Gang Sha, who brings this special mission to humanity. We are also very grateful to all students who support this divine mission. We are very grateful to every reader who experiences Divine Healing Hands to open your spiritual channels and to receive healing and blessing for every aspect of your life.*

*We always support everyone and bless everyone. You
are most loved and most blessed.
Your loving Divine.*

I will offer teaching and practices to apply Divine Healing
Hands to open your spiritual channels in chapter 7 of this book.
You will receive more blessings to open your spiritual channels.

In the next chapter I will lead you and every reader to do
more practices by applying Divine Healing Hands for boosting
energy, stamina, vitality, and immunity, and for rejuvenation and
longevity. Remember the teaching earlier in this book: do not
skip the practices. That would be a mistake.

Apply Divine Healing Hands to Boost Energy, Stamina, Vitality, and Immunity, and for Rejuvenation and Longevity

THIS IS A very unique book. This book carries Divine Healing Hands. Divine Healing Hands carry divine frequency and vibration with divine love, forgiveness, compassion, and light.

I emphasize this significant teaching again and again in all the books of my Soul Power Series as well as in all of my workshops and retreats:

- Divine Healing Hands carry divine frequency and vibration that can transform the frequency and vibration of all life, including health, relationships, finances, intelligence, and every aspect of all life.

- Divine Healing Hands carry divine love that melts all blockages and transforms all life.
- Divine Healing Hands carry divine forgiveness that brings inner joy and inner peace to all life.
- Divine Healing Hands carry divine compassion that boosts energy, stamina, vitality, and immunity of all life.
- Divine Healing Hands carry divine light that heals, prevents sickness, purifies and rejuvenates the soul, heart, mind, and body, and transforms health, relationships, finances, intelligence, and every aspect of life.
- Divine Healing Hands are divine sacred treasures to bring love, peace, and harmony to humanity, Mother Earth, Heaven, and countless planets, stars, galaxies, and universes.

In this chapter we will apply Divine Healing Hands to boost energy, stamina, vitality, and immunity, and for rejuvenation and longevity.

The two most important areas in the body for boosting energy, stamina, vitality, and immunity are the kundalini and Lower Dan Tian.

Develop the Kundalini

In ancient Chinese wisdom there is a very important energy center named Snow Mountain Area. This is a Buddhist term. In Taoist teaching it is named *golden urn*. In yoga it is named *kundalini*. In traditional Chinese medicine it is named *Ming*

Men area. "Ming" means *life*. "Men" means *gate*. "Ming Men" means *life gate*. The Ming Men area is divided into Ming Men fire and Ming Men water.

Millions of people suffer from hypertension or diabetes. Millions of women suffer from menopause. In traditional Chinese medicine, hypertension, diabetes, and menopause may be caused by insufficient Ming Men water. Some people may think that they should drink more water to correct the condition. This is not the case. Drinking more water will not correct the condition. You have to do special spiritual and energy practices or ingest proper herbs or other remedies to nourish the Ming Men water in order to balance Ming Men water.

If you do the next practice I will share with you, it could greatly assist you to heal hypertension, diabetes, menopause, and many other unhealthy conditions. There are so many sicknesses that are caused by insufficient Ming Men water or insufficient Ming Men fire.

Insufficient Ming Men fire can cause fatigue, cold extremities, sexual dysfunction, and issues within the reproductive system, urinary system, back, legs, and much more.

Increasing Ming Men fire and Ming Men water in order to balance them is the key for healing many sicknesses and for rejuvenation and longevity.

Here is how to locate the kundalini, which is the Ming Men area:

Make a straight line from your navel directly to your back. Divide this line into three equal parts. Go back two-thirds of the way from your navel and then go down 2.5 *cun* (one *cun* equals the width of the thumb joint). This is the center of the kundalini, which is a fist-sized area. See figure 3.

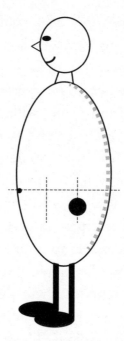

Figure 3. Location of kundalini/Ming Men area

The power and significance of the kundalini are as follows:

- Kundalini is the Ming Men area, which includes Ming Men fire and Ming Men water. Ming Men fire is the most important yang in the whole body. Ming Men water is the most important yin in the whole body.
- Kundalini is the key energy center for nourishing the kidneys.
- Kundalini provides energy food for the brain and Third Eye.
- Kundalini is a key center for rejuvenation and longevity.
- Kundalini is the prenatal energy center.

I will now lead you to develop your kundalini. Apply the Four Power Techniques:

Body Power. Sit up straight. Close your eyes. Place the tip of your tongue gently against the roof of your mouth. Place one palm over the navel and the other palm over the kundalini.

Soul Power. Say *hello*:

> *Dear soul mind body of my kundalini,*
> *I love you.*
> *You have the power to balance my Ming Men fire*
> *   and Ming Men water; nourish my kidneys;*
> *   brain; and Third Eye; rejuvenate my soul, heart,*
> *   mind, and body; and prolong my life.*
> *Do a good job.*
> *Thank you.*

On December 7, 2010, I received the Divine Love Peace Harmony Rainbow Light Ball[1] in India. The Divine created this priceless treasure for healing humanity, Mother Earth, and all universes. You can invoke this sacred divine treasure to develop your kundalini.

> *Dear Divine Love Peace Harmony Rainbow Light*
> *   Ball,*
> *I love you, honor you, and appreciate you.*

---

1. The Divine released this divine gift to humanity through Master Sha. Read more about this divine treasure and how to apply it in *Divine Love Peace Harmony Rainbow Light Ball: Transform You, Humanity, Mother Earth, and All Universes,* Heaven's Library Publication Corp., 2010 (available on www.DrSha.com).

Please come to my kundalini to develop my kundalini.
I am extremely grateful.
Please offer my kundalini a soul healing blessing as ap-
  propriate.
Thank you.

Mind Power. Visualize the Divine Love Peace Harmony Rainbow Light Ball rotating in your kundalini and radiating rainbow-colored light to your kidneys, spinal column, brain, and Third Eye.

Sound Power. Chant silently or aloud:

Develop my kundalini. Thank you.
Develop my kundalini. Thank you.
Develop my kundalini. Thank you.
Develop my kundalini. Thank you . . .

Divine Love Peace Harmony Rainbow Light Ball
  boosts my kundalini power. Thank you.
Divine Love Peace Harmony Rainbow Light Ball
  boosts my kundalini power. Thank you.
Divine Love Peace Harmony Rainbow Light Ball
  boosts my kundalini power. Thank you.
Divine Love Peace Harmony Rainbow Light Ball
  boosts my kundalini power. Thank you . . .

Put the book down and chant for fifteen minutes now. If you have chronic or life-threatening conditions related to the kundalini, chant two hours or more per day. The longer you chant and the more you chant, the better the results you could receive. Add all of your practice time together to total two hours or more per day.

I have thousands of students all over the world with all kinds of challenges. Thousands of soul healing miracles have happened in the last nine years since I was chosen as a divine servant, vehicle, and channel in July 2003. In recent years, the important divine teaching has been emphasized: **Chant two hours or more per day for chronic and life-threatening conditions.**

When people follow this guidance seriously, I have witnessed remarkable healing results and transformation in front of my eyes. When people do not follow the guidance, it truly affects their healing results. Soul healing works but one must follow the guidance.

Apply Divine Healing Hands to Develop the Kundalini

Now I will lead you to develop your kundalini by applying the Divine Healing Hands downloaded to this book. The Divine has guided me that the *first* time you do the following kundalini-boosting practice by applying the Divine Healing Hands downloaded to this book, it will *not* count toward the twenty times you can experience the power of the Divine Healing Hands within this book. However, the second (and any subsequent) time you use the Divine Healing Hands in this book to do the following practice *will* count toward the twenty times you can experience the power of Divine Healing Hands within this book.

I strongly suggest that each time you apply the Divine Healing Hands within this book, spend at least a half-hour practicing, because the Divine has guided me clearly that you cannot continue to use the Divine Healing Hands treasures in this book more than twenty times. Therefore, apply the Divine Healing

Hands within this book twenty times and practice for as long as you can each time to gain the greatest benefits. After that, you will need to connect with a Divine Healing Hands Soul Healer or one of my Worldwide Representatives to receive Divine Healing Hands blessings or to apply to receive Divine Healing Hands yourself.

Apply the Four Power Techniques:

Body Power. Sit up straight. Close your eyes. Place the tip of your tongue gently against the roof of your mouth. Place one palm over your navel and the other palm over your kundalini.

Soul Power. Say *hello:*

> *Dear Divine Healing Hands,*
> *I love you.*
> *You have the power to develop my kundalini.*
> *I am very grateful.*
> *Please offer an appropriate soul healing blessing to*
>   *develop my kundalini.*
> *Thank you.*

Mind Power. Visualize golden light shining in your kundalini area.

Sound Power. Chant silently or aloud:

> *Divine Healing Hands develop my kundalini.*
>   *Thank you.*
> *Divine Healing Hands develop my kundalini.*
>   *Thank you.*

Divine Healing Hands develop my kundalini.
Thank you.
Divine Healing Hands develop my kundalini.
Thank you . . .

Chant for as long as you can. If this is the first or second time you are doing this practice using the Divine Healing Hands downloaded to this book, chant for at least a half-hour. The more you chant, the more benefits you will receive from Divine Healing Hands. The kundalini is a very important energy center in the body. You should chant a half-hour to one hour per day to build this key foundational energy center. This is especially true if you have any condition related to insufficient Ming Men fire or insufficient Ming Men water as described above.

Develop the Lower Dan Tian

"Dan" means *light ball*. "Tian" means *field*. "Dan Tian" (pronounced *dahn tyen*) means *light ball field*. Human beings have three Dan Tians in the body: lower, middle, and upper.

The Lower Dan Tian is centered 1.5 *cun* directly below the navel and 2.5 *cun* inside the body. It is a fist-sized energy center.

The Lower Dan Tian has great power and significance. It is the:

- key foundational energy center for energy, stamina, vitality, and immunity
- key for rejuvenation
- key for longevity
- postnatal energy center

I will now lead you to develop your Lower Dan Tian.

Apply the Four Power Techniques to develop the Lower Dan Tian:

Body Power. Sit up straight. Close your eyes. Place the tip of your tongue gently against the roof of your mouth. Place both hands in the Yin Yang Palm Hand Position[2] below the navel on the lower abdomen. See figure 4.

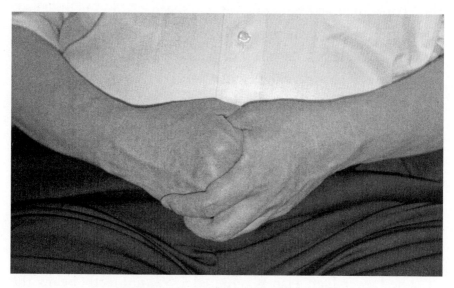

Figure 4. Yin Yang Palm Hand Position

Soul Power. Say *hello:*

> *Dear soul mind body of my Lower Dan Tian,*
> *I love you.*
> *You have the power to boost my energy, stamina, vital-*

---

2. Grip your left thumb with the fingers of your right hand and make a fist. Wrap all four fingers of the left hand over the right hand. Grip your left thumb with about 75–80 percent of your maximum strength. This is the Yin Yang Palm Hand Position.

ity, and immunity; rejuvenate my soul, heart, mind,
and body; and prolong my life.
Do a good job.
Thank you.

I will now offer a permanent divine treasure to every reader. I will offer Divine Purple Light Ball and Purple Liquid Spring of Divine Lower Dan Tian Soul Mind Body Transplants as a gift for the first time in any of my books.

Prepare!

Sit up straight. Close your eyes. Place the tip of your tongue gently against the roof of your mouth. Place your left hand over your Message Center (heart chakra) and your right hand in the traditional prayer position. This is called the Soul Light Era Prayer Position (figure 2).

Divine Order: Divine Purple Light Ball and Purple Liquid Spring of Divine Lower Dan Tian Soul Mind Body Transplants

Transmission!

Congratulations! You are extremely blessed. Humanity is extremely blessed.

Apply these divine treasures and the Four Power Techniques to boost your Lower Dan Tian power:

Soul Power. Say *hello:*

> *Dear Divine Purple Light Ball and Purple Liquid*
> *Spring of Divine Lower Dan Tian Soul Mind Body*
> *Transplants,*

I love you.
I am extremely honored to have received these priceless
divine treasures.
Please develop my Lower Dan Tian further and fur-
ther.
I cannot thank you enough.

Mind Power. Visualize the Divine Purple Light Ball and Purple Liquid Spring Lower Dan Tian Soul Mind Body Transplants rotating in your Lower Dan Tian.

Sound Power. Chant silently or aloud:

> *Divine Purple Light Ball and Purple Liquid Spring of*
> *Divine Lower Dan Tian Soul Mind Body Transplants*
> *boost my Lower Dan Tian power. Thank you.*
> *Divine Purple Light Ball and Purple Liquid Spring of*
> *Divine Lower Dan Tian Soul Mind Body Transplants*
> *boost my Lower Dan Tian power. Thank you.*
> *Divine Purple Light Ball and Purple Liquid Spring of*
> *Divine Lower Dan Tian Soul Mind Body Transplants*
> *boost my Lower Dan Tian power. Thank you.*
> *Divine Purple Light Ball and Purple Liquid Spring of*
> *Divine Lower Dan Tian Soul Mind Body Transplants*
> *boost my Lower Dan Tian power. Thank you . . .*

Put the book down and chant for fifteen minutes now.

The Lower Dan Tian is a very important foundational energy center for life. It is very important to spend a half-hour to one hour per practice to build the Lower Dan Tian. If you have chronic or life-threatening conditions, remember to chant two hours or more per day. The longer you chant and the more you chant, the better the results you could receive. You can add all of your practice time together to total two hours or more per day.

APPLY DIVINE HEALING HANDS TO DEVELOP
THE LOWER DAN TIAN

Now I will lead you to develop your Lower Dan Tian by applying the Divine Healing Hands downloaded to this book. As with the previous practice for the kundalini, the Divine has guided me that the *first* time you do the following Lower Dan Tian practice by applying the Divine Healing Hands downloaded to this book, it will *not* count toward the twenty times you can experience the power of the Divine Healing Hands within this book. However, the second (and any subsequent) time you use the Divine Healing Hands in this book to do the following practice *will* count toward the twenty times you can experience the power of Divine Healing Hands within this book.

I strongly suggest that each time you apply the Divine Healing Hands within this book, spend at least a half-hour practicing because the Divine has guided me clearly that you cannot continue to use the Divine Healing Hands treasures in this book more than twenty times. Therefore, apply the Divine Healing Hands within this book twenty times and practice for as long as you can each time to gain the greatest benefits. After that, you will need to connect with a Divine Healing Hands Soul Healer or one of my Worldwide Representatives to receive Divine Healing Hands blessings or to apply to receive Divine Healing Hands yourself.

Apply the Four Power Techniques:

Body Power. Sit up straight. Close your eyes. Place the tip of your tongue gently against the roof of your mouth. Place both hands in the Yin Yang Palm Hand Position on the lower abdomen (figure 4).

Soul Power. Say *hello:*

> *Dear Divine Healing Hands,*
> *I love you.*
> *You have the power to develop my Lower Dan Tian.*
> *I am very grateful.*
> *Please offer my Lower Dan Tian a soul healing bless-*
>   *ing as appropriate.*
> *Thank you.*

Mind Power. Visualize golden light shining in and around the Lower Dan Tian.

Sound Power. Chant silently or aloud:

> *Divine Healing Hands develop my Lower Dan Tian.*
>   *Thank you.*
> *Divine Healing Hands develop my Lower Dan Tian.*
>   *Thank you.*
> *Divine Healing Hands develop my Lower Dan Tian.*
>   *Thank you.*
> *Divine Healing Hands develop my Lower Dan Tian.*
>   *Thank you . . .*

Chant for as long as you can. If this is the first or second time you are doing this practice using the Divine Healing Hands downloaded to this book, chant for at least a half-hour. The longer you chant and the more you chant, the more benefits you will receive from the Divine Healing Hands.

Divine Sacred Circle for Healing All Sicknesses

In traditional Chinese medicine there is a most important yin yang circle in the body. This circle includes the Ren meridian and Du meridian. The Ren meridian starts from the genital area and flows up the front midline of the body to the face. It is the most important yin meridian. The Du meridian also starts from the genital area and flows up the back midline of the body to and over the top of the head and then down to the face. It is the most important yang meridian. The Ren meridian and Du meridian join as a circle.

In traditional Chinese medicine, sickness is caused by an imbalance of yin and yang. To balance the Ren and Du meridians is to balance yin and yang. This is a key to healing all sickness.

The Ren meridian includes the meridians of the yin organs: liver, heart, spleen, lungs, kidneys, and pericardium. The Du meridian includes the meridians of the yang organs: gallbladder, small intestine, stomach, large intestine, urinary bladder, and San Jiao (pronounced *sahn jee-yow*).

The World Health Organization standard name for the San Jiao is Triple Energizer. In traditional teaching it is called *Triple Heater, Triple Warmer,* or *Triple Burner.* The San Jiao is the pathway of qi and bodily fluids. San Jiao represents three areas inside the body: Upper Jiao, Middle Jiao, and Lower Jiao. The Upper Jiao is the space in the body above the diaphragm; it includes the heart, lungs, and brain. The Middle Jiao is the space in the body between the diaphragm and the level of the navel; it includes the liver, gallbladder, pancreas, stomach, and spleen. The Lower Jiao is the space in the body from the level of the navel down to the genital area; it includes the small and large intestines, urinary bladder, kidneys, reproductive organs, and sexual organs.

In traditional Chinese medicine, if qi and bodily fluids flow in the San Jiao, one is healthy. If the qi and bodily fluids do not flow in the San Jiao, one is sick.

The Ren and Du meridians form a vital circle in traditional Chinese medicine (TCM). One of the most important principles of TCM is to balance yin and yang. TCM uses Chinese herbs, acupuncture, and tui na (Chinese massage) to balance yin and yang. To balance the Ren and Du meridians is the key for healing in TCM because this balances yin and yang.

Traditional Chinese medicine began five thousand years ago. It has served billions of people in history. On May 8, 2008, the Divine gave me a sacred circle to balance yin and yang for healing all sicknesses. This sacred circle is named *Divine Inner Yin Yang Circle.*

This sacred circle starts from the Hui Yin (pronounced *hway yeen*) acupuncture point, which is located on the perineum between the genitals and anus. "Hui" means *accumulation.* "Yin" means *message energy matter of yin.* The Hui Yin acupuncture point gathers the soul, mind, and body of the yin of the entire body. It is the vital acupuncture point for healing all sickness. The sacred Divine Inner Yin Yang Circle flows from the Hui Yin up through the seven Soul Houses[3] in the center of the body to the top of the head, and flows down in front of the spinal column. See figure 5.

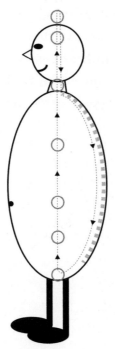

Figure 5. Divine Inner Yin Yang Circle

The Divine told me that this is the *inner* yin yang circle. The Ren and Du meridian circle in TCM is the *outer* yin yang circle. The relationship between the inner yin yang circle and the outer yin yang circle is: if the inner yin yang circle flows, the outer yin yang circle follows. See figure 6.

---

3. A human being lives in a house. Your beloved soul lives in your body. Your body is the house for your soul. There are seven Soul Houses where the soul can reside, which correspond to the chakras: at the bottom of the torso, in the lower abdomen, at the navel, in the center of the chest, in the throat, inside the brain, and on top of the head.

This inner yin yang circle includes the seven Soul Houses and Wai Jiao (pronounced *wye jee-yow*). The seven Soul Houses are also known as the seven energy chakras. The Wai Jiao was discovered in China by my spiritual mentor and father, Dr. and Master Zhi Chen Guo, after nearly fifty years of clinical research and practice with thousands of patients. The Wai Jiao is located in front of the spinal column and back ribs. It also extends up into the head. It is the biggest space inside the body.

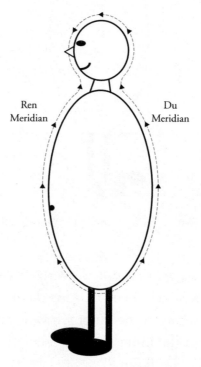

Figure 6. Outer Yin Yang Circle

The Wai Jiao and San Jiao connect. The San Jiao is like a river. The Wai Jiao is like the ocean. The river flows to the ocean. Blockages in the San Jiao that cause sickness will flow horizontally to the Wai Jiao. For example, if one has health issues in the heart, the related energy blockages will move from the Upper Jiao to the upper part of the Wai Jiao. Clearing soul mind body blockages in the Wai Jiao is the secret for healing all sickness.

How can you use this divine sacred inner yin yang circle to heal all sickness? I will lead you to do a practice now.

Body Power. Sit up straight. Close your eyes. Place the tip of your tongue gently against the roof of your mouth. If you are a male, sit with your left palm under the Hui Yin area, with fingers pointing backward. If you are a female, sit with your right palm under the Hui Yin area, with fingers pointing backward. Place your other palm on top of your head. See figure 7.

Figure 7. Body Power to develop the Divine Inner Yin Yang Circle

Soul Power. Say *hello:*

> *Dear my Divine Inner Yin Yang Circle,*
> *I love you.*
> *You have the power to heal all sickness.*
> *Do a good job.*
> *Thank you.*

> *Dear Divine Soul Song* Hei Heng Hong Ah Xi Yi
>   Weng You,[4]
> *I love you.*
> *Please remove soul mind body blockages in my seven*
>   *Soul Houses, Wai Jiao, and Divine Inner Yin Yang*
>   *Circle, which is the Divine Sacred Healing Circle.*
> *Please offer me a soul healing blessing as appropriate.*
> *I am extremely grateful.*
> *Thank you.*

Mind Power. Visualize golden light shining in the seven Soul Houses, Wai Jiao, and Divine Inner Yin Yang Circle.

Sound Power. Sing or chant silently or aloud:

> *Hei Heng Hong Ah Xi Yi Weng You* (pronounced *hey*
>   *hung hawng ah shee yee wung yoe*)
> *Hei Heng Hong Ah Xi Yi Weng You*
> *Hei Heng Hong Ah Xi Yi Weng You*
> *Hei Heng Hong Ah Xi Yi Weng You . . .*

---

4. See the fourth book in my Soul Power Series, *Divine Soul Songs: Sacred Practical Treasures to Heal, Rejuvenate, and Transform You, Humanity, Mother Earth, and All Universes,* pp. 117–119.

Put the book down and chant for five minutes now. Generally speaking, chant for three to five minutes per time, three to five times per day. If you have a chronic or life-threatening condition, remember to chant two hours or more per day. The longer you chant and the more you chant, the better the results you could receive. You can add all of your practice time together to total two hours or more per day.

APPLY DIVINE HEALING HANDS TO DEVELOP
THE SEVEN SOUL HOUSES, WAI JIAO,
AND DIVINE INNER YIN YANG CIRCLE

Now I will lead you to develop the seven Soul Houses, Wai Jiao, and Divine Inner Yin Yang Circle by applying the Divine Healing Hands downloaded to this book. Again, the Divine has guided me that the *first* time you apply the Divine Healing Hands within this book to do the following practice, it will *not* count toward the twenty times that you can use the Divine Healing Hands in this book. However, the second (and any subsequent) time you use the Divine Healing Hands in this book to do the following practice *will* count as one of the twenty times you can experience the power of the Divine Healing Hands in this book.

Body Power. Sit up straight. Close your eyes. Place the tip of your tongue gently against the roof of your mouth. Males, sit with your left palm under the Hui Yin area. Females, sit with your right palm under the Hui Yin area. Place the other palm on top of your head. (See figure 7.)

Soul Power. Say *hello:*

Dear Divine Healing Hands,
I love you.
You have the power to develop my seven Soul Houses,
    Wai Jiao, and Divine Inner Yin Yang Circle in
    order to heal all sickness.
Please offer a soul healing blessing as appropriate.
I am very grateful.
Thank you.

Mind Power. Visualize golden light from the Divine Healing Hands shining in the seven Soul Houses, Wai Jiao, and Divine Inner Yin Yang Circle.

Sound Power. Chant silently or aloud:

Divine Healing Hands clear soul mind body blockages
    in my seven Soul Houses, Wai Jiao, and Divine
    Inner Yin Yang Circle in order to heal all of my
    sicknesses. Thank you.
Divine Healing Hands clear soul mind body blockages
    in my seven Soul Houses, Wai Jiao, and Divine
    Inner Yin Yang Circle in order to heal all of my
    sicknesses. Thank you.
Divine Healing Hands clear soul mind body blockages
    in my seven Soul Houses, Wai Jiao, and Divine
    Inner Yin Yang Circle in order to heal all of my
    sicknesses. Thank you.
Divine Healing Hands clear soul mind body blockages
    in my seven Soul Houses, Wai Jiao, and Divine
    Inner Yin Yang Circle in order to heal all of my
    sicknesses. Thank you . . .

I emphasize again and again that you should chant for as long as you can. The longer you chant and the more you chant, the greater the benefits you will receive from Divine Healing Hands.

Divine Sacred Circle for Rejuvenation and Longevity

On May 8, 2008, the Divine also showed me the secret sacred circle for rejuvenation and longevity. The pathway of this sacred circle starts from the Hui Yin area. It moves toward the tailbone area, where there are two invisible holes. Energy flows along the circle through these two invisible holes to the spinal cord, and then up the spinal cord through the brain and to the top of the head. It then flows down through the seven Soul Houses in the center of the body, and finally back to the Hui Yin area and the Hui Yin acupuncture point in the perineum.

I will now lead you to develop the Divine Sacred Circle for Rejuvenation and Longevity. Apply the Four Power Techniques:

Body Power. Sit up straight. Close your eyes. Place the tip of your tongue gently against the roof of your mouth. Males, sit with your left palm under the Hui Yin area. Females, sit with your right palm under the Hui Yin area. Place the other palm on top of your head. (See figure 7.)

Soul Power. Say *hello*:

> *Dear Divine Sacred Circle for Rejuvenation and Longevity,*

I love you.
You have the power to rejuvenate my soul,
  heart, mind, and body and prolong my
  life.
I am very grateful.
Do a good job.
Thank you.

Dear Divine Soul Song You Weng Yi Xi Ah Hong
  Heng Hei,[5]
I love you.
Please activate my Divine Sacred Circle for Rejuvena-
  tion and Longevity.
I am extremely grateful.
Please offer me a soul healing blessing for rejuvenation
  and prolonging my life as appropriate.
Thank you.

Mind Power. Visualize golden light moving along the Divine Sacred Circle for Rejuvenation and Longevity—shining from the Hui Yin area to the tailbone, then up through the spinal cord and brain, and finally down through the seven Soul Houses and back to the Hui Yin area.

Sound Power. Sing or chant silently or aloud:

You Weng Yi Xi Ah Hong Heng Hei (pronounced *yoe*
  wung yee shee ah hawng hung hay)

---

5. See the fourth book in my Soul Power Series, *Divine Soul Songs: Sacred Practical Treasures to Heal, Rejuvenate, and Transform You, Humanity, Mother Earth, and All Universes*, p. 118.

You Weng Yi Xi Ah Hong Heng Hei
You Weng Yi Xi Ah Hong Heng Hei
You Weng Yi Xi Ah Hong Heng Hei . . .

Chant for as long as you can. The longer you chant and the more you chant, the better you can rejuvenate your soul, heart, mind, and body and prolong your life.

APPLY DIVINE HEALING HANDS TO DEVELOP
THE DIVINE SACRED CIRCLE FOR REJUVENATION
AND LONGEVITY

Now I will lead you to develop the Divine Sacred Circle for Rejuvenation and Longevity using the Divine Healing Hands downloaded to this book. The Divine has guided me that the *first* time you apply the Divine Healing Hands within this book to develop the Divine Sacred Circle for Rejuvenation and Longevity, it will *not* count toward the twenty times you can use the Divine Healing Hands downloaded to this book. However, the second (and any subsequent) time you use the Divine Healing Hands in this book to do the following practice *will* count toward the twenty times you can experience the power of Divine Healing Hands as a gift to readers of this book.

Body Power. Sit up straight. Close your eyes. Place the tip of your tongue gently against the roof of your mouth. Males, sit with your left palm under the Hui Yin area. Females, sit with your right palm under the Hui Yin area. Place the other palm on top of your head. (See figure 7.)

Soul Power. Say *hello:*

Dear Divine Healing Hands,
I love you.
You have the power to develop my Divine Sacred Cir-
*   cle for Rejuvenation and Longevity.*
I am very grateful.
Please offer a soul healing blessing to remove soul mind
*   body blockages in my Divine Sacred Circle for Reju-*
*   venation and Longevity as appropriate.*
Thank you.

Mind Power. Visualize golden light from the Divine Healing Hands shining around the entire Divine Sacred Circle for Rejuvenation and Longevity.

Sound Power. Chant silently or aloud:

Divine Healing Hands develop my Divine Sacred Cir-
*   cle for Rejuvenation and Longevity. I am so grateful.*
*   Thank you.*
Divine Healing Hands develop my Divine Sacred Cir-
*   cle for Rejuvenation and Longevity. I am so grateful.*
*   Thank you.*
Divine Healing Hands develop my Divine Sacred Cir-
*   cle for Rejuvenation and Longevity. I am so grateful.*
*   Thank you.*
Divine Healing Hands develop my Divine Sacred Cir-
*   cle for Rejuvenation and Longevity. I am so grateful.*
*   Thank you . . .*

Chant for as long as you can. Remember that the longer you chant and the more you chant, the greater the benefits you will receive from the Divine Healing Hands.

Millions of people worldwide need more energy, stamina, vitality, and immunity.

Millions of people are searching for rejuvenation and want to prolong their lives.

Practice and apply the Divine Inner Yin Yang Circle and Divine Sacred Circle for Rejuvenation and Longevity together. You can then receive healing, rejuvenation, and longevity at the same time. This is the way to practice:

Sing or chant silently or aloud for healing all sicknesses:

> *Hei Heng Hong Ah Xi Yi Weng You*
> *Hei Heng Hong Ah Xi Yi Weng You*
> *Hei Heng Hong Ah Xi Yi Weng You*
> *Hei Heng Hong Ah Xi Yi Weng You*

Then sing or chant for rejuvenation and longevity:

> *You Weng Yi Xi Ah Hong Heng Hei*
> *You Weng Yi Xi Ah Hong Heng Hei*
> *You Weng Yi Xi Ah Hong Heng Hei*
> *You Weng Yi Xi Ah Hong Heng Hei*

Continue to sing or chant the two sacred circles in alternation. Please spend at least ten minutes to sing or chant these two circles now. You could begin to feel their power. You can do this practice anytime, anywhere. You can sing or chant silently or aloud. Before you fall asleep you can sing or chant silently as you are lying in bed.[6] The moment you wake up you can sing or chant silently. You can sing or chant the two sacred circles

---

6. Always chant silently when lying down as chanting aloud while lying down drains your qi.

before and after meals. This is one of the most powerful daily practices. The Divine Inner Yin Yang Circle and Divine Sacred Circle for Rejuvenation and Longevity are treasures for humanity. Apply them often to experience their power and receive the benefits.

Thank you, Divine, for releasing these treasures to humanity. I wish millions and billions of people all over the world will receive great benefits by singing or chanting to promote the flow of these two sacred circles.

Sing or chant for ten minutes now:

Hei Heng Hong Ah Xi Yi Weng You
Hei Heng Hong Ah Xi Yi Weng You
Hei Heng Hong Ah Xi Yi Weng You
Hei Heng Hong Ah Xi Yi Weng You

You Weng Yi Xi Ah Hong Heng Hei
You Weng Yi Xi Ah Hong Heng Hei
You Weng Yi Xi Ah Hong Heng Hei
You Weng Yi Xi Ah Hong Heng Hei

Hei Heng Hong Ah Xi Yi Weng You
Hei Heng Hong Ah Xi Yi Weng You
Hei Heng Hong Ah Xi Yi Weng You
Hei Heng Hong Ah Xi Yi Weng You

You Weng Yi Xi Ah Hong Heng Hei
You Weng Yi Xi Ah Hong Heng Hei
You Weng Yi Xi Ah Hong Heng Hei
You Weng Yi Xi Ah Hong Heng Hei

Hei Heng Hong Ah Xi Yi Weng You
Hei Heng Hong Ah Xi Yi Weng You
Hei Heng Hong Ah Xi Yi Weng You
Hei Heng Hong Ah Xi Yi Weng You

You Weng Yi Xi Ah Hong Heng Hei
You Weng Yi Xi Ah Hong Heng Hei
You Weng Yi Xi Ah Hong Heng Hei
You Weng Yi Xi Ah Hong Heng Hei

Hei Heng Hong Ah Xi Yi Weng You
Hei Heng Hong Ah Xi Yi Weng You
Hei Heng Hong Ah Xi Yi Weng You
Hei Heng Hong Ah Xi Yi Weng You

You Weng Yi Xi Ah Hong Heng Hei
You Weng Yi Xi Ah Hong Heng Hei
You Weng Yi Xi Ah Hong Heng Hei
You Weng Yi Xi Ah Hong Heng Hei . . .

The practices in this chapter can help you and anyone who wants to boost energy, stamina, vitality, and immunity, as well as rejuvenate and prolong life.

Practice. Practice. Practice.

Benefit. Benefit. Benefit.

Boost your energy. Boost your energy. Boost your energy.

Boost your stamina. Boost your stamina. Boost your stamina.

Boost your vitality. Boost your vitality. Boost your vitality.

Boost your immunity. Boost your immunity. Boost your immunity.

Rejuvenate your soul, heart, mind, and body. Rejuvenate your soul, heart, mind, and body. Rejuvenate your soul, heart, mind, and body.

Prolong your life. Prolong your life. Prolong your life.

Hei Heng Hong Ah Xi Yi Weng You
Hei Heng Hong Ah Xi Yi Weng You
Hei Heng Hong Ah Xi Yi Weng You
Hei Heng Hong Ah Xi Yi Weng You

You Weng Yi Xi Ah Hong Heng Hei
You Weng Yi Xi Ah Hong Heng Hei
You Weng Yi Xi Ah Hong Heng Hei
You Weng Yi Xi Ah Hong Heng Hei

Apply Divine Healing Hands to Heal Human Beings

MILLIONS OF PEOPLE on Mother Earth are suffering with all kinds of sicknesses in their spiritual, mental, emotional, and physical bodies. I am extremely grateful that the Divine gives his soul healing hands to the chosen ones to remove the suffering of humanity.

Divine Healing Hands carry divine power for healing. They carry divine frequency and vibration that can transform the frequency and vibration of everyone and everything. There are not enough words to express the greatest gratitude to the Divine for the opportunity to receive Divine Healing Hands to assist humanity at this time. Anyone who has received Divine Healing Hands is extremely honored beyond comprehension.

The Divine Committee has told me that the Divine is planning to create two hundred thousand Divine Healing Hands Soul Healers on Mother Earth. After reaching this number, the Divine will no longer offer his soul healing hands to anyone else. Two hundred thousand chosen ones are the luckiest ones. They will assist humanity to pass through this difficult time on Mother Earth.

In this chapter you are going to learn, practice, and experience Divine Healing Hands to offer healing to your spiritual body, mental body, emotional body, and physical body. You will also read heart-touching and moving stories from people who have applied Divine Healing Hands in their lives and in the lives of others.

Spiritual Body

A human being has a spiritual body, a mental body, an emotional body, and a physical body. The spiritual body is the soul body. The important wisdom to share with you and humanity is that a human being has a body soul, souls of systems, souls of organs, and souls of cells. A cell includes cell units, DNA, RNA, and tiny matter. Every part of the cell has a soul. The spaces between the cells also have souls.

In conventional modern medicine there is a nerve chart. In traditional Chinese medicine there is a meridian chart. In my teaching of Soul Mind Body Medicine there is a soul chart. Scientists estimate that there are between eighty and one hundred twenty billion cells in a human being's brain. There are millions or billions of cells in every major organ. This means there are millions or billions of souls in one organ. There are countless souls in one's body.

The soul is a golden light being. The soul is the boss. Soul blockages are one of the major causes of sickness. Scientists and conventional modern medicine have not realized this yet. It will take some time for the scientific field to understand the soul and to recognize the soul. It could happen in the future.

The foundation teaching of Soul Mind Body Medicine is:

Heal the soul first; then healing of the mind and body will follow.

Before a person becomes sick, the soul was sick first. There is a spiritual reason for everything. Soul blockages are bad karma. Bad karma includes bad personal karma, bad ancestral karma, and more. Karma is cause and effect. Bad karma is the result of the mistakes that a human being and his or her ancestors have made in all lifetimes, including killing, harming, taking advantage of others, stealing, cheating, and more.

I shared the one-sentence secret about karma earlier in this book:

Karma is the root cause of success and failure in every aspect of life.

If a person has bad karma, this person could suffer all kinds of sicknesses and blockages in any aspect of life, including health, relationships, finances, business, and more.

Since July 2003 I have offered divine healing blessings for hundreds of thousands of people all over the world. Thousands of soul healing miracles have occurred. More and more soul healing miracles have made me understand further and further that soul blockages are the key cause for sickness. To heal many sicknesses, removing soul blockages is vital, especially for chronic and life-threatening conditions.

Divine Healing Hands are extremely powerful because they can remove soul blockages. Divine Healing Hands cannot remove all soul blockages in one session. Divine Healing Hands remove soul blockages little by little, but this removal of soul blockages little by little has created thousands of soul healing miracles already.

I would like to share an extremely powerful story of the spiritual journey and one person's deep desire to receive Divine Healing Hands and become a Divine Healing Hands Soul Healer:

> *I am so grateful for all the people I attracted into my life, for all the occurrences and struggles, as they have all brought me to our beloved Master Sha, whom I'm honored and humbled to have as my spiritual master and father.*
>
> *I was baptized a Roman Catholic and was very devoted, especially in my teenage years in high school. I was part of the school and church choirs and attended daily rosary devotions. Though I didn't have much money, I offered my services wherever needed, assisting in all church and school activities, devoting my free time to the children in the convalescent home on the school grounds.*
>
> *It has always been my greatest desire to serve, my mantra being that I am an empty vessel asking the Divine to use me for service, to show me how I can best offer service to others.*
>
> *Now being a massage therapist and having studied holistic disciplines like Ayurveda, my desire to assist people has deepened; to educate and provide them with the opportunity to enhance their own abilities to experience*

health in spirit, body, mind, and emotions and to restore the triad of soul, mind, and body. I am so grateful to have found a spiritual master to teach me such divine and Tao teaching and wisdom, for I can heal myself, my loved ones, and all souls.

I have strongly desired to communicate with my soul, with the Divine, Jesus, and Mary, who have walked with me and carried me through many dark struggles in my life, as well as all saints. I wanted to know my purpose in life, which I learned through Master Sha's divine and Tao teaching. My purpose is to serve, and my soul wanted to open up!

I began my search for "truth" and started reading many books of the previous era of mind over matter and, though grateful for these teachings, I never experienced significant or permanent transformation in my life.

In January 2008 I was diagnosed with Stage II vaginal cancer. I recognized that my cancer was caused by a lack of forgiveness, holding onto past hurts, pain, and guilt from hurting others. I began my journey of forgiveness, asking for forgiveness from those I have hurt knowingly and unknowingly, and offering forgiveness to those who had hurt me knowingly and unknowingly, and hardest of all, forgiving myself. Through these practices, my holistic treatments coupled with five sessions of chemo, and my unwavering faith in the Divine, Jesus, and Mary, within six months there was no sign of ever having had cancer. To this day I am cancer free.

In October 2010 I finally had all of my spiritual desires realized, and my search for a spiritual master/teacher came to an end. I found my master and spiritual father, beloved Master Sha.

My aunt Kathleen, who lives in Canada, is also a massage therapist and very holistic. She offered me great support during my cancer treatment, had attended a few of Master Sha's retreats, and sent me three of his books: Divine Soul Songs, Soul Wisdom, *and* Soul Communication. *My soul was immediately drawn to them, as it recognized them as truth. Though I was a bit hesitant at first because I felt I was not worthy, even though I was holding the tools to my heart's and soul's desire, I began to overcome these blockages. Though I still have some of these blockages of lack of self-worth, which prevent me from opening my soul communication channels further, I have brought out my Soul Language, Soul Song, and Tao Song.*

I started reading Divine Soul Songs *and focused on the practices to heal my relationships and to bless my finances and business as I was starting a new holistic service preparing organic meals for clients. I sang the Divine Soul Songs* Love, Peace and Harmony *and* God Gives His Heart to Me. *I hit a stumbling block when after eight months of blockages, my business ceased. I fell into a depressive state and sadly stopped practicing and even contemplated suicide, as well as taking my son's life with me as I didn't want him to suffer in life as I did. But how could I ever bring myself to hurt my son and take his life?*

I remember just falling to the floor in my bedroom, lying there in a ball, sobbing uncontrollably for what could have been hours. The only words I could utter were "Jesus, help me! Jesus, help me! Jesus, help me!" Then I heard a clear voice say, "Pick up the Divine Soul Songs *book again. Read it and practice devotedly and persistently." I found the strength to pick myself up off the floor and retrieved* Divine Soul Songs *from my desk and practiced and sang* Love, Peace and Harmony *and* God Gives His Heart to Me, *reading and practicing from cover to cover throughout the night. From the next day I continued to practice daily, devotedly and persistently for four, six, and sometimes eight hours, as I wasn't working. I practiced, I chanted, I offered service, and I continued to read* Soul Wisdom *and* Soul Communication.

As I write this, the realization just hit me that Master Sha saved my life that night. How can I ever thank and honor beloved Master Sha, the Divine, Tao, and Da Tao enough? Countless thank yous are not enough. Countless bowdowns are not enough.

I connected with Master Sha's Facebook page and our beloved soul family and listened daily to the Tao Songs. I was gifted a guest pass to attend an Opening Your Spiritual Channels workshop via webcast, and the participants were further gifted with passes to attend a Tao Soul Healing and Enlightenment Retreat. Again I was gifted two additional passes to attend Tao Soul Healing and Enlightenment Retreats, and this year I attended the Tao Soul Healing and Enlightenment Retreat by webcast as well.

I was further gifted the Divine Transformation, Power of Soul, Tao I, Tao II, *and* Tao Song and Tao Dance *books. I also received thirty copies of the* Tao Song and Tao Dance *book, which I distributed to the National Library in Trinidad, which further distributed them to their other libraries, the prison, and homes for battered women. I also showed the books of the Soul Power Series to the main bookstore chains in Trinidad, requesting that they carry these sacred treasures. One of the major chains is carrying the Soul Power Series at this time. And I also shared books and Master Sha's divine and Tao teaching and wisdom and the Divine Healing Hands and Love Peace Harmony Movements with friends and family.*

I attend the weekly Saturday Free Soul Healing Blessings and Daily Divine Healing Hands teleconferences, the daily Tao Practice calls, and the Sunday Divine Blessings teleconference as often as I can, as well as doing my daily Xiu Lian practices. I'm presently reading Tao II *after completing* Tao I.

It is my greatest soul's and heart's desire to receive Divine Healing Hands, for which I have been approved, to become a Soul Healer and Soul Teacher, a Worldwide Representative and Disciple of beloved Master Sha with approval so I can join, serve, and spread the Love Peace Harmony Movement and the Divine Healing Hands Movement. My deepest desire is to be a Total GOLD servant to the Divine, Tao, Da Tao, to humanity, Mother Earth, all universes, and wan ling, and to meld with Tao.

I have recently moved from my birth country of Trinidad and Tobago to Barbados, as it is my desire and intention to spread Master Sha's divine and Tao teachings and wisdom, books, and the Love Peace Harmony Movement and Divine Healing Hands mission here in Barbados and by extension, in all of the islands of the Caribbean. It is my desire to bring Master Sha and Master Sha's Worldwide Representatives to the Caribbean islands and to establish a Love Peace Harmony Center in the Caribbean where appropriate.

I had never known the love of a father or parent until I found Master Sha. Since I began writing this letter I have been gifted the Divine Healing Hands Soul Mind Body Transplants! I am so grateful for every struggle, every lesson, every person I've ever attracted into my life because they all brought me to Master Sha and my journey as a Divine Healing Hands Soul Healer. There are no words to express my deepest love and gratitude for Master Sha for his love and generosity, for the love and generosity of the Divine and Tao for saving my life, yet again. I am so grateful to him and our beloved soul family for all the blessings and divine and Tao treasures that I have received. I am so humbled, honored, and blessed. I release all attachment, fear, doubt, and worry. I trust that I will receive everything that I need from the Divine, Tao, and Da Tao to further advance my divine and Tao journey to become a greater unconditional Total GOLD servant.

With endless love and gratitude.

Thank you! Thank you! Thank you!

I love you. I love you. I love you.

Countless bowdowns. Countless bowdowns. Countless bowdowns.

K. R.
Barbados

APPLY DIVINE HEALING HANDS TO HEAL THE SPIRITUAL BODY

Now let me lead you to do a practice to heal the spiritual body.

First I will offer priceless permanent divine treasures to every reader.

Prepare!

Sit up straight. Close your eyes. Place the tip of your tongue gently against the roof of your mouth. Place your left hand over your Message Center (heart chakra) and your right hand in prayer position. This is called the Soul Light Era Prayer Position.

Divine Order: Divine Purple Light Ball and Purple Liquid Spring of Divine Forgiveness Soul Mind Body Transplants

Transmission!

Congratulations! You are extremely blessed. Humanity is extremely blessed.

Now let us apply these divine treasures to heal and transform your spiritual body.

Apply the Four Power Techniques:

Body Power. Sit up straight. Close your eyes. Place the tip of your tongue gently against the roof of your mouth. Put your hands in the Soul Light Era Prayer Position.

Soul Power. Say *hello:*

> *Dear soul mind body of my spiritual body,*
> *I love you.*
> *Dear soul mind body of Divine Purple Light Ball and*
>   *Purple Liquid Spring of Divine Forgiveness Soul*
>   *Mind Body Transplants,*
> *I love you.*
> *You have the power to heal and transform the soul*
>   *blockages in my spiritual body.*

Please offer a soul healing blessing as appropriate.
I am extremely grateful.
Thank you.

Mind Power. Visualize purple light radiating in your inner souls: the souls of your systems, organs, and cells, including cell units, DNA, RNA, spaces between the cells, and tiny matter inside the cells.

Sound Power. Chant silently or aloud:

Divine treasures heal and transform my spiritual body.
  Thank you.
Divine treasures heal and transform my spiritual body.
  Thank you.
Divine treasures heal and transform my spiritual body.
  Thank you.
Divine treasures heal and transform my spiritual body.
  Thank you . . .

Put the book down and chant for five minutes now. Generally speaking, chant for three to five minutes per time, three to five times per day. If you have a chronic or life-threatening condition, chant two hours or more per day. The longer you chant and the more you chant, the better the results you could receive. You can add all of your practice time together to total two hours or more per day.

Now I will lead you to heal the spiritual body by applying Divine Healing Hands. Again, the Divine has guided me that the first time you apply the Divine Healing Hands in this book to heal the spiritual body does not count toward the twenty times you can experience the power of Divine Healing Hands downloaded to this book. However, if you use the Divine Healing Hands in this book again to heal the spiritual body it *will* count toward the twenty times you can experience the power of Divine Healing Hands as a gift to every reader.

I strongly suggest that you spend at least a half-hour practicing every time you apply the Divine Healing Hands downloaded to this book for any kind of healing and transformation because you cannot continue to use the Divine Healing Hands in this book more than twenty times. The Divine is not responsible for Divine Healing Hands healing beyond this.

Apply the Four Power Techniques:

Body Power. Sit up straight. Close your eyes. Place the tip of your tongue gently against the roof of your mouth. Place one palm over the navel and the other palm over the heart.

Soul Power. Say *hello:*

> *Dear Divine Healing Hands,*
> *I love you.*
> *You have the power to heal my spiritual body.*
> *I am extremely grateful.*
> *Please offer a soul healing blessing as appropriate.*
> *Thank you.*

Mind Power. Visualize golden light from the Divine Healing Hands shining in your heart and soul.

Sound Power. Chant silently or aloud:

Divine Healing Hands heal my spiritual body.
   Thank you.
Divine Healing Hands heal my spiritual body.
   Thank you.
Divine Healing Hands heal my spiritual body.
   Thank you.
Divine Healing Hands heal my spiritual body.
   Thank you . . .

Chant for as long as you can. The more you chant and the longer you chant, the more benefits you will receive from Divine Healing Hands.

Now read a story about a chance meeting that opened up a priceless opportunity to become a Divine Healing Hands Soul Healer:

> *My name is Claudia Thompson. I am a humble Universal Servant and would like to share my story as a Divine Healing Hands recipient and a new Divine Healing Hands Soul Healer. I hope that my story may offer some inspiration to someone out there who can benefit from these examples of Master Sha's beautiful and powerful mission.*
>
> *I first came to know about Master Sha's work from a lady who came into my antique shop in Atlanta a little over two years ago. She was listening to a teleconference and shared it with me. The chants sounded foreign to me, but I was open-minded. After becoming friends she shared more and told me she was a healer.*

I play soccer and constantly put my body to the test. I had really hurt my right foot, and after being in pain for about a week I gladly accepted her offer of a healing blessing. Expecting her to massage my feet, I found it amazing that she did not even touch them, but was doing a type of prayer over them. I felt a rush of heat and afterward my foot felt 100 percent better. This was extraordinary and it opened my eyes to more of Master Sha's gifts.

Being a slow learner, I applied a few principles but had put most of this information on the back burner. If someone had told me that two years later I myself would be a Divine Healing Hands Soul Healer, I would have laughed.

About a year after this angel of Master Sha's just happened to walk into my life (there are no accidents), I found my life in a tough transition. I had closed my business after twenty years. I had lost my mom from a long illness, and my knee was badly injured, which kept me from playing soccer, which I love. Somehow I received information that Master Sha would be in Atlanta, and I knew that I needed to see him and get some serious external help to get me through this rough time.

I attended and was blown away at this giant of a soul and knew that my life would never be the same. I received some extraordinary treasures and became more familiar with the mission. In August, one of Master Sha's Worldwide Representatives came to Atlanta and was kind enough to give me a Soul Operation and Divine Soul Mind Body Healing and Transmission System for my knee. Within minutes it was better and within days it was as if I had a new knee.

Well, this was extraordinary proof of the power of Master Sha's work. I experienced playing soccer like I was twenty years old for many, many months. Since then I have had a few setbacks that I know are due to heavy karma and I am working on these, but I have living proof of the power of Master Sha.

Being healed is not enough for me, but sharing this experience and helping people who have no hope is so important to me. This past February I was counseled by one of Master Sha's Worldwide Representatives, Master Bill Thomas, in Atlanta, and he did a soul reading that mentioned that I could be a powerful healer. This floored me, but I knew deep down I did want to serve my fellow man and to share the same opportunities that I had been given to transform mentally, physically, and spiritually. I had to push my insecurities to the side and take a leap of faith.

I attended a three-day workshop in Atlanta this past June and received my Divine Healing Hands, and all I can say is it feels so natural. I tell people it is like praying, except you have the "big guns" behind you to help with your healing. I can never bow down enough to the Divine for allowing me to be one of his Universal Servants and to offer help the best way I can to my fellow man, animals, plants, and more.

I have two cases that clearly demonstrate the power of Divine Healing Hands. The first healing was for my French bulldog, Hector. He had an eye infection for a few weeks that would drain throughout the day. Literally the first time I offered him a Divine Healing Hands blessing during the daily Divine Healing Hands teleconference, his eye was clear and has stayed clear.

The second healing was for a friend I visited in Los Angeles who was about to perform onstage the next day but was suffering from severe bladder pains (a problem she has dealt with her whole life). I offered a soul healing as appropriate and she agreed. Afterward, she said her pain was gone. Of course I bowed down to thank the Divine for helping my best friend. What makes this even better is that I am able to teach her some of Master Sha's soul wisdom to further her journey.

These are two very clear cases that I experienced my first month as a Divine Healing Hands Soul Healer. With the Divine's help, I hope to have many more healing experiences with those I come in contact with who are in need. I know I have a l-o-n-g way to go in my evolution, but I am proud of myself that I stepped up and put my ego aside to let the Divine take over. This has given my life such a beautiful purpose and I am so grateful to all who helped me get to where I am now.

Thank you. Thank you. Thank you.

Claudia R. Thompson
Atlanta, Georgia

Mental Body

A human being has a mental body. The mental body is the mind body. Mind means consciousness. People understand the mind is related to the brain. People may not understand that the mind is in every system, every organ, and every cell. Everything has a soul, mind, and body.

The mental body has blockages that can include negative mind-sets, negative attitudes, negative beliefs, ego, attachments, and more. To heal the mental body is to remove all of them.

Divine Healing Hands have the power to remove mind blockages.

APPLY DIVINE HEALING HANDS TO HEAL THE MENTAL BODY

Now let me lead you to do a practice to heal the mental body.

First I will offer priceless permanent divine treasures to every reader.

Prepare!

Sit up straight. Close your eyes. Place the tip of your tongue gently against the roof of your mouth. Place your left hand over your Message Center (heart chakra) and your right hand in the traditional prayer position.

Divine Order: Divine Purple Light Ball and Purple Liquid Spring of Divine Clarity of Mind Soul Mind Body Transplants

Transmission!

Congratulations! You are extremely blessed. Humanity is extremely blessed.

Apply these divine treasures to heal and transform your mental body.

Apply the Four Power Techniques:

Body Power. Sit up straight. Close your eyes. Place the tip of your tongue gently against the roof of your mouth. Place your hands in the Soul Light Era Prayer Position.

Soul Power. Say *hello:*

> *Dear soul mind body of my mental body,*
> *I love you.*
> *Dear soul mind body of Divine Purple Light Ball and*
>   *Purple Liquid Spring of Divine Clarity of Mind*
>   *Soul Mind Body Transplants,*
> *I love you.*
> *You have the power to heal and transform the nega-*
>   *tive mind-sets, negative attitudes, negative be-*
>   *liefs, ego, attachments, and more in my mental*
>   *body.*
> *Please offer a soul healing blessing as appropriate.*
> *I am extremely grateful.*
> *Thank you.*

Mind Power. Visualize purple light radiating in your mind at the body, systems, organs, and cellular levels.

Sound Power. Chant silently or aloud:

> *Divine treasures heal and transform my mental body.*
>   *Thank you.*
> *Divine treasures heal and transform my mental body.*
>   *Thank you.*
> *Divine treasures heal and transform my mental body.*
>   *Thank you.*

> *Divine treasures heal and transform my mental body.*
> *Thank you . . .*

Put the book down and chant for five minutes now. Generally speaking, chant for three to five minutes per time, three to five times per day. If you have a chronic or life-threatening condition, chant for two hours or more per day. The longer you chant and the more you chant, the better the results you could receive. Add all of the practice time together to total two hours or more per day.

Now I will lead you to heal and transform the mental body by applying Divine Healing Hands. Again, the Divine has guided me that to apply the Divine Healing Hands for the first time in this book to heal and transform the mental body does not count toward the twenty times the reader can experience the power of Divine Healing Hands downloaded to this book. However, if you use the Divine Healing Hands in this book again to heal and transform the mental body it *will* count toward the twenty times you can experience the power of Divine Healing Hands as a gift to every reader.

I strongly suggest that you spend at least a half-hour practicing every time you apply the Divine Healing Hands downloaded to this book for any kind of healing and transformation because the Divine has clearly guided me that you cannot apply the Divine Healing Hands in this book more than twenty times.

Apply the Four Power Techniques:

Body Power. Sit up straight. Close your eyes. Place the tip of your tongue gently against the roof of your mouth. Place one palm over your navel and the other palm over your heart.

Soul Power. Say *hello:*

> *Dear Divine Healing Hands,*
> *I love you.*
> *You have the power to heal and transform my mental*
>   *body by removing my negative mind-sets, negative*
>   *attitudes, negative beliefs, ego, attachments, and*
>   *more.*
> *Please offer a soul healing blessing as appropriate.*
> *I am extremely grateful.*
> *Thank you.*

Mind Power. Visualize golden light from the Divine Healing Hands shining in your heart and soul.

Sound Power. Chant silently or aloud:

> *Divine Healing Hands bring clarity to my mind and*
>   *transform my negative mind-sets, negative attitudes,*
>   *negative beliefs, ego, attachments, and more.*
>   *Thank you.*
> *Divine Healing Hands bring clarity to my mind and*
>   *transform my negative mind-sets, negative attitudes,*
>   *negative beliefs, ego, attachments, and more.*
>   *Thank you.*
> *Divine Healing Hands bring clarity to my mind and*
>   *transform my negative mind-sets, negative attitudes,*
>   *negative beliefs, ego, attachments, and more.*
>   *Thank you.*
> *Divine Healing Hands bring clarity to my mind and*

transform my negative mind-sets, negative attitudes,
negative beliefs, ego, attachments, and more.
Thank you . . .

Chant for as long as you can. The longer you chant and the more you chant, the more benefits you will receive from Divine Healing Hands.

Emotional Body

Five thousand years ago, traditional Chinese medicine clearly shared the profound wisdom and connection between the physical body and the emotional body:

- The Wood element (liver) connects with anger in the emotional body.
- The Fire element (heart) connects with anxiety and depression in the emotional body.
- The Earth element (spleen) connects with worry in the emotional body.
- The Metal element (lungs) connects with grief and sadness in the emotional body.
- The Water element (kidneys) connects with fear in the emotional body.

Anger, depression, anxiety, worry, grief, sadness, and fear are the major emotional imbalances for humanity. There are other emotional issues as well. They all can be categorized in the Five Elements. They can all be balanced by balancing the Five Elements.

Enjoy this heart-touching story of Divine Healing Hands healing end-stage liver cirrhosis.

My name is Arti Patil, and I am an optometrist. We are a family of eye doctors and have an eye hospital in Mumbai, India.

Since I have been practicing with my Divine Healing Hands I have started to believe more and more that the Divine is so very generous in granting sincere healing requests from anybody. This is just one classic story where the results were just fabulous.

A very young chronic alcoholic was diagnosed with the final stage of liver cirrhosis, severe anemia, loss of appetite, and poor liver and kidney functions. All his blood chemistry was very discouraging. Despite these conditions, he kept asking for alcohol and got violent if he was refused a drink.

A request for healing came to me and I started working on him immediately. After giving him five-minute Divine Healing Hands blessings twice a day for two days, I was told that he asked for food, ate it, and could retain it. On the fourth day he stopped demanding alcohol and did not get violent.

The following days his appetite picked up and his sleep pattern also improved. I continued the Divine Healing Hands soul healings. His blood tests were repeated after two weeks and showed remarkable improvement. The doctors were shocked, but I as a Divine Healing Hands Soul Healer was not because we know that they really are the Divine's soul healing hands that are healing and blessing each one who requests.

This patient has not had alcohol ever since and has

recovered to an extent of eighty percent since we started to offer him healing blessings.

I hope this motivates more and more people to become Divine Healing Hands Soul Healers in order to offer service to humanity and in the transition period.

Thank you. Thank you. Thank you.

Mrs. Arti Patil
Mumbai, India

I will lead you in some practices to heal emotional imbalances.

ANGER

Apply the Four Power Techniques to heal anger:

Body Power. Sit up straight. Close your eyes. Place the tip of your tongue gently against the roof of your mouth. Place one palm below the navel on the lower abdomen. Place the other palm over the liver.

Soul Power. Say *hello:*

> *Dear soul mind body of my liver,*
> *I love you.*
> *You have the power to heal my anger.*
> *Do a good job.*
> *Thank you.*
>
> *Dear Divine,*
> *Dear Tao,*

Please forgive the mistakes that my ancestors and I
have made in all lifetimes that are related with the
liver and anger.
In order to receive forgiveness I will serve humanity,
Mother Earth, and all souls unconditionally.
Thank you.

Mind Power. Visualize green light radiating in the liver.

Sound Power. Chant or sing silently or aloud:

Jiao Ya Shu Gan (pronounced *jee-yow yah shoo gahn*)
Jiao Ya Shu Gan
Jiao Ya Shu Gan
Jiao Ya Shu Gan
Jiao Ya Shu Gan . . .

"Jiao Ya" is the sacred Tao Song mantra to vibrate and radiate in the liver. "Tao Song" means *the song from the Source.* "Shu" means *smooth.* "Gan" means *liver.* "Jiao Ya Shu Gan" means *Tao Song smoothes the liver.*

Stop reading now. Chant *Jiao Ya Shu Gan* for five minutes. Generally speaking, chant for three to five minutes per time, three to five times per day. If you have a chronic or life-threatening condition, chant for two hours or more per day. The longer you chant and the more often you chant, the better the results you could receive. Add all of the practice time together to total two hours or more per day.

DEPRESSION AND ANXIETY

Apply the Four Power Techniques to heal depression and anxiety:

Body Power. Sit up straight. Close your eyes. Place the tip of your tongue to the roof of your mouth. Place one palm below the navel on the lower abdomen. Place the other palm over the heart.

Soul Power. Say *hello:*

> *Dear soul mind body of my heart,*
> *I love you.*
> *You have the power to heal depression and anxiety.*
> *Do a good job.*
> *Thank you.*

> *Dear Divine,*
> *Dear Tao,*
> *Please forgive the mistakes that my ancestors and I*
>   *have made in all lifetimes related to the heart, de-*
>   *pression, and anxiety.*
> *In order to receive forgiveness I will serve humanity,*
>   *Mother Earth, and all souls unconditionally.*
> *Thank you.*

Mind Power. Visualize red light radiating in the heart.

Sound Power. Chant or sing silently or aloud:

> *Zhi Ya Yang Xin* (pronounced *jr yah yahng sheen*)
> *Zhi Ya Yang Xin*

Zhi Ya Yang Xin
Zhi Ya Yang Xin
Zhi Ya Yang Xin . . .

"Zhi Ya" is the sacred Tao Song mantra to vibrate and radiate in the heart. "Yang" means *nourish*. "Xin" means *heart*. "Zhi Ya Yang Xin" means *Tao Song nourishes the heart*.

Stop reading now. Chant *Zhi Ya Yang Xin* for five minutes. Generally speaking, chant for three to five minutes per time, three to five times per day. If you have a chronic or life-threatening condition, chant for two hours or more per day. The longer you chant and the more you chant, the better the results you could receive. Add all of the practice time together to total two hours or more per day.

Following is a story of a Divine Healing Hands healing blessing clearing a home of negativity and stagnant energy and improving family relationships:

My name is Leslie H. and I have been fortunate to receive Divine Healing Hands training in December 2011 in San Francisco. I had not been practicing for very long when I decided to invoke this blessing for my family home where my elderly father still resides.

Unfortunately, growing up in this house was not a pleasant experience as my parents had a troubled marriage and there were many arguments in the household. My dad has lived alone these past few years and has been very depressed. Every time my brother Dave and I would visit the family home, we dreaded it as we could feel the negativity and stagnant energy.

In mid-December I was asked to help my brother prepare a vacant bedroom in this house for rental. When I came over one Saturday afternoon, Dave was in the garage working on his car and my father was in the living room watching television. Before I began cleaning the bedroom, I closed the door and privately invoked my Divine Healing Hands to bless our family home, to clear it of any remaining negativity and unhappiness, and to replace any energetic disturbances with divine love and light.

When I began washing the bedroom walls, I decided to sing and send love to the souls of the walls. I also asked the divine love souls in the bedroom to turn on. What would ordinarily have been a chore became an act of love and a joyful experience. Soon afterward my brother ran from the garage into the bedroom that I was cleaning. In amazement he asked me, "Leslie, what did you do? The energy of the whole house just changed!" Dave could actually feel the difference and that the negativity had been cleared. I briefly explained to him that I just asked my new Divine Healing Hands to bless the home.

After cleaning the bedroom, I then showed my Dad how to use the remote control to play his favorite music channels since he likes the oldies. I began dancing to one of these oldies and invited him to sing along with me, which he did. We had a marvelous happy time together. Our family dynamics have since changed, and our relationships are now more cooperative, loving, and harmonious. I have taken courses in space/energy clearing before, but the vibration and power of Divine Healing Hands is exceptional. I highly recommend Divine Healing Hands not only for individual healing, but for creating a healthy, happy home environment.

> *Leslie H.*
> *Penngrove, California*

WORRY

Apply the Four Power Techniques to heal worry:

Body Power. Sit up straight. Close your eyes. Place the tip of your tongue gently against the roof of your mouth. Place one palm below the navel on the lower abdomen. Place the other palm over the spleen.

Soul Power. Say *hello:*

> *Dear soul mind body of my spleen,*
> *I love you.*
> *You have the power to heal worry.*
> *Do a good job.*
> *Thank you.*

> *Dear Divine,*
> *Dear Tao,*
> *Please forgive the mistakes that my ancestors and I have*
> *made in all lifetimes related to the spleen and worry.*

In order to receive forgiveness I will serve humanity,
   Mother Earth, and all souls unconditionally.
Thank you.

Mind Power. Visualize golden light radiating in the spleen.

Sound Power. Chant or sing silently or aloud:

Gong Ya Jian Pi (pronounced *gawng yah jyen pee*)
Gong Ya Jian Pi
Gong Ya Jian Pi
Gong Ya Jian Pi
Gong Ya Jian Pi . . .

"Gong Ya" is the sacred Tao Song mantra to vibrate and radiate in the spleen. "Jian" means *strengthen*. "Pi" means *spleen*. "Gong Ya Jian Pi" means *Tao Song strengthens the spleen*.

Stop reading now. Chant *Gong Ya Jian Pi* for five minutes. Generally speaking, chant for three to five minutes per time, three to five times per day. If you have a chronic or life-threatening condition, chant for two hours or more per day. The longer you chant and the more you chant, the better the results you could receive. Add all of the practice time together to total the two hours or more per day.

GRIEF AND SADNESS

Apply the Four Power Techniques to heal grief and sadness:

Body Power. Sit up straight. Close your eyes. Place the tip of your tongue gently against the roof of your mouth. Place your right palm over your left lung. Place your left palm over your right lung. Your arms should cross each other.

Soul Power. Say *hello:*

> *Dear soul mind body of my lungs,*
> *I love you.*
> *You have the power to heal grief and sadness.*
> *Do a good job.*
> *Thank you.*

> *Dear Divine,*
> *Dear Tao,*
> *Please forgive the mistakes that my ancestors and I*
> *have made in all lifetimes related to the lungs, grief,*
> *and sadness.*
> *In order to receive forgiveness I will serve humanity,*
> *Mother Earth, and all souls unconditionally.*
> *Thank you.*

Mind Power. Visualize white light radiating in the lungs.

Sound Power. Chant or sing silently or aloud:

> *Shang Ya Xuan Fei* (pronounced *shahng ya shwen*
> *fay*)
> *Shang Ya Xuan Fei*
> *Shang Ya Xuan Fei*
> *Shang Ya Xuan Fei*
> *Shang Ya Xuan Fei . . .*

"Shang Ya" is the sacred Tao Song mantra to vibrate and radiate in the lungs. "Xuan" means *disperse*. "Fei" means *lungs*. "Shang Ya Xuan Fei" means *Tao Song promotes the function of the lungs*.

Put the book down and chant *Shang Ya Xuan Fei* for five minutes. Generally speaking, chant for three to five minutes per time, three to five times per day. If you have a chronic or life-threatening condition, chant for two hours or more per day. The longer you chant and the more you chant, the better the results you could receive. Add all of the practice time together to total two hours or more per day.

FEAR

Apply the Four Power Techniques to heal fear:

Body Power. Sit up straight. Close your eyes. Place the tip of your tongue gently against the roof of your mouth. Place one palm on the lower abdomen. Place the other palm over the kundalini.

Soul Power. Say *hello:*

> *Dear soul mind body of my kidneys,*
> *I love you.*
> *You have the power to heal fear.*
> *Do a good job.*
> *Thank you.*
>
> *Dear Divine,*
> *Dear Tao,*

Please forgive the mistakes that my ancestors and I
     have made in all lifetimes related to the kidneys and
     fear.
In order to receive forgiveness I will serve humanity,
     Mother Earth, and all souls unconditionally.
Thank you.

Mind Power. Visualize blue light radiating in the kidneys.

Sound Power. Chant or sing silently or aloud:

> *Yu Ya Zhuang Shen* (pronounced *yü yah jwahng shun*)
> *Yu Ya Zhuang Shen*
> *Yu Ya Zhuang Shen*
> *Yu Ya Zhuang Shen*
> *Yu Ya Zhuang Shen . . .*

"Yu Ya" is the sacred Tao Song mantra to vibrate and radiate in the kidneys. "Zhuang" means *make strong*. "Shen" means *kidneys*. "Yu Ya Zhuang Shen" means *Tao Song makes the kidneys strong*.

Put the book down and chant *Yu Ya Zhuang Shen* for five minutes. Generally speaking, chant for three to five minutes per time, three to five times per day. If you have a chronic or life-threatening condition, chant for two hours or more per day. The longer you chant and the more you chant, the better the results you could receive. Add all of the practice time together to total two hours or more per day.

OTHER EMOTIONAL IMBALANCES

There are other emotional imbalances such as guilt, shame, unworthiness, and more. All of them connect with the Five Elements. All of them can be balanced by balancing the Five Elements.

Apply the Four Power Techniques to heal other emotional imbalances:

Body Power. Sit up straight. Close your eyes. Place the tip of your tongue gently against the roof of your mouth. Take your left hand and place all of the fingers together. Grasp the fingers of your left hand with your right hand. Place both hands on the lower abdomen below the navel. This is the Five Elements Hand Position. See figure 8.

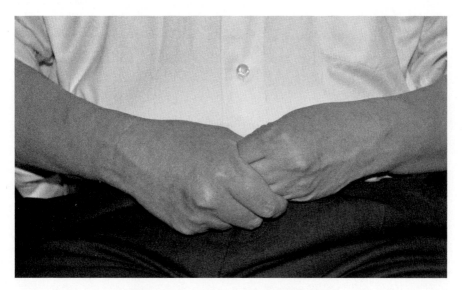

Figure 8. Five Elements Hand Position

Soul Power. Say *hello:*

Dear soul mind body of my liver, heart, spleen, lungs,
*   and kidneys,*
I love you all.
You have the power to heal all of my emotional imbal-
*   ances.*
Do a good job.
Thank you.

Dear Divine,
Dear Tao,
Please forgive the mistakes that my ancestors and I
*   have made in all lifetimes related to the Five Ele-*
*   ments and all emotional imbalances.*
In order to receive forgiveness I will serve humanity,
*   Mother Earth, and all souls unconditionally.*
Thank you.

Mind Power. Visualize rainbow light radiating in the liver, heart, spleen, lungs, and kidneys.

Sound Power. Chant or sing silently or aloud:

Jiao Zhi Gong Shang Yu (pronounced *jee-yow jr*
*   gawng shahng yü*)
Jiao Zhi Gong Shang Yu
Jiao Zhi Gong Shang Yu
Jiao Zhi Gong Shang Yu
Jiao Zhi Gong Shang Yu . . .

"Jiao" is the sacred Tao Song mantra to vibrate and radiate in the liver. "Zhi" is the sacred Tao Song mantra to vibrate and radiate in the heart. "Gong" is the sacred Tao Song mantra to vibrate and radiate in the spleen. "Shang" is the sacred Tao Song mantra to vibrate and radiate in the lungs. "Yu" is the sacred Tao Song mantra to vibrate and radiate in the kidneys. Chanting this Tao Song mantra vibrates all the major organs. Therefore, it balances all Five Elements.

Put the book down and stop reading now. Chant *Jiao Zhi Gong Shang Yu* for five minutes. Generally speaking, chant for three to five minutes per time, three to five times per day. If you have a chronic or life-threatening condition, chant for two hours or more per day. The longer you chant and the more you chant, the better the results you could receive. Add all of the practice time together to total two hours or more per day.

APPLY DIVINE PURPLE LIGHT BALL AND PURPLE
LIQUID SPRING OF DIVINE LOVE TO HEAL
EMOTIONAL IMBALANCES

Now I will offer priceless permanent divine treasures to heal the emotional body.

Prepare!

Divine Order: Divine Purple Light Ball and Purple Liquid Spring of Divine Love Soul Mind Body Transplants

Transmission!

Congratulations! You are extremely blessed. Humanity is extremely blessed.

Divine Love melts all blockages and transforms all life. Let me lead you to practice to heal the emotional imbalances of anger, depression, anxiety, worry, grief, sadness, fear, and more together.

Apply the Four Power Techniques:

Body Power. Sit up straight. Close your eyes. Place the tip of your tongue gently against the roof of your mouth. Place your hands in the Five Elements Hand Position (figure 8).

Soul Power. Say *hello:*

> *Dear soul mind body of my emotional body,*
> *I love you.*
> *Dear soul mind body of Divine Purple Light Ball and*
> *Purple Liquid Spring of Divine Love Soul Mind*
> *Body Transplants,*
> *I love you.*
> *You have the power to heal my emotional imbalances,*
> *including anger, depression, anxiety, worry, grief,*
> *sadness, fear, and more.*
> *Please offer a soul healing blessing as appropriate.*
> *Thank you.*

Mind Power. Visualize purple light radiating in the liver, heart, spleen, lungs, and kidneys.

Sound Power. Chant or sing silently or aloud:

> *Divine Purple Light Ball and Purple Liquid Spring of*
> *Divine Love heal and transform my emotional body.*
> *Thank you.*
> *Divine Purple Light Ball and Purple Liquid Spring of*

> *Divine Love heal and transform my emotional body.*
> *Thank you.*
> *Divine Purple Light Ball and Purple Liquid Spring of*
> *Divine Love heal and transform my emotional body.*
> *Thank you.*
> *Divine Purple Light Ball and Purple Liquid Spring of*
> *Divine Love heal and transform my emotional body.*
> *Thank you . . .*

Now put the book down and chant *Divine Purple Light Ball and Purple Liquid Spring of Divine Love heal and transform my emotional body* for five minutes. Generally speaking, chant for three to five minutes per time, three to five times per day. If you have a chronic or life-threatening condition, chant for two hours or more a day. The longer you chant and the more you chant, the better the results you could receive. Add all of the practice time together to total the two hours or more a day.

APPLY DIVINE HEALING HANDS TO HEAL THE EMOTIONAL BODY

Now I will lead you to heal the emotional body by applying Divine Healing Hands. Again, the Divine has guided me that the first time you apply the Divine Healing Hands in this book to heal the emotional body does not count toward the twenty times you can experience the power of Divine Healing Hands downloaded to this book. However, the second (and subsequent) time you use the Divine Healing Hands in this book to heal the emotional body it *will* count toward the twenty times you can experience the power of Divine Healing Hands as a gift to every reader.

Apply the Four Power Techniques:

Body Power. Sit up straight. Close your eyes. Place the tip of your tongue gently against the roof of your mouth. Place one palm over the lower abdomen below the navel. Place the other palm over the kundalini.

Soul Power. Say *hello*:

> *Dear Divine Healing Hands,*
> *I love you.*
> *You have the power to heal my emotional body.*
> *Please offer a soul healing blessing as appropriate.*
> *I am extremely grateful.*
> *Thank you.*

Mind Power. Visualize Divine Healing Hands radiating golden light in your kundalini area and in your liver, heart, spleen, lungs, and kidneys.

Sound Power. Chant or sing silently or aloud:

> *Divine Healing Hands heal and transform my emotional body. Thank you.*
> *Divine Healing Hands heal and transform my emotional body. Thank you.*
> *Divine Healing Hands heal and transform my emotional body. Thank you.*
> *Divine Healing Hands heal and transform my emotional body. Thank you . . .*

Chant for as long as you can. The longer you chant and the more you chant, the more benefits you will receive from Divine Healing Hands.

Read how one Divine Healing Hands Soul Healer healed her unbalanced emotions:

> *My family has had ongoing conflicts since I was a young teenager. I am now thirty. These conflicts can include verbal abuse, psychological abuse, threats, and even physical violence at times. My brother has significant mental health problems, including unbalanced emotions, impulse control issues, explosive anger, and drug addictions.*
>
> *It was not easy growing up with a brother who suffers from these issues. It has always been a struggle for me to cope with this. Even though I now live multiple states away from my family, every time I talk to a family member and they give accounts of the most recent episode with my brother, I am deeply affected. I worry about the lives of my parents and brother.*
>
> *After I talk with my parents about the most recent altercation they had with my brother, I usually become very upset for days, worrying about my family, feeling great sadness for their suffering, and feeling much grief that my brother continues to live this way.*
>
> *After the last phone call, I decided to ask my Divine Healing Hands to heal my emotions. I shed some tears at the beginning of the healing, and at the end I felt as if something inside of me had healed. I felt whole and balanced inside. I was able to enjoy the rest of the evening and*

did not suffer for days like I did in the past. This is a miracle. I am so very grateful.

Thank you, Master Sha. Thank you, Divine. Thank you, Tao.

Shelly Stum
Daytona Beach, Florida

Physical Body

Five Elements is one of the most important practices and theories in traditional Chinese medicine. It uses the five elements of nature—wood, fire, earth, metal, and water—to summarize and categorize the organs, bodily tissues, emotional body, and more.

Five Elements theory has been the guiding principle for millions of people to heal and rejuvenate the soul, heart, mind, and body. In traditional Chinese medicine, balancing the Five Elements is one of the keys to healing.

The Five Elements are:

- Wood, which includes the liver, gallbladder, tendons, and eyes in the physical body, and anger in the emotional body
- Fire, which includes the heart, small intestine, blood vessels, and tongue in the physical body, and depression and anxiety in the emotional body
- Earth, which includes the spleen, stomach, muscles, mouth, lips, gums, and teeth in the physical body, and worry in the emotional body
- Metal, which includes the lungs, large intestine, skin,

and nose in the physical body, and grief and sadness in the emotional body

- Water, which includes the kidneys, urinary bladder, bones, and ears in the physical body, and fear in the emotional body

There are many sicknesses of the physical body, including pain, stiffness, numbness, injuries, inflammation, infections, growths such as cysts, tumors, and cancer, organ dysfunction and failure, and much more.

There are many sicknesses of the mental body, including mental confusion, loss of memory, mental disorders, and much more.

There are many sicknesses of the emotional body, including depression, anxiety, fear, anger, worry, sadness, grief, guilt, shame, and much more.

There are many sicknesses of the spiritual body, including negative memories, curses, wrong vows, all kinds of bad karma, and much more.

I am sharing sacred wisdom with you and humanity:

Every sickness is due to soul mind body blockages in one or more of the Five Elements.

In this book I am sharing profound sacred wisdom and practical techniques to heal all kinds of sickness, including sicknesses in the physical body, emotional body, mental body, and spiritual body.

The power of Divine Healing Hands cannot be expressed enough. Here is a story of the power of Divine Healing Hands to heal a serious nosebleed:

My husband and I both received our Divine Healing Hands in June 2011. It was during that workshop that I had a major healing of an episode of atrial fibrillation, a potentially life-threatening condition.

Since then, on more than one occasion, my husband has felt that his Divine Healing Hands was not very powerful because there were times when he clearly felt the Divine come through his hand while offering a Divine Healing Hands blessing, and there were many times when he felt nothing.

He now realizes that his Divine Healing Hands is indeed powerful.

I take blood thinner medication and several nights ago as I was fixing our evening meal I leaned over the trash can to dispose of some trash. As I stood up, I felt my nose running and when I lifted my hand to my nose, my hand was full of blood. I crossed the kitchen to the sink and it was clear to me that blood was not just dripping from my nose, it was a steady stream. I leaned over the sink and tried to reach for a towel or anything within my reach in an effort to keep the blood from spattering all over the cabinets and the wall above the sink. Nothing was within my reach so I called for my husband to come and help me.

When he first walked into the kitchen he thought he was going to have to take me to the emergency room because of the blood thinner I am taking to prevent a stroke in case my heart goes into A-fib again. He grabbed a towel and a couple of clean dishcloths, ran cold water over them, placed a cold towel on the back of my neck, and asked me to raise my head to help stop the flow of blood. When I raised my head upright, I began to choke on the blood run-

ning down my throat. My husband handed me a cold rag to put on my forehead and one to put on my nose to hold it closed, but even that did not slow the steady flow of blood.

He then asked if he should invoke his Divine Healing Hands. I said, "Please do." As soon as he invoked his Divine Healing Hands, the blood flow slowed enough that I could stand up straight, and as soon as he began singing his Soul Song, the blood stopped immediately. He continued singing and I was able to feel a clot form in my nose.

Afterward he sent me to the living room to rest while he cleaned up the mess in the kitchen. After he finished cleaning up, he came into the living room and said, "I cannot believe what just happened. I didn't feel anything in my hands yet you were healed. I guess my Divine Healing Hands are more powerful than I believed they were!"

It was so strange as I have never had a nosebleed like that, especially without warning such as a sneeze or an itchy nose. All I did was lean over the trashcan and blood began to gush from my nose.

While this is not a really spectacular healing, I believe the Divine gave me that severe nosebleed to show my husband that his Divine Healing Hands is in fact truly powerful. We both were truly amazed at the sight of the kitchen when my nose quit bleeding. There was blood on the wall, above the trash can, and on the floor, the countertops beside the sink, and the wall and window above the sink. I know this is a bit graphic, but I have never before witnessed a nosebleed as bad as the one I had that evening for no apparent reason. The only time I have seen a nose bleed that badly is when a friend broke his nose in an accident.

I am so very grateful that this happened to me, if for no other reason than to validate the power we have been given—especially to my husband—as a vehicle of the Divine with our Divine Healing Hands.

Thank you. Thank you. Thank you.

Judy Sisk
Charles Sisk
Arvada, Colorado

Now I will lead you to practice to heal the physical body.

Apply the Four Power Techniques:

Body Power. Sit up straight. Close your eyes. Place the tip of your tongue gently against the roof of your mouth. Place one palm on the lower abdomen below the navel. Place the other palm on your back, directly behind the navel.

Soul Power. Say *hello:*

> *Dear soul mind body of my physical body,*
> *Dear soul mind body of the Five Elements inside my*
>   *body,*
> *I love you.*
> *You have the power to heal and transform my physical*
>   *body.*
> *Do a good job.*
> *Thank you.*

Dear Divine,

Dear Tao,

I love you.

*Please forgive all of the mistakes that my ancestors and
I have made in all lifetimes.*

*In order to receive your forgiveness I will serve human-
ity, Mother Earth, and all souls unconditionally.*

I am very grateful.

Thank you.

Mind Power. Visualize golden light radiating in your Zhong (pronounced *jawng*). See figure 9.

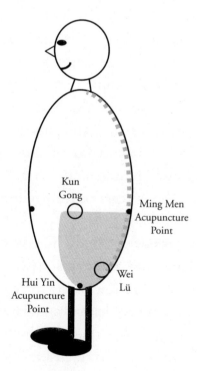

Figure 9. Location of Zhong

Zhong is an area in the lower abdomen that includes four major sacred areas. They are the Kun Gong, Ming Men acupuncture point, Wei Lü, and Hui Yin acupuncture point. "Zhong" means *core*.

The Kun Gong (pronounced *kwun gawng*) is the place where Yuan Qi and Yuan Jing are produced. "Yuan" means *origin*. "Yuan Qi" (pronounced *ywen chee*) means *original energy*. "Yuan Jing" (pronounced *ywen jing*) means *original matter*. Yuan Qi and Yuan Jing are the keys for life. The Kun Gong includes the area immediately around the navel.

The Ming Men acupuncture point lies on the back, directly behind the navel.

The Wei Lü (pronounced *way lü*) is the tailbone area.

The Hui Yin acupuncture point lies on the perineum, between the genitals and the anus.

I am releasing a major divine and Tao secret to you now.

You may have heard of ear acupuncture. A human being's ear has many acupuncture points that reflect and connect with every part of the body. You may also have heard of foot reflexology. A human being's feet reflect and connect with every part of the body. This *ear reflection* and *feet reflection* are physical reflections and connections. The ears and feet are part of the physical body. Part of the body (ears or feet) reflects an image of the entire body.

Zhong is a *space* inside the body. The sacred wisdom is that **Zhong space reflects and connects with every part of the body.** I will name this reflection *Zhong space reflection*.

Therefore, to visualize golden light radiating in the Zhong is to heal the whole body. This is the deep divine and Tao wisdom I am releasing now. In particular, focusing your mind on Zhong could balance the Five Elements, which include every system, organ, and cell in the body.

Sound Power. Chant or sing silently or aloud:

> *Zhong Zhong Zhong Zhong Zhong Zhong Zhong*
> *Zhong Zhong Zhong Zhong Zhong Zhong Zhong*
> *Zhong Zhong Zhong Zhong Zhong Zhong Zhong*
> *Zhong Zhong Zhong Zhong Zhong Zhong Zhong . . .*

Put the book down and sing or chant *Zhong* for five minutes now. Generally speaking, chant for three to five minutes per time, three to five times per day. If you have a chronic or life-threatening condition, chant for two hours or more per day. The longer you chant and the more you chant, the better the results you could receive. Add all of your practice time together to total two hours or more a day.

APPLY DIVINE HEALING HANDS TO HEAL THE PHYSICAL BODY

Now I will lead you to heal the physical body by applying Divine Healing Hands. I strongly suggest that each time you apply the Divine Healing Hands within this book, spend at least a half-hour practicing because the Divine has guided me clearly that you cannot use the Divine Healing Hands treasures in this book more than twenty times. Therefore, apply the Divine Healing Hands within this book twenty times and practice for as long as you can each time to gain the greatest benefits. After that, you will need to connect with a Divine Healing Hands Soul Healer or one of my Worldwide Representatives to receive Divine Healing Hands blessings or to apply to receive Divine Healing Hands yourself.

Apply the Four Power Techniques along with Divine Healing Hands to heal the physical body:

Body Power. Sit up straight. Close your eyes. Place the tip of your tongue gently against the roof of your mouth. If you are a Divine Healing Hands Soul Healer, put your hands in the Soul Light Era Prayer Position and shake your right hand. If you are not a Divine Healing Hands Soul Healer, simply put your hands in the Soul Light Era Prayer Position.

Soul Power. Say *hello*:

> *Dear Divine Healing Hands,*
> *I love you.*
> *You have the power to heal my physical body.*
> *I am extremely grateful.*
> *Please offer my physical body a soul healing blessing as*
>   *appropriate.*
> *Thank you.*

Mind Power. Visualize Divine Healing Hands radiating golden light in your Zhong.

Sound Power. Chant or sing silently or aloud:

> *Divine Healing Hands heal and transform my physi-*
>   *cal body. Thank you.*

Divine Healing Hands heal and transform my physical body. Thank you.
Divine Healing Hands heal and transform my physical body. Thank you.
Divine Healing Hands heal and transform my physical body. Thank you . . .

Chant for as long as you can. The longer you chant and the more you chant, the more benefits you will receive from Divine Healing Hands.

You have read about the power of Divine Healing Hands. You have also experienced the power of Divine Healing Hands. There are thousands of miraculous soul healing stories from Divine Healing Hands. Here is one heart-touching story of transformation for two people who were diagnosed with cancer.

> *In the fall of 2010 I received two phone calls within a couple days. The first one was from a dear nursing friend in Canada to let me know that she'd been diagnosed with terminal lung cancer. She had two lesions in her lungs. I don't know why she reached out to me because she didn't know that I had Divine Healing Hands. I haven't seen her for three years.*
>
> *Two days later I received a phone call from an aunt to let me know that an uncle had been diagnosed with cancer of the stomach and that he would be having surgery just before Christmas. I quickly packaged him up some of Master Sha's books and sent them to him.*

I let my friend and uncle know that I was going on a vacation and that I wouldn't be able to touch base with them until I returned. I took Master Sha's books with me on vacation and faithfully offered Divine Healing Hands blessings to both of them every eight hours. No excuse, no work; I just did Divine Healing Hands.

Early in 2011 both of them went to the doctor for their follow-up appointments and were told that, for some miraculous reason, there was no cancer left. They had surgery but neither of them had to follow up or go to the cancer clinic. Both of them questioned that because they had been told they would need chemo and radiation, but both of them were told no, there was nothing there. They didn't even have to follow up with one appointment at the cancer clinic. They were cured.

I just want to say thank you and that Divine Healing Hands truly does work.

Brenda Gartner, RN, CEN
Waimanalo, Hawaii

Divine Healing Hands often bring unexpected blessings. This is one such story:

This experience happened at my workplace. A colleague of mine asked for a healing blessing because she had an intense headache. We found a quiet place where I immediately started to offer a Divine Healing Hands blessing along with my Soul Song. I instantly felt a very strong golden bright healing light coming out from my hand. My whole body was vibrating and moving, and we were in the company of many healing angels, archangels, Jesus, Mary, and many saints.

After the healing, I asked her, "How do you feel?" Her answer surprised me. She told me that she saw two dark shadows inside her that were very confused. They didn't know what to do or where to go. The shadows disappeared when the light came into her. She also understood those dark shadows to be related to the hatred and resentment she had toward some individuals.

The next day, I asked her how she was and she told me that her husband fights with her every evening when she goes home, but on that particular night she had the realization that it is better to love and accept her spouse than to fight. She felt peace and stopped fighting.

I asked her about her headache and she replied that she had forgotten about it. Not only did she have these insights, but her headache was gone as well.

Thank you, Divine Healing Hands. Thank you, Soul Song. Thank you, Heaven's Team. Thank you, all souls. Love you all.

Carmen C. Ferlan
Sahuarita, Arizona

Here is another miraculous story about Divine Healing Hands healing heart valves that needed replacement, thus avoiding heart surgery:

My brother's mother-in-law had a heart problem. It was a heart valve issue, and they didn't think she was going to make it. My sister and I both turned on our Divine

Healing Hands every day. We did a practice where we would send our Divine Healing Hands out to be with her for twelve hours, and then we would call them back to rest twelve hours later.

To make a long story short, she is fine now. Not only did she recover fully, but the last email I received said that her heart problem is gone. She needed new heart valves but the doctor said her heart is fine now.

David H.
Akron, Ohio

Divine Healing Hands are priceless treasures to heal the spiritual, mental, emotional, and physical bodies. Divine Healing Hands are permanent divine treasures. This book offers you an opportunity to experience Divine Healing Hands soul healing blessings twenty times. You could receive great healing and transformation from these twenty Divine Healing Hands blessings. This is divine generosity.

To become a Divine Healing Hands Soul Healer is to serve. Those who receive the permanent download of Divine Healing Hands Soul Mind Body Transplants can apply Divine Healing Hands anytime, anywhere to serve themselves, their loved ones, pets, and more.

In this chapter I have given you some of the most powerful and profound sacred soul secrets, soul wisdom, soul knowledge, and practical soul techniques to heal the spiritual, mental, emotional, and physical bodies. Apply them again and again to heal you and your loved ones, family, friends, colleagues, and more.

In reading this chapter, you have received permanent divine

treasures of Divine Purple Light Ball and Purple Liquid Spring of Divine Forgiveness Soul Mind Body Transplants, Divine Purple Light Ball and Purple Liquid Spring of Divine Clarity of Mind Soul Mind Body Transplants, and Divine Purple Light Ball and Purple Liquid Spring of Divine Love Soul Mind Body Transplants. These are all priceless permanent divine treasures to bring you divine assistance for healing all sickness and transforming all life. Use them as much as you can for the rest of your life to heal and transform every aspect of your life.

You and humanity are extremely blessed that the Divine is giving these incredible and powerful treasures as gifts to you and any reader. We cannot thank the Divine enough. We cannot be grateful to the Divine enough.

> *Heal. Heal. Heal.*
> *Transform. Transform. Transform.*
> *Thank you, Divine Healing Hands.*
> *Thank you, all permanent divine treasures.*
> *Thank you, Divine.*
> *Thank you, Tao.*
> *Thank you. Thank you. Thank you.*

5

Apply Divine Healing Hands for Life Transformation

$\mathcal{R}$ELATIONSHIPS, FINANCES, AND intelligence are three very important aspects of human life. Divine Healing Hands have the power and ability to heal and transform relationships, finances, and intelligence. God's soul healing hands carry Divine Soul Power that can heal and transform any aspect of all life.

Relationships

Human beings have all kinds of relationships. Some of our most important relationships are those with our spouse or partner, with other family members, with colleagues and coworkers, and with friends. There are many challenges in all kinds of relationships around the world. Family relationships between husband and wife, partners, siblings, parent and child, and more could be challenging. Workplace relationships between boss and employees or between coworkers could be challenging. In society there could be challenges between organizations. Each of us is deeply affected by relationships between organizations and relationships between countries. Many books, seminars, workshops, and teachings on improving relationships are available. I will share how to transform relationships at the soul level.

Transform the soul of a relationship first; then transformation of the relationship will follow.

Everyone and everything has a soul, including a relationship between individuals, organizations, cities, countries, and more. You can apply soul healing and, especially, Divine Healing Hands to transform every aspect of life, including relationships, finances, and much more.

I will share a story of the power of Divine Healing Hands to heal relationships:

> *Dear my beloved teacher and spiritual father, Master Sha,*
>
> *I would like to express my great gratitude to you, the Divine, and Tao for the extreme generosity to give the Divine's soul hands to humanity and Mother Earth.*
>
> *Being a Divine Healing Hands Soul Healer accomplished my father's wish for me. The recommendations my dad had given to me before I went to university were two: one was to be a doctor and the other was to be a teacher. Because I am a very sensitive person, it is very hard for me to see people in pain and suffering, so I didn't manage to go to medical school.*

As time went by I saw so many people around me suffering from all kinds of sickness every day. My heart was so painful. At the same time, my heart was even more painful because I knew that even if I were to become a doctor, there would be so many hopeless cases I couldn't help.

I received the Divine Healing Hands download in January 2012. So many miracles have happened in my life. Now my dad in Heaven must be very proud and happy for me. As a soul healer I can help people and myself much more than I could as a physical doctor.

As many of us know, Divine Healing Hands can remove blockages and transform all aspects of life. The most profound benefits I have received from Divine Healing Hands are remote healing and transformation of relationships.

Like many new Chinese immigrants in Canada, most of our beloved close family members are still in China. It is very sad when some of them get sick. We are on the other side of the world and there is nothing that we can do to help and support them in a practical way.

My father-in-law is eighty-two years old. His health is a big concern for my husband and me. Since last summer he has had leg and foot problems. Walking has become more and more difficult for him. Since I received Divine Healing Hands, I have called his soul to join the free Divine Healing Hands Blessings teleconference every day. His legs and feet became much better after a month and there is no problem with his walking. I am so grateful that I can give my love and care to my loved ones in this way.

My husband has had serious work relationship prob-

lems for many years. He hardly worked in one unit for more than two years over the last twenty years. In January 2011 he got a new job and that was a big jump for his career. I offered a relationship blessing practice for him when he went on the interview and when he started to work, everything went on very nice and sound. Afterward I forgot to keep offering the blessings. His working situation became harder and harder. He didn't let me know until one day this past March when he was laid off.

I was shocked when I got his phone call from work. I right away realized he needed a Divine Healing Hands blessing for finding a new job. I turned on my Divine Healing Hands Soul Healer treasures and practiced for two to three hours in the evening. The next day we printed his résumé, wrote down a few addresses, and started job hunting.

The first place we went offered him a job right away. This job offered him approximately a one-third increase in his salary. I was shocked again by the results. Divine Healing Hands blessings are truly beyond words and imagination.

Since then I call his soul to join in the daily Divine Healing Hands Blessings teleconference often for the relationships with his coworkers, boss, the materials, and tools. Now everything in his workplace has become wonderful. He has never been so happy at work.

The healing stories pile up every day through serving with my Divine Healing Hands. Divine Healing Hands made my dreams come true. I cannot thank you enough, Master Sha and the Divine.

Please accept my deepest gratitude and love in Chinese:

无限感恩, Wu xian gan en, *which means "boundless gratitude, cannot thank you enough."*

> *Zhu Lu*
> *Toronto, Ontario, Canada*

Let us start to practice to transform relationships.

RELATIONSHIPS BETWEEN PEOPLE

First let us practice to transform the relationship between people. Apply the Four Power Techniques to transform all types of relationships. I will also lead you to apply your divine treasures. The same practice can be used for relationships of any type.

Body Power. Sit up straight. Close your eyes. Place the tip of your tongue gently against the roof of your mouth. Place one palm on the abdomen below the navel. Place the other palm over the heart.

Soul Power. Say *hello*:

> *Dear soul mind body of* _____ (name the person with
>   whom you wish to transform your relationship),
> *I love you.*
> *Please come.*
> *Let us offer forgiveness to each other.*
> *Dear soul mind body of Divine Purple Light Ball and*
>   *Purple Liquid Spring of Divine Forgiveness Soul*
>   *Mind Body Transplants,*[1]
> *I love you.*

---

1. You received these in chapter 4. See page 94.

You have the power to heal my relationship with
_____ (name).
Please transform our relationship.
Thank you.

Mind Power. Visualize the divine treasure of Divine Purple Light Ball and Purple Liquid Spring of Divine Forgiveness radiating between you and the other person.

Sound Power. Chant or sing silently or aloud:

> *Divine Purple Light Ball and Purple Liquid Spring of Divine Forgiveness heal and transform our relationship. Thank you.*
> *Divine Purple Light Ball and Purple Liquid Spring of Divine Forgiveness heal and transform our relationship. Thank you.*
> *Divine Purple Light Ball and Purple Liquid Spring of Divine Forgiveness heal and transform our relationship. Thank you.*
> *Divine Purple Light Ball and Purple Liquid Spring of Divine Forgiveness heal and transform our relationship. Thank you . . .*

Stop reading now. Chant *Divine Purple Light Ball and Purple Liquid Spring of Divine Forgiveness heal and transform our relationship. Thank you* for five minutes. Generally speaking, chant for three to five minutes per time, three to five times per day. If you have very challenging relationships, chant for one to two hours a day. The longer you chant and the more you chant, the better the results you could receive.

In my teaching, forgiveness brings inner peace and inner joy. Doing a regular forgiveness practice is key to self-clearing karma and removing blockages in every aspect of life, including relationships.

Forgiveness is two-sided. If "A" and "B" have issues in a relationship, "A" needs to forgive "B" and "B" also needs to forgive "A." The forgiveness practice is as follows:

> *Dear* _____ (name the person with whom you
>   wish to transform your relationship),
> *I love you.*
> *Please forgive all of the mistakes I have made against*
>   *you in this lifetime and in all lifetimes.*
> *I sincerely apologize for all of the pain and suffering I*
>   *have caused you.*
> *If you have made any mistakes against me in this life-*
>   *time and in all lifetimes, I forgive you completely.*

Chant or sing repeatedly silently or aloud:

> *I forgive you.*
> *You forgive me.*
> *Bring love, peace, and harmony.*
> *Bring love, peace, and harmony . . .*

This mantra and practice have power beyond words. This is soul transformation of relationships. Practice more and more. You will understand the benefits more and more.

Stop reading now. Chant *I forgive you. You forgive me. Bring love, peace, and harmony. Bring love, peace, and harmony.* for five minutes. Generally speaking, chant for three to five minutes per time, three to five times per day. If you have very challenging relationships you should chant for one to two hours a day. The longer you chant and the more you chant, the better the results you could receive. Add all of your practice time together to total one hour or more a day.

Many people experience relationship challenges of all kinds in their workplace. Divine Healing Hands can transform these challenges—between manager and staff, between coworkers, and more. Here is one story that is a good example:

> I am a Divine Healing Hands Soul Healer who works in a public agency in a highly charged political atmosphere. We recently lost the top three executives in the agency in a political test of wills that left many ducking for cover.
>
> We were appointed an interim General Manager whose focus was to run the agency as a means to promote his own agenda: he wants the job permanently. There was a great push from above to increase both production and output of staff and work.
>
> This created a great deal of stress for everyone involved. This is a professional organization with many highly qualified, highly motivated individuals.
>
> I have been sending Divine Healing Hands blessings to the interim General Manager and the agency every day for the past few weeks as the energy has been quite heavy and dull.
>
> I have noticed a great shift in the energy in the workplace. There has been a noticeable change of attitude and support from all of the workers. I am aware that what will unfold in the future will be exactly what the agency needs in order to move forward.

I thank Master Sha, the Divine, and Divine Healing Hands for this great gift. It is so wonderful to have the darkness and clouds dissipated and the light shining again in my workplace.

Christopher Keehn
Monterey, California

RELATIONSHIPS BETWEEN ORGANIZATIONS

Relationships between organizations can also have challenges, conflict, communication blockages, and more.

Now let us practice to transform a relationship between organizations by applying the Divine Purple Light Ball and Purple Liquid Spring of Divine Forgiveness Soul Mind Body Transplants that you received in chapter 4.

Apply the Four Power Techniques:

Body Power. Sit up straight. Close your eyes. Place the tip of your tongue gently against the roof of your mouth. Place one palm on your abdomen below the navel. Place the other palm over your heart.

Soul Power. Say *hello:*

> *Dear soul mind body of* _____ *and* _____ (give names of organizations that need transformation),
> *I love you.*
> *Let us do a forgiveness practice together.*
> *Dear soul mind body of Divine Purple Light Ball and Purple Liquid Spring of Divine Forgiveness Soul Mind Body Transplants,*
> *I love you.*

You have the power to heal the relationship between
these two organizations.
Please transform their relationship.
Thank you.

Mind Power. Visualize the divine treasures of Divine Purple Light Ball and Purple Liquid Spring of Divine Forgiveness radiating between the organizations.

Sound Power. Chant or sing silently or aloud:

Divine Purple Light Ball and Purple Liquid Spring of
Divine Forgiveness heal and transform the relation-
ship between the organizations. Thank you.
Divine Purple Light Ball and Purple Liquid Spring of
Divine Forgiveness heal and transform the relation-
ship between the organizations. Thank you.
Divine Purple Light Ball and Purple Liquid Spring of
Divine Forgiveness heal and transform the relation-
ship between the organizations. Thank you.
Divine Purple Light Ball and Purple Liquid Spring of
Divine Forgiveness heal and transform the relation-
ship between the organizations. Thank you . . .

Stop reading and put the book down. Chant *Divine Purple Light Ball and Purple Liquid Spring of Divine Forgiveness heal and transform the relationship between the organizations. Thank you* for five minutes. Generally speaking, chant for three to five minutes per time, three to five times per day. If the two organizations have heavy challenges between them, chant for one to two hours a day. The longer you chant and the more you chant, the better the results you could receive.

APPLY DIVINE HEALING HANDS
TO TRANSFORM RELATIONSHIPS

Now I will lead you to heal a relationship between two organizations by applying Divine Healing Hands. I strongly suggest that each time you apply the Divine Healing Hands within this book, spend at least a half-hour practicing because the Divine has guided me clearly that you cannot use the Divine Healing Hands treasures in this book more than twenty times. Therefore, apply the Divine Healing Hands within this book twenty times and practice for as long as you can each time to gain the greatest benefits. After that, you will need to connect with a Divine Healing Hands Soul Healer or one of my Worldwide Representatives to receive Divine Healing Hands blessings or to apply to receive Divine Healing Hands yourself.

Body Power. Sit up straight. Close your eyes. Place the tip of your tongue gently against the roof of your mouth. If you are a Divine Healing Hands Soul Healer, put your hands in the Soul Light Era Prayer Position and shake your right hand. If you are not a Divine Healing Hands Soul Healer, simply put your hands in the Soul Light Era Prayer Position.

Soul Power. Say *hello:*

> *Dear Divine Healing Hands,*
> *I love you.*
> *You have the power to heal and transform the relationship between the organizations _____ and*
> _____.
> *I am extremely grateful.*

Please offer a soul healing blessing as appropriate.
Thank you.

Mind Power. Visualize Divine Healing Hands radiating golden light between the two organizations.

Sound Power. Chant or sing silently or aloud:

> *Divine Healing Hands heal and transform the rela-*
>   *tionship between _____ and _____.*
>   *Thank you.*
> *Divine Healing Hands heal and transform the rela-*
>   *tionship between _____ and _____.*
>   *Thank you.*
> *Divine Healing Hands heal and transform the rela-*
>   *tionship between _____ and _____.*
>   *Thank you.*
> *Divine Healing Hands heal and transform the rela-*
>   *tionship between _____ and _____.*
>   *Thank you . . .*

Chant for as long as you can. The longer you chant and the more you chant, the more benefits your request will receive from Divine Healing Hands.

Next I will lead you to apply Divine Healing Hands to transform the relationship between you and another person. Use the Four Power Techniques:

Body Power. Sit up straight. Close your eyes. Place the tip of your tongue gently against the roof of your mouth. If you are a Divine Healing Hands Soul Healer, put your hands in the Soul

Light Era Prayer Position and shake your right hand. If not, simply put your hands in the Soul Light Era Prayer Position.

Soul Power. Say *hello:*

> *Dear Divine Healing Hands,*
> *I love you.*
> *You have the power to heal and transform the relationship between* _____ (name the person with whom you wish to transform your relationship) *and me.*
> *I am extremely grateful.*
> *Please offer a soul healing blessing as appropriate.*
> *Thank you.*

Mind Power. Visualize Divine Healing Hands radiating golden light between you and the other person.

Sound Power. Chant or sing silently or aloud:

> *Divine Healing Hands heal and transform the relationship between* _____ *and me.*
> *Thank you.*
> *Divine Healing Hands heal and transform the relationship between* _____ *and me.*
> *Thank you.*
> *Divine Healing Hands heal and transform the relationship between* _____ *and me.*
> *Thank you.*
> *Divine Healing Hands heal and transform the relationship between* _____ *and me.*
> *Thank you . . .*

Chant for as long as you can. The longer and the more you chant, the more benefits your relationships will receive from Divine Healing Hands.

Finances

Most people think about their finances every day. Many people have financial challenges they wish to transform. The last eight years have brought more and more financial challenges and other challenges on Mother Earth. This is part of Mother Earth's transition period. For millions of people, transforming finances is vital.

I will now offer priceless permanent divine treasures that can be applied to transform finances.

Prepare!

Divine Order: Divine Purple Light Ball and Purple Liquid Spring of Divine Light Soul Mind Body Transplants

Transmission!

Congratulations! You are blessed. Humanity is blessed.

Divine Light heals, prevents sickness, purifies and rejuvenates soul, heart, mind, and body, and transforms relationships, finances, intelligence, and every aspect of life.

I will lead you to practice to transform finances by applying the Four Power Techniques and Divine Purple Light Ball and Purple Liquid Spring of Divine Light Soul Mind Body Transplants:

Body Power. Sit up straight. Close your eyes. Place the tip of your tongue gently against the roof of your mouth. Place one palm on your abdomen below the navel. Place the other palm over your Message Center.

Soul Power. Say *hello:*

> *Dear soul mind body of my finances,*
> *I love you.*
> *Dear soul mind body of Divine Purple Light Ball and*
>   *Purple Liquid Spring of Divine Light Soul Mind*
>   *Body Transplants,*
> *I love you.*
> *You have the power to transform my finances.*
> *I am extremely grateful.*
> *Please offer my finances a soul healing blessing as*
>   *appropriate.*
> *Thank you.*

Mind Power. Visualize the divine treasure of Divine Purple Light Ball and Purple Liquid Spring of Divine Light transforming your financial situation.

Sound Power. Chant or sing silently or aloud:

> *Divine Purple Light Ball and Purple Liquid Spring of*
>   *Divine Light transform my finances. Thank you.*
> *Divine Purple Light Ball and Purple Liquid Spring of*
>   *Divine Light transform my finances. Thank you.*
> *Divine Purple Light Ball and Purple Liquid Spring of*
>   *Divine Light transform my finances. Thank you.*
> *Divine Purple Light Ball and Purple Liquid Spring of*
>   *Divine Light transform my finances. Thank you . . .*

Stop reading now. Chant *Divine Purple Light Ball and Purple Liquid Spring of Divine Light transform my finances. Thank you* for five minutes. Generally speaking, chant for three to five minutes per time, three to five times per day. If you have heavy financial challenges, chant for one to two hours a day. The longer you chant and the more you chant, the better the results you could receive.

APPLY DIVINE HEALING HANDS
TO TRANSFORM FINANCES

Now I will lead you to transform your finances by applying Divine Healing Hands. The Divine has guided me clearly that you cannot continue to use the Divine Healing Hands within this book more than twenty times. Therefore, practice for as long as you can each time you apply the Divine Healing Hands downloaded to this book in order to gain the greatest benefits from the twenty sessions. After that, you will need to connect with a Divine Healing Hands Soul Healer or one of my Worldwide Representatives to receive Divine Healing Hands blessings or apply to receive Divine Healing Hands yourself.

Body Power. Sit up straight. Close your eyes. Place the tip of your tongue gently against the roof of your mouth. If you are a Divine Healing Hands Soul Healer, put your hands in the Soul Light Era Prayer Position and shake your right hand. If you are not a Divine Healing Hands Soul Healer, simply put your hands in the Soul Light Era Prayer Position.

Soul Power. Say *hello:*

Dear Divine Healing Hands,
I love you.
You have the power to transform my finances.
I am extremely grateful.
Please offer my finances a soul healing blessing as
*   appropriate.*
Thank you.

Mind Power. Visualize Divine Healing Hands radiating golden light and transforming your finances.

Sound Power. Chant or sing silently or aloud:

Divine Healing Hands transform my finances.
*   Thank you.*
Divine Healing Hands transform my finances.
*   Thank you.*
Divine Healing Hands transform my finances.
*   Thank you.*
Divine Healing Hands transform my finances.
*   Thank you . . .*

Chant for as long as you can. The longer you chant and the more you chant, the more benefits you will receive from Divine Healing Hands.

Increasing Intelligence

Many people talk about increasing and developing intelligence. Most people think intelligence comes from the mind. I want to share with humanity that intelligence does come from the mind, but the most important sources of intelligence are the heart and the soul.

There are three kinds of intelligence:

- mind intelligence
- heart intelligence
- soul intelligence

Traditional Chinese medicine teaches that the heart houses the mind and soul. If one has heart problems, one's brain and intelligence could be seriously affected. Memory, comprehension, realization, and more could be affected.

Soul is the boss for a human being. Our beloved soul has experiences and memories from many lifetimes. Our beloved soul communicates with and learns from our spiritual fathers and mothers in Heaven. Our beloved soul carries great wisdom and knowledge. Soul intelligence is beyond words. Generally speaking, soul intelligence is hidden. Developing soul intelligence is the key to highly developing one's intelligence.

Let me first lead you in a practice to develop mind intelligence.

MIND INTELLIGENCE

My spiritual father and mentor, Dr. and Master Zhi Chen Guo, discovered a sacred number code for developing the power of the mind. It is:

01777—908—01777—92244

You can chant this code in English, one digit at a time. You can chant this code in any language because the message is the same. I recommend chanting it in Chinese because the Chinese also carries a special vibration:

01777	Ling Yao Chi Chi Chi (pronounced *ling yow chee chee chee*)
908	Jiu Ling Ba (pronounced *jeo ling bah*)
01777	Ling Yao Chi Chi Chi
92244	Jiu Er Er Si Si (pronounced *jeo ar ar sz sz*)

What is the significance of these numbers? They are three separate subcodes:

01777 stimulates the corpus callosum, the tissue connecting the right brain and the left brain. The cells in this area transport messages from one side of the brain to the other.

908 stimulates the left brain.

92244 stimulates the right brain. See figure 10.

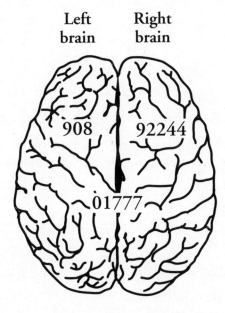

Figure 10. Sacred number code to develop the entire brain

To develop the entire brain—left, right, and corpus callosum—the practice is very simple. Just learn the subcodes and chant them rapidly in the special pattern. You can do this practice almost anywhere and anytime. As you chant this code, you are stimulating the central brain cells between the right and left brain (the corpus callosum), then stimulating the left brain, next going back to the center of the brain, and then stimulating the right brain. Repeat this pattern rapidly to stimulate all of the cells in the brain and to develop the connections among them. This is a major secret to develop mind intelligence.

Apply the Four Power Techniques with this sacred number code to develop mind intelligence:

Body Power. Sit up straight. Close your eyes. Place the tip of your tongue gently against the roof of your mouth. Place one palm over your kundalini. Remember, kundalini energy nourishes the brain. Place the other palm on the top of your head.

Soul Power. Say *hello*:

> *Dear soul mind body of my brain and my mind,*
> *I love you.*
> *You have the power to boost your intelligence.*
> *Do a good job.*
> *Thank you.*
> *Dear 01777—908—01777—92244,*
> *I love you.*
> *You have the power to increase my mind intelligence.*
> *I am very grateful.*
> *Thank you.*

Mind Power. Visualize golden light radiating in your entire brain.

Sound Power. Chant or sing silently or aloud:

> *01777 (ling yow chee chee chee)—908 (jeo ling*
> *bah)—01777 (ling yow chee chee chee)—92244*
> *(jeo ar ar sz sz)*
> *01777—908—01777—92244*
> *01777—908—01777—92244*
> *01777—908—01777—92244 . . .*

Or simply chant in English (or your native language):

> *01777 (zero one seven seven seven)—908 (nine zero*
> *eight)—01777(zero one seven seven seven)—92244*
> *(nine two two four four)*
> *01777—908—01777—92244*
> *01777—908—01777—92244*
> *01777—908—01777—92244 . . .*

Stop reading and put the book down. Chant *01777 (ling yow chee chee chee)—908 (jeo ling bah)—01777 (ling yow chee chee chee)—92244 (jeo ar ar sz sz)* or chant in English, *01777– 908– 01777–92244* for five minutes.

Generally speaking, chant for three to five minutes per time, three to five times per day. If you have major challenges with mind intelligence, such as poor comprehension, brain fog, dyslexia, injury, or other brain blockages, chant for one to two hours a day. The longer you chant and the more you chant, the better the results you could receive.

APPLY DIVINE HEALING HANDS TO INCREASE
MIND INTELLIGENCE

Now I will lead you to increase mind intelligence by applying Divine Healing Hands. I strongly suggest that each time you apply the Divine Healing Hands within this book, spend at least a half-hour practicing because the Divine has guided me clearly that you cannot use the Divine Healing Hands treasures in this book more than twenty times. Therefore, apply the Divine Healing Hands within this book twenty times and practice for as long as you can each time to gain the greatest benefits. After that, you will need to connect with a Divine Healing Hands Soul Healer or one of my Worldwide Representatives to receive Divine Healing Hands blessings or apply to receive Divine Healing Hands yourself.

Body Power. Sit up straight. Close your eyes. Place the tip of your tongue gently against the roof of your mouth. If you are a Divine Healing Hands Soul Healer, put your hands in the Soul Light Era Prayer Position and shake your right hand. If you are not a Divine Healing Hands Soul Healer, simply put your hands in the Soul Light Era Prayer Position.

Soul Power. Say *hello:*

> *Dear Divine Healing Hands,*
> *I love you.*
> *You have the power to increase my mind intelligence.*
> *I am extremely grateful.*
> *Please offer my mind a soul healing blessing for intel-*
>   *ligence as appropriate.*
> *Thank you.*

Mind Power. Visualize Divine Healing Hands radiating golden light within your brain.

Sound Power. Chant or sing silently or aloud:

> *Divine Healing Hands increase my mind intelligence.*
>   *Thank you.*
> *Divine Healing Hands increase my mind intelligence.*
>   *Thank you.*
> *Divine Healing Hands increase my mind intelligence.*
>   *Thank you.*
> *Divine Healing Hands increase my mind intelligence.*
>   *Thank you . . .*

Chant for as long as you can. The longer you chant and the more you chant, the more benefits you will receive from Divine Healing Hands.

HEART INTELLIGENCE

The nature of the heart is love. One of the best ways to develop heart intelligence is to apply Divine Purple Light Ball and Purple Liquid Spring of Divine Love Soul Mind Body Transplants, which you received when you read chapter 4.

Now let me lead you to develop heart intelligence by applying the Four Power Techniques and the Divine Love Soul Mind Body Transplants:

Body Power. Sit up straight. Close your eyes. Place the tip of your tongue gently against the roof of your mouth. If you are a Divine Healing Hands Soul Healer, put your hands in the Soul

Light Era Prayer Position and shake your right hand. If you are
not a Divine Healing Hands Soul Healer, simply put your hands
in the Soul Light Era Prayer Position.

Soul Power. Say *hello:*

> *Dear soul mind body of my heart,*
> *I love you.*
> *You have the power to increase your intelligence.*
> *Do a good job.*
> *Thank you.*

> *Dear soul mind body of Divine Purple Light Ball and*
>   *Purple Liquid Spring of Divine Love Soul Mind*
>   *Body Transplants,*
> *I love you.*
> *You have the power to increase my heart intelligence.*
> *I am extremely grateful.*
> *Thank you.*

Mind Power. Visualize purple light radiating in your heart.

Sound Power. Chant or sing silently or aloud:

> *Divine Purple Light Ball and Purple Liquid Spring of*
>   *Divine Love increase my heart intelligence.*
>   *Thank you.*
> *Divine Purple Light Ball and Purple Liquid Spring of*
>   *Divine Love increase my heart intelligence.*
>   *Thank you.*
> *Divine Purple Light Ball and Purple Liquid Spring of*

> *Divine Love increase my heart intelligence.*
> *Thank you.*
> *Divine Purple Light Ball and Purple Liquid Spring of*
> *Divine Love increase my heart intelligence.*
> *Thank you . . .*

Now put the book down and chant *Divine Purple Light Ball and Purple Liquid Spring of Divine Love increase my heart intelligence. Thank you* for ten minutes. Generally speaking, chant for three to five minutes per time, three to five times per day. If you have major challenges with heart intelligence, chant for two hours or more a day. The longer you chant and the more you chant, the better the results you could receive. Add all of the practice time together to total two hours or more a day.

APPLY DIVINE HEALING HANDS TO INCREASE
HEART INTELLIGENCE

Now I will lead you to develop heart intelligence using Divine Healing Hands. As a reminder, the Divine has clearly guided me that you cannot use the Divine Healing Hands downloaded to this book more than twenty times. I strongly suggest that you practice for as long as you can each time you apply the Divine Healing Hands in this book in order to gain the greatest benefits. After applying them twenty times, you will need to connect with a Divine Healing Hands Soul Healer or one of my Worldwide Representatives to receive Divine Healing Hands blessings or to apply to receive Divine Healing Hands yourself.

Body Power. Sit up straight. Close your eyes. Place the tip of your tongue gently against the roof of your mouth. If you are a

Divine Healing Hands Soul Healer, put your hands in the Soul Light Era Prayer Position and shake your right hand. If you are not a Divine Healing Hands Soul Healer, simply put your hands in the Soul Light Era Prayer Position.

Soul Power. Say *hello:*

> *Dear Divine Healing Hands,*
> *I love you.*
> *You have the power to increase my heart intelligence.*
> *I am extremely grateful.*
> *Please offer my heart a soul healing blessing for intelligence as appropriate.*
> *Thank you.*

Mind Power. Visualize Divine Healing Hands radiating golden light within your heart.

Sound Power. Chant or sing silently or aloud:

> *Divine Healing Hands increase my heart intelligence.*
>   *Thank you.*
> *Divine Healing Hands increase my heart intelligence.*
>   *Thank you.*
> *Divine Healing Hands increase my heart intelligence.*
>   *Thank you.*
> *Divine Healing Hands increase my heart intelligence.*
>   *Thank you . . .*

Chant for as long as you can. The longer you chant and the more you chant, the more benefits you will receive from Divine Healing Hands.

SOUL INTELLIGENCE

Your body soul has reincarnated for hundreds or thousands of lifetimes. Your beloved soul has had many experiences and gained great wisdom over all of these lifetimes. For most people, only a little of the wisdom of the soul has been conveyed to the mind and heart. Our soul's wisdom and knowledge remain largely hidden. Developing your soul intelligence can make you extremely intelligent.

Now let me lead everyone to develop soul intelligence by applying the Four Power Techniques and the divine sacred code *3396815*.

The divine sacred code 3396815 was given by the Divine to my spiritual father and mentor, Dr. and Master Zhi Chen Guo, nearly forty years ago. This sacred code unites the spiritual world and the physical world. It has tremendous spiritual power.

When spoken in Chinese, the sound of each number in 3396815 stimulates cellular vibration in a specific area of the body. Chanting 3396815 repeatedly causes energy to flow continuously through the main organs and systems of the body. The pattern of this flow promotes energy and healing in a powerful way. See figure 11.

- 33 (pronounced *sahn sahn*) stimulates the chest and lungs
- 9 (pronounced *jeo*) stimulates the lower abdomen
- 6 (pronounced *leo*) stimulates the sides and ribs
- 8 (pronounced *bah*) stimulates the navel area
- 1 (pronounced *yow*) stimulates the head and neck
- 5 (pronounced *woo*) stimulates the stomach area

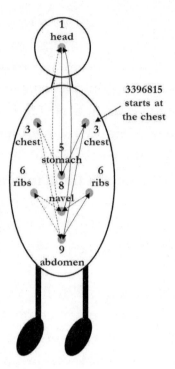

Figure 11. The divine sacred code 3396815

Therefore, 3396815 promotes energy flow in the following pattern:

- starts at the chest area (33)
- flows down to the lower abdomen (9)
- flows to the rib area on both sides (6)
- flows to the navel area (8)
- flows up to the neck and head (1)
- flows down to the stomach area (5)

The significance and power of 3396815 are that it is a divine sacred code to:

- remove soul mind body blockages for healing and transforming all life, including health, relationships, finances, intelligence, children, and every aspect of life
- develop the four major spiritual channels, which are the Soul Language Channel, Direct Soul Communication Channel, Third Eye Channel, and Direct Knowing Channel
- develop soul, heart, and mind intelligence
- purify and rejuvenate soul, heart, mind, and body
- prolong life

Now let me lead you to develop soul intelligence by applying the Four Power Techniques and the divine sacred code 3396815:

Body Power. Sit up straight. Close your eyes. Place the tip of your tongue gently against the roof of your mouth. Put your hands in the Soul Light Era Prayer Position.

Soul Power. Say *hello:*

> *Dear soul mind body of my soul,*
> *I love you.*
> *You have the power to increase my soul intelligence.*
> *Do a good job.*
> *Thank you.*
> *Dear soul mind body of 3396815 (sahn sahn jeo leo*
>   *bah yow woo),*
> *I love you.*
> *You have the power to increase my soul intelligence.*
> *I am very grateful.*
> *Thank you.*

Mind Power. Visualize rainbow light radiating in your soul.

Sound Power. Chant *3396815—San San Jiu Liu Ba Yao Wu* (*sahn sahn jeo leo bah yow woo*) out loud and as fast as you can.

> *San San Jiu Liu Ba Yao Wu*
> *San San Jiu Liu Ba Yao Wu*
> *San San Jiu Liu Ba Yao Wu*
> *San San Jiu Liu Ba Yao Wu . . .*

Put the book down and chant this sacred code for several minutes now. Chant as fast as you can. Relax and let the words flow naturally. Release the desire to pronounce the code correctly. Chant very fast! Suddenly a special voice or sound could flow out. This voice could sound very strange; you may not have heard it before. Do not be surprised. This is your Soul Language.

How do you know that you are speaking Soul Language? When a special voice or sound comes out, stop chanting. Then start to chant *3396815* (*sahn sahn jeo leo bah yow woo*) again as fast as you can. The special voice or sound will flow out again. Then you will know that the special voice or sound is your Soul Language. Congratulations!

Soul Language carries soul frequency and vibration with soul love, soul forgiveness, soul compassion, and soul light.

Soul frequency and vibration can transform the frequency and vibration of the mind and body.

Soul love can melt all blockages and transform all life, including health, relationships, finances, intelligence, and every aspect of all life.

Soul forgiveness can bring inner joy and inner peace to all life.

Soul compassion can boost energy, stamina, vitality, and immunity of all life.

Soul light can heal, prevent sickness, purify and rejuvenate soul, heart, mind, and body, and transform all life.

Stop reading now. Chant *3396815* (*sahn sahn jeo leo bah yow woo*) for ten minutes. If your Soul Language flows out, wonderful! If your Soul Language does not flow out, continue to chant *3396815*. Practice. Suddenly your Soul Language could come out.[2]

Generally speaking, chant for three to five minutes per time, three to five times per day. If you have heavy challenges with soul intelligence or if you want to open your spiritual channels further, chant one to two hours a day. The longer you chant and the more you chant, the better the results you could receive. Add all of the practice time together to total one to two hours or more a day.

APPLY DIVINE HEALING HANDS TO INCREASE
SOUL INTELLIGENCE

Now I will lead you to develop soul intelligence by applying Divine Healing Hands. The Divine has guided me that to apply the Divine Healing Hands downloaded to this book is very powerful, and I strongly suggest that each time you apply the Divine Healing Hands within this book, spend at least a half-hour practicing because you cannot use the Divine Healing Hands treasures in this book more than twenty times. Therefore, apply the Divine

---

2. To learn more about Soul Language, see *Soul Wisdom: Practical Soul Treasures to Transform Your Life* (Toronto/New York: Heaven's Library/Atria Books, 2008) and *Soul Communication: Opening Your Spiritual Channels for Success and Fulfillment* (Toronto/New York: Heaven's Library/Atria Books, 2008).

Healing Hands within this book twenty times and practice for as long as you can each time to gain the greatest benefits. After that, you will need to connect with a Divine Healing Hands Soul Healer or one of my Worldwide Representatives to receive Divine Healing Hands blessings or to apply to receive Divine Healing Hands yourself.

Body Power. Sit up straight. Close your eyes. Place the tip of your tongue gently against the roof of your mouth. If you are a Divine Healing Hands Soul Healer, put your hands in the Soul Light Era Prayer Position and shake your right hand. If you are not a Divine Healing Hands Soul Healer, simply put your hands in the Soul Light Era Prayer Position.

Soul Power. Say *hello*:

> *Dear Divine Healing Hands,*
> *I love you.*
> *You have the power to increase my soul intelligence.*
> *I am extremely grateful.*
> *Please offer my soul a soul healing blessing for intelligence as appropriate.*
> *Thank you.*

Mind Power. Visualize Divine Healing Hands radiating golden light within your soul.

Sound Power. Chant silently or aloud:

> *Divine Healing Hands increase my soul intelligence.*
> *Thank you.*

Divine Healing Hands increase my soul intelligence.
  Thank you.
Divine Healing Hands increase my soul intelligence.
  Thank you.
Divine Healing Hands increase my soul intelligence.
  Thank you . . .

Chant for as long as you can. The longer you chant and the more you chant, the more benefits you will receive from Divine Healing Hands.

I have explained and led every reader in practices to develop mind intelligence, heart intelligence, and soul intelligence. If humanity learns how to develop these three intelligences, humanity's intelligence will increase beyond words, comprehension, and imagination.

The practices in this section are very important. To increase your mind intelligence, heart intelligence, and soul intelligence, practice more and more. Apply the divine sacred code 3396815. Apply Divine Healing Hands. Practice. Practice. Practice. Increasing your intelligence brings unlimited benefits to transform your life.

APPLY DIVINE HEALING HANDS TO INCREASE
CHILDREN'S INTELLIGENCE

Intelligence is vital for a child's success. Knowing how to develop and increase children's intelligence is very important. All parents want their children to be healthy, happy, and intelligent.

Divine Healing Hands carry divine power. They can not only offer healing, but can transform every aspect of life, including intelligence and much more.

Let me lead you to apply Divine Healing Hands to increase children's intelligence. If children's intelligence is increased, the quality of humanity will be transformed. The significance of developing children's intelligence cannot be overstated.

Let us practice now by applying the Four Power Techniques and Divine Healing Hands to increase children's intelligence:

Body Power. Sit up straight. Close your eyes. Place the tip of your tongue gently against the roof of your mouth. If you are a Divine Healing Hands Soul Healer, put your hands in the Soul Light Era Prayer Position and shake your right hand. If you are not a Divine Healing Hands Soul Healer, simply put your hands in the Soul Light Era Prayer Position.

Soul Power. Say *hello:*

> *Dear Divine Healing Hands,*
> *I love you.*
> *You have the power to increase my child's (or children's) mind, heart, and soul intelligence.*
> *I am extremely grateful.*
> *Please offer a soul healing blessing for all three intelligences as appropriate.*
> *Thank you.*

Mind Power. Visualize Divine Healing Hands radiating golden light to your child's (or children's) mind, heart, and soul.

Sound Power. Chant silently or aloud:

> *Divine Healing Hands increase my child's (or*
> *children's) mind, heart, and soul intelligence.*
> *Thank you.*
> *Divine Healing Hands increase my child's (or*
> *children's) mind, heart, and soul intelligence.*
> *Thank you.*
> *Divine Healing Hands increase my child's (or*
> *children's) mind, heart, and soul intelligence.*
> *Thank you.*
> *Divine Healing Hands increase my child's (or*
> *children's) mind, heart, and soul intelligence.*
> *Thank you . . .*

Chant for as long as you can. The longer you chant and the more you chant, the more benefits your child or children will receive from Divine Healing Hands.

APPLY DIVINE HEALING HANDS TO INCREASE STUDENTS' INTELLIGENCE

There are hundreds of millions of students worldwide. There are elementary school, middle school, high school, and university students. Many people return to school as adults in order to complete or further their education. There are master's degree students, doctoral degree students, postgraduate students, and more.

Divine Healing Hands has the power to increase mind, heart, and soul intelligence for all levels of students. If students at all levels were to increase their intelligence, the world would be different. Parents make great efforts in many ways to help their children increase their intelligence: tutors, software programs and study aids, study groups, classes, and more. Divine Healing

Hands can increase a student's intelligence. How blessed humanity is to have the opportunity to receive Divine Healing Hands to heal, transform, and bless every aspect of life.

Let us practice now by applying the Four Power Techniques and Divine Healing Hands to increase a student's or students' intelligence:

Body Power. Sit up straight. Close your eyes. Place the tip of your tongue gently against the roof of your mouth. If you are a Divine Healing Hands Soul Healer, put your hands in the Soul Light Era Prayer Position and shake your right hand. If not, simply put your hands in the Soul Light Era Prayer Position.

Soul Power. Say *hello:*

> *Dear Divine Healing Hands,*
> *I love you.*
> *You have the power to increase the intelligence of*
> _____ (give the name of the student[s]).
> *I am extremely grateful.*
> *Please offer a soul healing blessing to increase intelligence as appropriate.*
> *Thank you.*

Mind Power. Visualize Divine Healing Hands radiating golden light to the mind, heart, and soul of the student(s).

Sound Power. Chant silently or aloud:

> *Divine Healing Hands increase the student's (or students') mind, heart, and soul intelligence.*
> *Thank you.*

> *Divine Healing Hands increase the student's (*or
> *students') mind, heart, and soul intelligence.*
> *Thank you.*
> *Divine Healing Hands increase the student's (*or
> *students') mind, heart, and soul intelligence.*
> *Thank you.*
> *Divine Healing Hands increase the student's (*or
> *students') mind, heart, and soul intelligence.*
> *Thank you . . .*

Chant for as long as you can. The longer and more often you chant, the more benefits the student or students will receive from Divine Healing Hands.

APPLY DIVINE HEALING HANDS TO INCREASE
ADULTS' AND SENIORS' INTELLIGENCE

Everyone can benefit from increased intelligence. Adults and seniors need intelligence. As they age, many adults become concerned about Alzheimer's disease or other types of dementia and losing cognitive and other abilities.

I will offer major permanent divine treasures to help adults and seniors increase their brain function.

Prepare!

**Divine Order: Divine Purple Light Ball and
Purple Liquid Spring of Divine Compassion for Brain,
Heart, and Soul Soul Mind Body Transplants**

Transmission!

Congratulations! You are blessed. Humanity is blessed.

Divine Compassion boosts energy, stamina, vitality, and immunity, and can transform all life.

Let us practice now by applying the Four Power Techniques, Divine Healing Hands, and Divine Purple Light Ball and Purple Liquid Spring of Divine Compassion for Brain, Heart, and Soul Soul Mind Body Transplants to increase brain function and intelligence for adults and seniors.

Body Power. Sit up straight. Close your eyes. Place the tip of your tongue gently against the roof of your mouth. If you are a Divine Healing Hands Soul Healer, put your hands in the Soul Light Era Prayer Position and shake your right hand. If you are not a Divine Healing Hands Soul Healer, simply put your hands in the Soul Light Era Prayer Position.

Soul Power. Say *hello*:

> *Dear soul mind body of my mind, heart, and soul,*
> *I love you.*
> *You have the power to increase your intelligence.*
> *Do a good job.*
> *Thank you.*
> *Dear soul mind body of Divine Purple Light Ball and*
>   *Purple Liquid Spring of Divine Compassion for*
>   *Brain, Heart, and Soul Soul Mind Body Trans-*
>   *plants,*
> *I love you.*
> *Dear Divine Healing Hands,*
> *I love you.*
> *You have the power to increase my brain function and*

> *the intelligence of my* (or name of person)
> *mind, heart, and soul.*
> *I am extremely grateful.*
> *Please offer a soul healing blessing as appro-*
>   *priate.*
> *Thank you.*

Mind Power. Visualize Divine Healing Hands radiating golden light to your mind, heart, and soul.

Sound Power. Chant silently or aloud:

> *Divine Healing Hands increase the brain function*
>   *and intelligence of my* (or name of person) *mind,*
>   *heart, and soul. Thank you.*
> *Divine Healing Hands increase the brain function*
>   *and intelligence of my* (or name of person) *mind,*
>   *heart, and soul. Thank you.*
> *Divine Healing Hands increase the brain function*
>   *and intelligence of my* (or name of person) *mind,*
>   *heart, and soul. Thank you.*
> *Divine Healing Hands increase the brain function*
>   *and intelligence of my* (or name of person) *mind,*
>   *heart, and soul. Thank you . . .*

Chant for as long as you can. The longer and the more you chant, the more benefits you will receive from Divine Healing Hands and other divine treasures.

As I have written many times throughout this book, Divine Healing Hands carry divine frequency and vibration that can transform any aspect of life. The following story is one of great transformation for the parents of one of my students.

My mother and father used to suffer quite terribly from many health conditions. Both of them suffered from lung difficulties; they were diagnosed with emphysema, and my mother was having quite a bit of difficulty breathing, along with extreme fatigue. Her balance was off and she used a cane to get around. I was always quite concerned about her falling as she had fallen quite a bit in the past few years and broke a few large bones.

One of the worst problems for my mother was her fear that her memory was failing. She had constant concern that she was getting Alzheimer's like her mother. She worried constantly about this.

My parents were aging quite quickly. Each day was saddening for me to watch as my father struggled to hold my mother up as she hobbled along next to him and they both struggled to breathe and move along.

About two months ago I began calling their souls into the daily free Divine Healing Hands Blessings teleconference to receive Divine Healing Hands soul healing blessings. I did not tell them that they were receiving these daily healing blessings.

After two months, neither parent has any difficulty with breathing! I accompanied my mother to her doctor, and both she and her doctor were remarking at her incredible improvement in her respiratory challenges as she seems to be completely free of any difficulty.

Her balance has taken an almost complete turnaround and she no longer uses a cane, although she cannot under-

stand the meaning of it. As a matter of fact, my parents are now going out dancing two times a week! I have not seen them this happy in twenty years. They are both ecstatically happy and enjoying life like two youngsters in love again.

And the best result of all is that my mother said to me, "I don't know why I was ever afraid that I had Alzheimer's. I just decided to let that go one day a few weeks ago. I'm absolutely fine. That was so silly."

Thank you, Divine. Thank you, Master Sha.

G. G.
Florida

Millions of people want to transform their lives. Humanity faces so many challenges in relationships, finances, intelligence, and every aspect of life. The divine treasures and practices in this chapter are vital to transform every aspect of life. Divine Healing Hands have the power to transform all life. We cannot honor the Divine enough for giving his soul hands to transform every aspect of life for humanity.

After you receive Divine Healing Hands, you have a direct connection with the Divine. When you offer healing, blessing, and life transformation with Divine Healing Hands, the Divine is there for you. There are no words to express our greatest gratitude and honor that we can receive Divine Healing Hands.

Thank you. Thank you. Thank you.

6

Apply Divine Healing Hands to Heal Animals and Nature

MANY FAMILIES HAVE pets. When I came from China to North America I realized more and more that many people treat their pets like a family member. I very often hear them call their dog or cat their son, daughter, or baby. They think of themselves as the mother or father.

Healing Animals

When their animals are sick, people take very good care of them. People love animals. Animals bring happiness, harmony, companionship, and health to the family.

I saw in a Chinese television news program where a renowned movie star had a blood clot in one of his legs. He had an operation and two years later another artery was blocked in the same leg. He had difficulty walking and had many other sicknesses. A friend of this movie star gave him a dog. Every day, the movie star had to walk the dog. As he did, he realized his ability to walk got better and better. Many of his health conditions improved. He said that walking his dog transformed his health and life. This story clearly shows one of the benefits of having a pet.

Now let me lead everyone to offer soul healing to heal animals.

First I will offer major permanent divine treasures to heal you, your loved ones, and your beloved pets.

Prepare!

Divine Order: Divine Purple Light Ball and Purple Liquid Spring of Divine Balance of Soul, Heart, Mind, and Body Soul Mind Body Transplants

Transmission!

Congratulations! You are blessed. Humanity is blessed. Your pets are blessed.

Let me lead you in a practice to apply the divine treasures you have just received to bless your pets. Apply the Four Power Techniques:

Body Power. Sit up straight. Close your eyes. Place the tip of your tongue gently against the roof of your mouth. Put your hands in the Soul Light Era Prayer Position.

Soul Power. Say *hello*:

> *Dear soul mind body of* _____ (give name of pet),
> *Dear soul mind body of* _____ (give name of the
>   system, organ, or condition that needs healing
>   within the pet),

I love you.
Dear soul mind body of Divine Purple Light Ball and
   Purple Liquid Spring of Divine Balance of Soul,
   Heart, Mind, and Body Soul Mind Body
   Transplants,
I love you.
You have the power to heal _____'s (name of pet)
   _____(give name of the system, organ, or con-
   dition for which you are requesting soul healing
   blessings).
I am very grateful.
Thank you.

Mind Power. Visualize purple light radiating in your pet.

Sound Power. Chant silently or aloud:

Divine Purple Light Ball and Purple Liquid Spring of
   Divine Balance of Soul, Heart, Mind, and Body
   Soul Mind Body Transplants heal and rejuvenate
   my pet. Thank you.
Divine Purple Light Ball and Purple Liquid Spring of
   Divine Balance of Soul, Heart, Mind, and Body
   Soul Mind Body Transplants heal and rejuvenate
   my pet. Thank you.
Divine Purple Light Ball and Purple Liquid Spring of
   Divine Balance of Soul, Heart, Mind, and Body
   Soul Mind Body Transplants heal and rejuvenate
   my pet. Thank you.
Divine Purple Light Ball and Purple Liquid Spring of
   Divine Balance of Soul, Heart, Mind, and Body

*Soul Mind Body Transplants heal and rejuvenate
my pet. Thank you . . .*

Put the book down and stop reading now. Chant *Divine
Purple Light Ball and Purple Liquid Spring of Divine Balance of
Soul, Heart, Mind, and Body Soul Mind Body Transplants heal and
rejuvenate my pet. Thank you* for ten minutes. Generally speaking, chant for three to five minutes per time, three to five times
per day. If your pet has serious challenges or chronic or life-
threatening conditions, chant for one to two hours a day. The
longer you chant and the more you chant, the better the results
your pet could receive.

Now I will lead you to offer a healing blessing to your pet by
applying Divine Healing Hands. I strongly suggest that each time
you apply the Divine Healing Hands within this book, spend
at least a half-hour practicing because the Divine has guided
me clearly that you cannot continue to use the Divine Healing
Hands treasures in this book more than twenty times. Therefore,
apply the Divine Healing Hands within this book twenty times
and practice for as long as you can each time to gain the greatest
benefits. After that, you will need to connect with a Divine Healing Hands Soul Healer or one of my Worldwide Representatives
to receive Divine Healing Hands blessings or to apply to receive
Divine Healing Hands yourself.

APPLY DIVINE HEALING HANDS TO HEAL ANIMALS

Our beloved pets and other animals can become injured or sick.
Apply the Four Power Techniques and Divine Healing Hands to
offer soul healing blessings:

Body Power. Sit up straight. Close your eyes. Place the tip of your tongue gently against the roof of your mouth. If you are a Divine Healing Hands Soul Healer, put your hands in the Soul Light Era Prayer Position and shake your right hand. If you are not a Divine Healing Hands Soul Healer, simply put your hands in the Soul Light Era Prayer Position.

Soul Power. Say *hello:*

> *Dear Divine Healing Hands,*
> *I love you.*
> *You have the power to heal* _____ (name of pet
>   and the unhealthy condition).
> *I am extremely grateful.*
> *Please offer a soul healing blessing as appropriate.*
> *Thank you.*

Mind Power. Visualize Divine Healing Hands radiating golden light within the pet.

Sound Power. Chant silently or aloud:

> *Divine Healing Hands heal* _____ (name the pet
>   and the unhealthy condition). *Thank you.*
> *Divine Healing Hands heal* _____ (name the pet
>   and the unhealthy condition). *Thank you.*
> *Divine Healing Hands heal* _____ (name the pet
>   and the unhealthy condition). *Thank you.*
> *Divine Healing Hands heal* _____ (name the pet
>   and the unhealthy condition). *Thank you . . .*

Chant for as long as you can. The longer and the more you chant, the more benefits your pet will receive from Divine Healing Hands.

I would like to emphasize that it is not proper to ask Divine Healing Hands or any permanent divine treasures to heal all animals on Mother Earth, in Heaven, or in countless planets, stars, galaxies, and universes.

Dr. Rulin Xiu, a physicist from Pahoa, Hawaii, shares her personal stories of healing her beloved dog and others.

> *My beloved dog Buga did not eat for about a week. He became weaker and weaker. He had severe constipation. I thought he would be able to overcome it himself. I gave him mineral oil and herbs. He did not get better and continued to get worse. One morning I saw him in the woods. His spirit was very low, and it occurred to me that he was dying. I knew I needed to do something.*
>
> *I offered Buga a Divine Healing Hands blessing. I walked toward him and held him in my arms. As I was offering the Divine Healing Hands blessing he looked at me and I saw the spirit come back to him. He started to get up as I continued to offer the blessing. As the blessing continued, he started to run after some animals. I wondered if I needed to take him to the doctor, but decided not to. After a couple of days he was completely healed and returned to eating normally.*
>
> *I will share another story of offering a Divine Healing Hands blessing to a friend. I offered her a blessing because her neck and shoulder had been out of place for over twelve years. She was in constant pain. I started to offer her Di-*

vine Healing Hands along with my Soul Song while at the beach. After the blessing she said her neck and shoulder were much better.

As I was offering the Divine Healing Hands blessing and Soul Song there were a number of dolphins that came. We started to dance by the ocean because she felt so much better. We danced the most beautiful amazing dance that we had ever done. She said, "There was no pain at all after the Divine Healing Hands blessing." I will continue to offer her a few more blessings so she can be completely healed.

One more story I would like to share is about my plumber, Mark. About six months ago I called him to do some work at my home and he said that he could not come because he was in so much pain that he was incapacitated. A few months later I called him again to do some work and he said that his condition had not changed and he could not work. He said he would instruct me over the phone how to do the plumbing. I then thought of Divine Healing Hands. I offered him a blessing over the phone. Amazingly, he did not experience any more pain after the Divine Healing Hands healing. He was so thankful. He started to do the plumbing work for me right away.

People always thank me for the amazing healing that I offer to them. It is an incredible gift that the Divine and Master Sha have given us. I am not doing the healing. I feel great while doing the work. It is like I am being healed. I am always grateful to the people and to the Divine as I offer the healing blessing. I feel better after offering the Divine Healing Hands healing blessings. I cannot thank the Divine enough for this gift and for being able to serve others.

I realize the power of Divine Healing Hands deeper and deeper in my heart. I deeply appreciate that Master Sha offered Divine Healing Hands to me so that I can serve my beloved dogs and my friends.

Healing Nature

Millions of people enjoy gardening and nature. People grow fruit trees and vegetables. Some grow flowers and keep houseplants. Farmers cultivate acres of land with various crops. Many people feel a deep connection with nature and enjoy spending time outdoors hiking, enjoying views, breathing fresh air, camping, swimming, boating, running, rock climbing, bird watching, and more. Nature is filled with trees, flowers and other plants, gardens, rivers, lakes, mountains, rocks, and much more.

Most people understand that a human being has a body, mind, and spirit. Spirit is soul. Everything has a soul, mind, and body. Pets and animals have souls. Everything in nature has a soul. Many people do not understand that inanimate things such as mountains, rivers, and oceans also have a soul. Countless fish, plants, insects, and other living things make their home on the land or in the water. Each of them has a soul. Soul healing can be applied to anyone and anything because everyone and everything has a soul.

In ancient spiritual teaching, *wan wu jie you ling*. "Wan" means *ten thousand*. "Wu" means *thing*. "Jie" means *all*. "You" means *to have*. "Ling" means *soul*. "Wan wu jie you ling" (pronounced *wahn woo jyeh yoe ling*) means *everything has a soul*. Soul is a golden light being. Everyone and everything in Mother Earth, Heaven, and countless planets, stars, galaxies, and universes has a soul. A mountain could have thousands of trees.

Every tree has a soul. Every leaf on each tree has a soul. Our body carries countless souls.

Mind is consciousness. Everyone and everything has consciousness.

Body consists of energy and tiny matter. Everyone and everything has a body.

Everything has a soul, mind, and body.

I will now offer another set of priceless permanent divine treasures to you. I will then lead you to apply these treasures to heal yourself, your loved ones, and nature.

Prepare!

Divine Order: Divine Purple Light Ball and Purple Liquid Spring of Divine Nourishment and Balance Soul Mind Body Transplants

Transmission!

Congratulations! You are blessed. Humanity is blessed. Nature is blessed.

Now let us offer soul healing blessings to nature by applying the Four Power Techniques and the Divine Purple Light Ball and Purple Liquid Spring of Divine Nourishment and Balance Soul Mind Body Transplants together:

Body Power. Sit up straight. Close your eyes. Place the tip of your tongue gently against the roof of your mouth. Put your hands in the Soul Light Era Prayer Position.

Soul Power. Say *hello:*

Dear soul mind body of _____ (name the part of
   nature for which you are requesting a healing
   blessing),
I love you.
*Dear soul mind body of Divine Purple Light Ball and
   Purple Liquid Spring of Divine Nourishment and
   Balance Soul Mind Body Transplants,*
I love you.
You have the power to nourish and balance _____
   (name the part of nature that you are requesting
   a healing for).
Please heal and bless as appropriate.
I am very grateful.
Thank you.

Mind Power. Visualize purple light radiating in the part of nature for which you are requesting a healing blessing.

Sound Power. Chant silently or aloud:

*Divine Purple Light Ball and Purple Liquid Spring of
   Divine Nourishment and Balance Soul Mind Body
   Transplants nourish and balance* _____
   (name the part of nature for which you are
   requesting a healing blessing). *Thank you.*
*Divine Purple Light Ball and Purple Liquid Spring of
   Divine Nourishment and Balance Soul Mind Body
   Transplants nourish and balance* _____
   (name the part of nature for which you are
   requesting a healing blessing). *Thank you.*

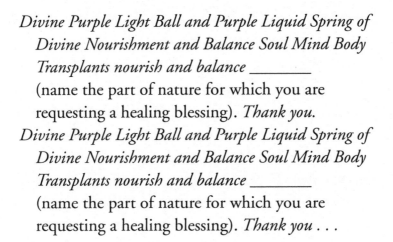

> *Divine Purple Light Ball and Purple Liquid Spring of*
> *Divine Nourishment and Balance Soul Mind Body*
> *Transplants nourish and balance* _____
> (name the part of nature for which you are
> requesting a healing blessing). *Thank you.*
> *Divine Purple Light Ball and Purple Liquid Spring of*
> *Divine Nourishment and Balance Soul Mind Body*
> *Transplants nourish and balance* _____
> (name the part of nature for which you are
> requesting a healing blessing). *Thank you . . .*

Put the book down and stop reading now. Chant *Divine Purple Light Ball and Purple Liquid Spring of Divine Nourishment and Balance Soul Mind Body Transplants nourish and balance* _____. *Thank you* for ten minutes. Generally speaking, chant for three to five minutes per time, three to five times per day. If there are serious challenges with nature, chant for one to two hours a day. The longer you chant and the more you chant for your request(s), the better the results your request(s) could receive.

It is very important to understand that it is not proper to ask the Divine Purple Light Ball and Purple Liquid Spring of Divine Nourishment and Balance Soul Mind Body Transplants or any divine treasures to bless all nature in Mother Earth, Heaven, or countless planets, stars, galaxies, and universes, as well as in any area affected by natural or man-made disasters.

This next story shows the power of a Divine Healing Hands soul healing blessing to transform flowers.

My experience since having been honored with the Divine Healing Hands Soul Healer transmission in 2010 has been wide-ranging; from angry spider bite pustules clearing and leaving no scars; a knot on the spine dissolving; excruciating pain reduced to little or no pain; balancing emotions; and awe-inspiring cellular vibration.

I feel very humbled to be able to offer this blessing from the Divine. My hand vibrates as a wave of light and vibration emanates from my hand, which appears to be grander than the size of the room at times. I am in constant awe as the Divine allows me to be a vehicle for healing, rejuvenation, and transformation. The multitude of souls who come to serve during a Divine Healing Hands blessing is phenomenal by reports of those who feel and sense and those who see.

One of the highlights of my day is joining the daily Divine Healing Hands teleconference and to be able to serve globally with my Divine Healing Hands family, inspired and led by my spiritual father, Dr. and Master Zhi Gang Sha. Thank You. Thank You. Thank You.

Of the many stories I could share, there is one that stands out and is asking to be shared.

I was honored to join Master Elaine Ward and Rick Riecker in the Catskill Mountains in New York to serve on their team for the first global Divine Healing Hands Certification Training. This training was offered worldwide in twenty cities simultaneously, March 30–April 1, 2012.

Master Elaine and Rick had prepared beautifully the setting for the training. The altar was simple and elegant, and a vase of fresh-cut flowers had been placed in service and honor of our master and teacher at the event.

The training was held in a yurt dwelling on five wooded acres. Though the yurt was quite comfortable and provided an amazing spiritual setting for the training, being early spring in New York, temperatures inside the yurt dipped each night as we slept comfortably in another building. The flowers suffered and appeared lifeless, drooping, and beyond recuperation the next morning. There was no time to replace them. I heard, "This is great teaching. Offer Divine Healing Hands blessings." I thanked the flowers for their service, asked that we be forgiven for our misunderstanding of the dangers they might encounter in the coolness of the yurt at night. I offered the blessing as appropriate and sadly forgot this teaching as we began to busy ourselves with the day's activities.

At some point I became aware that the flowers were no longer drooping. They were restored to their former beauty and shined adoringly throughout the training. As the day came to a close, we took the flowers with us to the guest accommodations, where they could continue to serve and enjoy our newly developing Divine Healing Hands community each night. At the close of our training on the third day, we took the flowers and left them in the big guest house at Miriam's Well for all newcomers to enjoy their high vibrational healing service. These flowers had transformed. They were wide open, faces fully beaming from serving and from having been given a second chance at life against all odds.

For me, this is a metaphor for the power of Divine

Healing Hands soul healing, to offer healing, rejuvenation, and transformation against all limitations of human thinking and understanding by allowing the Divine to perform miracles.

Thank you, Master Sha, for allowing me to be a humble servant and Certified Divine Healing Hands Soul Healer.

Frances Anne Brown
Suffolk, Virginia

APPLY DIVINE HEALING HANDS TO HEAL NATURE

Now I will lead you to offer healing blessings to nature by applying Divine Healing Hands. I strongly suggest that each time you apply the Divine Healing Hands within this book, spend at least a half-hour practicing because the Divine has guided me clearly that you cannot continue to use the Divine Healing Hands treasures in this book more than twenty times. Therefore, practice for as long as you can each time you apply the Divine Healing hands downloaded to this book in order to gain the greatest benefits. After that, you will need to connect with a Divine Healing Hands Soul Healer or one of my Worldwide Representatives to receive Divine Healing Hands blessings or to apply to receive Divine Healing Hands yourself.

Apply the Four Power Techniques:

Body Power. Sit up straight. Close your eyes. Place the tip of your tongue gently against the roof of your mouth. If you are a

Divine Healing Hands Soul Healer, put your hands in the Soul Light Era Prayer Position and shake your right hand. If you are not a Divine Healing Hands Soul Healer, simply put your hands in the Soul Light Era Prayer Position.

Soul Power. Say *hello:*

> *Dear Divine Healing Hands,*
> *I love you.*
> *You have the power to heal _____* (name the part
>   of nature for which you are requesting a healing
>   blessing).
> *I am extremely grateful.*
> *Please offer a soul healing blessing as appropriate.*
> *Thank you.*

Mind Power. Visualize Divine Healing Hands radiating golden light within the part of nature for which you are requesting a healing blessing.

Sound Power. Chant silently or aloud:

> *Divine Healing Hands heal _____* (name the part
>   of nature for which you are requesting a healing
>   blessing). *Thank you.*
> *Divine Healing Hands heal _____* (name the part
>   of nature for which you are requesting a healing
>   blessing). *Thank you.*
> *Divine Healing Hands heal _____* (name the part
>   of nature for which you are requesting a healing
>   blessing). *Thank you.*

Divine Healing Hands heal _____ (name the part
of nature for which you are requesting a healing
blessing). *Thank you . . .*

Chant for as long as you can for your request(s). The longer
and more you chant, the more benefits your request(s) will receive from applying Divine Healing Hands.

As before, it is very important to understand that it is not
proper to ask any divine treasures, including Divine Healing
Hands, to bless all nature in Mother Earth, Heaven, or countless planets, stars, galaxies, and universes, as well as in any area
affected by natural or man-made disasters.

Pets and animals play an important role in many people's lives,
and human beings cannot survive without nature, including
plants and water. Animals and nature could be deeply affected in
Mother Earth's transition. Therefore, to learn how to offer soul
healing for animals and nature is vital. To learn how to apply
Divine Healing Hands to offer soul healing blessings to animals
and nature is extremely important also.

The more you think about Divine Healing Hands, the deeper
the honor you could feel in your heart and soul. In chapter 4 we
learned, practiced, and experienced how to apply Divine Healing
Hands to heal the spiritual body, mental body, emotional body,
and physical body of a human being. We also learned, practiced,
and experienced how to apply Divine Healing Hands to transform relationships, finances, intelligence, and every aspect of life
in chapter 5. In chapter 6 we have learned, practiced, and experienced how to apply Divine Healing Hands to heal animals and
nature.

The applications of soul healing, including Divine Healing Hands, are vast. Everyone and everything has a soul. Everyone and everything can receive healing and transformation from soul healing and Divine Healing Hands.

I want to express again my greatest gratitude from the bottom of my heart to the Divine. Thank you, Divine, for your generosity to offer your soul healing hands to the chosen ones. Anyone who receives Divine Healing Hands Soul Mind Body Transplants is given the honor and privilege forever to apply Divine Healing Hands anytime, anywhere to offer soul healing blessings to humanity, animals, and nature for healing, rejuvenation, and transformation of all life.

I repeat:

> *Words are not enough.*
> *Thoughts are not enough.*
> *Imagination is not enough.*
> *Comprehension is not enough.*
> *Appreciation is not enough.*
> *Gratitude is not enough.*
> *Honor is not enough for Divine Healing Hands.*
> *We are extremely blessed.*
> *Thank you. Thank you. Thank you.*

Apply Divine Healing Hands to Open Your Spiritual Channels

MILLIONS OF PEOPLE on the spiritual journey want to open their spiritual channels. They want to connect more deeply with the Divine, their guides, angels, saints, buddhas, and other high-level spiritual beings. They desire to communicate with these beings in order to gain insight and wisdom that will benefit their spiritual journey.

There have been many teachings in history about how to open your spiritual channels. In my teaching there are four spiritual channels. They are:

- Soul Language Channel
- Direct Soul Communication Channel
- Third Eye Channel
- Direct Knowing Channel

I have taught thousands of people all over the world to open their spiritual channels. I have hundreds of students who have opened their advanced spiritual channels.

Why does a person need to open their spiritual channels?

To open your spiritual channels serves your soul journey in a profound way. Opening your spiritual channels empowers you to communicate with the Soul World, including your spiritual fathers and mothers in Heaven, the Divine, and Tao to receive the guidance and wisdom you need to fulfill your soul journey. The Divine is the spiritual father and mother for all souls. Tao is the Source that creates Heaven, Mother Earth, and countless planets, stars, galaxies, and universes.

To open your spiritual channels also serves your physical life. The normal stages of a human being's life are: birth, infant, toddler, child, teenager, adult, senior, and transition to the Soul World. The earlier your spiritual channels open, the better. The guidance from your spiritual fathers and mothers, the Divine, and Tao can benefit every aspect of your physical life. It can guide you to the right study in school. It can guide you to choose the proper occupation. It can guide you to flourish in your business. It can guide you to find your true love and right partner. It can guide you to educate your children and grandchildren in the right direction. You can receive guidance for every aspect of life.

In one sentence:

To open your spiritual channels is to help you to fulfill your soul journey and physical journey in order to benefit your health, relationships, finances, intelligence, and more to bring success in every aspect of life.

Let me share the secrets, wisdom, knowledge, and practical techniques to open your four spiritual channels by applying Divine Healing Hands.

Open Your Soul Language Channel

What is the Soul Language Channel?

By now many of you have brought out your Soul Language. If not, you can always go back and re-read chapter 5 and repeat the practice there to bring out your Soul Language. The Soul Language Channel is the path for your Soul Language to flow out. Opening this channel is vital to opening the other three spiritual channels.

The path of the Soul Language Channel is as follows:

The Soul Language Channel starts from the Hui Yin acupuncture point, which lies on the perineum between the genitals and anus. It flows straight up through the seven Soul Houses in the center of the body to the top of the head and Bai Hui[1] (pronounced *bye hway*) acupuncture point. From there it flows down in front of the center of the spinal column and back to the Hui Yin acupuncture point. See figure 12.

Why does a person need to open the Soul Language Channel?

To open the Soul Language Channel is to bring out your Soul Language. Bringing out your Soul Language has many benefits.

Soul Language carries your own sacred soul healing power because:

---

1. To locate the Bai Hui acupuncture point, imagine a line from the top of one ear going over the head to the top of the other ear. Imagine another line from the tip of the nose going up and over the top of the head to the nape of the neck. The Bai Hui acupuncture point is located where these two lines intersect.

- Soul Language carries soul frequency and vibration that can transform the frequency and vibration of the mind and body.
- Soul Language carries soul love that melts all blockages and transforms all life, including health, relationships, finances, and intelligence, and brings success in every aspect of life.
- Soul Language carries soul forgiveness that brings inner joy and inner peace to all life.
- Soul Language carries soul compassion that boosts energy, stamina, vitality, and immunity of all life.
- Soul Language carries soul light that heals, prevents sickness, purifies and rejuvenates the soul, heart, mind, and body, and transforms relationships, finances, and every aspect of life.

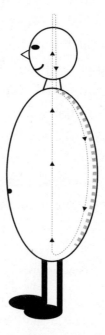

Figure 12. Soul Language Channel

Soul Language has incredible healing power. Applying Soul Language has created thousands of soul healing miracles. I will share one story of Soul Language healing that took place in Toronto, Ontario, Canada, during one of my Soul Healing and Enlightenment Retreats.

Hundreds of people attended this retreat. I led the participants to speak or to bring out their Soul Language. I called an acupuncturist who had just brought out his Soul Language for the first time to the stage. I asked for a volunteer to receive a healing blessing from the acupuncturist's Soul Language. Many people raised their hands. I chose one woman who had suffered from slipped discs and back pain for years; she also had difficulty bending her legs. The acupuncturist offered a soul healing blessing to the woman using his Soul Language. For Body Power, he extended his right arm and pointed his fingers at the woman's back. For Soul Power I taught him to say the following:

Dear my Soul Language,
I love you.
Please heal the back pain and other issues caused by
*   this woman's slipped discs.*
Thank you.

That was an extremely simple and direct way to offer soul healing through Soul Language. Then he chanted his Soul Language for approximately five minutes. After the healing the woman bent completely over, touching her hands to the floor. The pain had completely disappeared. She said, "Wow! This is amazing!"

Soul Language is the language of your soul. Soul Language is every human being's own sacred soul treasure to heal themselves and others. I strongly recommend to every reader and all humanity to bring out your own Soul Language and to practice Soul Language regularly. Ask your Soul Language to heal your spiritual, mental, emotional, and physical bodies. I have practiced Soul Language for eighteen years. I have taught Soul Language to thousands and thousands of people all over the world. There are thousands of soul healing miracles from using Soul Language. I would like you, every reader, and humanity to pay great attention to Soul Language. The soul healing power of Soul Language is beyond words.

How do you develop your Soul Language?

I shared some of this practice in chapter 5. Now I will summarize the essence of how to develop your Soul Language.

Apply the Four Power Techniques to develop your Soul Language Channel:

Body Power. Sit up straight. Close your eyes. Place the tip of your tongue gently against the roof of your mouth. Put your hands in the Soul Light Era Prayer Position.

Soul Power. Say *hello:*

> *Dear my Message Center,*
> *I love you.*
> *Dear my Soul Language Channel,*
> *I love you.*
> *Dear 3396815* (pronounced *sahn sahn jeo leo*
>   *bah yow woo*),
> *I love you.*
> *You have the power to develop my Soul Language.*

Please remove soul mind body blockages in my Soul
Language Channel in order to bring out my Soul
Language.
I am extremely grateful.
Thank you.

The Message Center is a fist-sized energy center located in the center of the chest, behind the sternum. It is also known as the heart chakra.

The Message Center has great power and significance. It is:

- the key center for opening and developing the four spiritual channels, which are the Soul Language Channel, Direct Soul Communication Channel, Third Eye Channel, and Direct Knowing Channel
- the love, forgiveness, compassion, and light center
- the life transformation center
- the soul enlightenment center (When a soul reaches the level of the Message Center, it is an enlightened soul.)
- the key center for developing mind intelligence, heart intelligence, and soul intelligence
- the healing center
- the karma center

Soul Language is a powerful tool that one can apply for:

- healing
- rejuvenation
- purification of soul, heart, mind, and body
- prolonging life
- reaching immortality

3396815 (San San Jiu Liu Ba Yao Wu) is a divine sacred code with the following power and significance:

- 3396815 removes soul mind body blockages to develop the Soul Language Channel.
- 3396815 removes soul mind body blockages to develop the Direct Soul Communication Channel.
- 3396815 removes soul mind body blockages to develop the Third Eye Channel.
- 3396815 removes soul mind body blockages to develop the Direct Knowing Channel.
- 3396815 is a sacred soul healing treasure for healing the spiritual, mental, emotional, and physical bodies.
- 3396815 is a sacred soul healing treasure to transform the physical body to a light body.
- 3396815 is a sacred soul healing treasure to rejuvenate soul, heart, mind, and body.
- 3396815 is a sacred soul healing treasure for longevity.
- 3396815 is a sacred soul healing treasure for immortality.

Let us continue the practice to develop your Soul Language Channel. Even if you have already brought out your Soul Language, you can always open this channel more to receive the benefits. Remember the teaching: do not skip the practices.

Mind Power. Visualize golden light radiating in your Message Center and Soul Language Channel. Visualize your Message

Center and Soul Language Channel opening to bring out your Soul Language.

Sound Power. Chant *3396815* (*sahn sahn jeo leo bah yow woo*) as fast as you can.

> *San San Jiu Liu Ba Yao Wu*
> *San San Jiu Liu Ba Yao Wu*
> *San San Jiu Liu Ba Yao Wu*
> *San San Jiu Liu Ba Yao Wu . . .*

Stop reading and put the book down. Chant *San San Jiu Liu Ba Yao Wu* as fast as you can for five minutes. Suddenly a special voice or sound could flow out from your mouth. This is your Soul Language.

How do you know whether you are really speaking Soul Language? First, you must have trust and avoid trying to analyze your Soul Language. Second, you must have no expectation and no embarrassment. Everyone's Soul Language sounds different. Let your Soul Language come out, whatever it sounds like. Third, you can apply this technique:

When the special sound or voice flows out, stop and chant *San San Jiu Liu Ba Yao Wu* again as fast as you can. Your special sound or voice may come out again. Congratulations! If the special sound flows out each time you try to chant *San San Jiu Liu Ba Yao Wu,* you have confirmed that the special sound or voice is your Soul Language.

Your Soul Language could sound the same for weeks or months. Your Soul Language could sound different each time you speak it. Again, have no expectation. Whatever happens, do not be surprised or disappointed.

APPLY SOUL LANGUAGE FOR HEALING AND REJUVENATION

I will now offer another set of priceless permanent divine treasures to every reader.

Prepare!

Divine Order: Divine Purple Light Ball and Purple Liquid Spring of Divine Soul Language Soul Mind Body Transplants

Transmission!

Congratulations! You are blessed. Humanity is blessed.

Now I will lead you to apply the Four Power Techniques, Soul Language, and the Divine Purple Light Ball and Purple Liquid Spring of Divine Soul Language Soul Mind Body Transplants together to offer healing to the spiritual, mental, emotional, and physical bodies:

Body Power. Sit up straight. Close your eyes. Place the tip of your tongue gently against the roof of your mouth. Place one palm over your navel. Place the other palm over your kundalini area.

Soul Power. Say *hello:*

> *Dear my Soul Language,*
> *I love you.*
> *You have the power to heal my spiritual, mental, emotional, and physical bodies.*
> *Do a good job.*
> *Thank you.*
> *Dear Divine Purple Light Ball and Purple Liquid*

> *Spring of Divine Soul Language Soul Mind Body*
> *Transplants,*
> *I love you.*
> *Please turn on to heal my spiritual, mental, emotional,*
> *and physical bodies.*
> *Thank you.*

Mind Power. Visualize purple light radiating in your spiritual, mental, emotional, and physical bodies.

Sound Power. Chant silently or aloud:

> *Divine Purple Light Ball and Purple Liquid Spring of*
> *Divine Soul Language Soul Mind Body Transplants*
> *heal my spiritual, mental, emotional, and physical*
> *bodies. Thank you.*
> *Divine Purple Light Ball and Purple Liquid Spring of*
> *Divine Soul Language Soul Mind Body Transplants*
> *heal my spiritual, mental, emotional, and physical*
> *bodies. Thank you.*
> *Divine Purple Light Ball and Purple Liquid Spring of*
> *Divine Soul Language Soul Mind Body Transplants*
> *heal my spiritual, mental, emotional, and physical*
> *bodies. Thank you.*
> *Divine Purple Light Ball and Purple Liquid Spring of*
> *Divine Soul Language Soul Mind Body Transplants*
> *heal my spiritual, mental, emotional, and physical*
> *bodies. Thank you . . .*

Stop reading and put the book down. Chant *Divine Purple Light Ball and Purple Liquid Spring of Divine Soul Language Soul*

Mind Body Transplants heal my spiritual, mental, emotional, and physical bodies. Thank you for five minutes.

Then chant Soul Language for an additional five minutes. Start by chanting *3396815 (sahn sahn jeo leo bah yow woo)*. Then flow out your Soul Language.

Generally speaking, chant for three to five minutes per time, three to five times per day. If you have serious challenges in your spiritual, mental, emotional, or physical bodies, chant one to two hours a day. The longer you chant and the more you chant, the better the results you could receive.

APPLY SOUL LANGUAGE WITH FORGIVENESS PRACTICE
IN ORDER TO SELF-CLEAR BAD KARMA

Bad karma is the soul's record of unpleasant services from all lifetimes, current and past. We accumulate bad karma by hurting, harming, taking advantage of others, stealing, cheating, and more. *Karma is the root cause of success and failure in every aspect of life.* This includes blockages in health, relationships, finances, business, and more.

Forgiveness is the key to self-clearing bad karma. True forgiveness brings inner joy and inner peace. If you have challenges with a family member or colleague, you probably have bad karma between you. One key to forgiveness is to always check yourself for any mistakes you have made that contribute to the challenges in your relationship. If you and the other person are each aware of your own mistakes and sincerely ask for forgiveness, love, peace, and harmony could easily happen.

It is important that both sides forgive each other. *I forgive you. You forgive me. Bring love, peace, and harmony.* If both sides apply unconditional forgiveness, love, peace, and harmony could happen very quickly. This would be a great way to self-clear bad karma.

Sincerely ask for forgiveness for any mistakes you have made, and offer unconditional forgiveness to those who have hurt or harmed you in any way in this lifetime and in past lifetimes. Some souls we have harmed will forgive right away; others will take time. Do a forgiveness practice daily if possible, especially if you have major blockages in any aspect of life. *Heal and transform the soul first; then healing and transformation of every aspect of life will follow.* This is the power of forgiveness.

Let me guide you to do a forgiveness practice with Soul Language to self-clear bad karma.

Apply the Four Power Techniques:

Body Power. Sit up straight. Close your eyes. Place the tip of your tongue gently against the roof of your mouth. Put your hands in the Soul Light Era Prayer Position.

Soul Power. Say *hello:*

> *Dear soul mind body of* _____ (name systems, organs, or parts of the body that need healing),
> *I love you.*
> *Dear soul mind body of my Soul Language,*
> *I love you.*
> *You have the power to heal* _____ (repeat your healing request).
> *Do a good job.*
> *Thank you.*
> *Dear Divine Purple Light Ball and Purple Liquid*
>   *Spring of Divine Forgiveness Soul Mind Body*

Transplants and Divine Soul Language Soul Mind
Body Transplants,
I love you.
Please turn on to clear soul mind body blockages in
order to heal my _____ (repeat your request).
Thank you.

Mind Power. Visualize purple light radiating in the area of your request.

Sound Power. Chant silently or aloud:

Divine Purple Light Ball and Purple Liquid Spring of
Divine Forgiveness Soul Mind Body Transplants and
Divine Soul Language Soul Mind Body Transplants
clear soul mind body blockages to heal _____
(repeat your request). *Thank you.*
Divine Purple Light Ball and Purple Liquid Spring of
Divine Forgiveness Soul Mind Body Transplants and
Divine Soul Language Soul Mind Body Transplants
clear soul mind body blockages to heal _____
(repeat your request). *Thank you.*
Divine Purple Light Ball and Purple Liquid Spring of
Divine Forgiveness Soul Mind Body Transplants and
Divine Soul Language Soul Mind Body Transplants
clear soul mind body blockages to heal _____
(repeat your request). *Thank you.*
Divine Purple Light Ball and Purple Liquid Spring of
Divine Forgiveness Soul Mind Body Transplants and
Divine Soul Language Soul Mind Body Transplants
clear soul mind body blockages to heal _____
(repeat your request). *Thank you . . .*

Stop reading now. Chant *Divine Purple Light Ball and Purple Liquid Spring of Divine Forgiveness Soul Mind Body Transplants and Divine Soul Language Soul Mind Body Transplants clear soul mind body blockages to heal* _____. *Thank you* for five minutes.

Then chant your Soul Language for an additional five minutes. Start by chanting *3396815* (*sahn sahn jeo leo bah yow woo*). Then flow out your Soul Language.

Generally speaking, chant for three to five minutes per time, three to five times per day. If you have serious health challenges such as a chronic or life-threatening condition, chant one to two hours a day. The longer and the more you chant, the better the results you could receive. You can add all of your practice time together to total two hours a day.

APPLY SOUL LANGUAGE TO PURIFY YOUR SOUL, HEART, MIND, AND BODY IN ORDER TO UPLIFT YOUR SOUL STANDING IN HEAVEN

Billions of people are on the spiritual journey. Every human's soul has been on its journey for hundreds, thousands, or even more lifetimes. Today many people are consciously searching for soul secrets, soul wisdom, soul knowledge, and practical soul techniques to fulfill their soul journey.

I am honored to share my insights about the soul journey with you. You do not need to change your belief system at all. I respect your belief system. It is a privilege to share what I have learned from the Divine, Tao, and my spiritual fathers and mothers.

What is the purpose of the soul journey? The purpose of the soul journey is to uplift your soul standing in Heaven. Everyone and everything has a soul. Every soul has its standing in Heaven. Heaven has layers. Why does a spiritual being want to uplift his or her soul standing? The higher one's soul standing, the greater one's soul power. The greater one's soul power, the greater one's healing and blessing power, and the greater one's abilities to serve. The higher one's soul standing, the closer one is to the divine realm.

Humanity and the Divine do not occupy the same realm in Heaven. Human beings, animals, and countless souls live in the realm of Jiu Tian (pronounced *jeo tyen*). "Jiu" means *nine*. "Tian" means *Heaven*. "Jiu Tian" means *nine layers of Heaven*. Each soul in Jiu Tian resides in one of nine main layers or levels. The lowest level is the ninth one, level 9.

See figure 13 to understand what souls can be found in each layer.

Tian Wai Tian (Divine Realm)

Jiu Tian (nine layers of Heaven)

Layer 1
Layer 2 } Saints

Layer 3
Layer 4 } Human beings

Layer 5
Layer 6 } Animals, insects, bacteria, etc.

Layer 7
Layer 8 } Plants, fungi, nature, objects, etc.
Layer 9

Figure 13. Nine layers of Heaven (Jiu Tian)

Generally speaking, the souls of inanimate things reside in layer 9. The souls of plants and nature, including mountains, oceans, rivers, trees, and more, reside in layers 7, 8, and 9. The souls of animals reside in layers 5 and 6. Most human beings' souls reside in layers 3 and 4. Layers 1 and 2 in Jiu Tian are the saints' layers.

Souls that reside in Jiu Tian must continue to reincarnate. A human being reincarnates as long as his or her soul is in Jiu Tian. A human being has two lives: physical life and soul life. The purpose of physical life is to serve the soul life. Physical life is limited. Soul life is eternal. Souls reincarnate again and again.

The important wisdom is that the purpose of physical life is to purify your soul, heart, mind, and body further in order to fulfill your soul journey. Human beings on Mother Earth have the greatest opportunity to purify their souls. Mother Earth is filled with much pollution of all kinds, including killing, harming, taking advantage of others, cheating, stealing, power struggles, ego, control, and much more.

In ancient spiritual teaching, Mother Earth is the "bitter sea" or place of "red dust." This is to explain that Mother Earth is a polluted world. In this polluted world it is very important to purify our soul, heart, mind, and body. Mother Earth is a special place where we come to purify our soul, heart, mind, and body.

If your Third Eye is open, you could see many saints in Heaven who sit or stand in a lotus flower. The lotus flower represents purity. The lotus flower grows from the mud and yet it radiates such purity and beauty. Similarly, our purpose is to rise out of and above the mud and radiate purity, love, care, compassion, forgiveness, and more.

A spiritual being must understand deeply the importance of purifying the soul, heart, mind, and body. The purpose of the spiritual journey can be summarized in one sentence:

The purpose of the spiritual journey is to purify your soul, heart, mind, and body in order to uplift your soul standing in Heaven.

The saints have a higher level of purity than normal human beings. Therefore, they have reached layers 1 and 2 in Jiu Tian. Even the saints whose souls reside in Jiu Tian must continue to reincarnate. Purification of the soul, heart, mind, and body continues in every lifetime. The purer a human being is, the higher his or her soul standing in Heaven. The ultimate goal of the soul journey is to be uplifted to Tian Wai Tian (literally the "Heaven beyond Heaven," pronounced *tyen wye tyen*), which is the divine realm. A soul that is uplifted to Tian Wai Tian stops reincarnation.

A soul that is so pure that it is uplifted to Tian Wai Tian will stay in Heaven in soul form. This soul no longer has to return in a physical form. This soul will continue to serve in a special way. We know that the Divine serves continuously. All souls in Tian Wai Tian serve continuously. When a human being needs help from the Divine or another soul in the divine realm, the Divine or another soul in the divine realm will instantly offer service.

How do you purify your soul, heart, mind, and body to uplift your soul standing? The best way to purify is to offer unconditional universal service. Unconditional universal service is service without asking for anything in return. It is selfless service. Many of you do volunteer work. You may serve children, the poor, the homeless, spiritual groups, hospitals, disaster areas, and more without asking for anything in return. You may donate money to these groups and causes. You may offer unconditional service in other ways.

In the physical world, if you work for a company you receive a salary. This compensation is physical payment in the physical world. When you offer unconditional universal service, Heaven offers you spiritual payment with virtue. Virtue is spiritual currency. Instead of coins, virtue is Heaven's beautiful flowers that flow to your Akashic Record book.[2] Heaven's flowers include all kinds of colors: red, golden, rainbow, purple, crystal, and beyond crystal, each representing a different frequency.

Remember the Universal Law of Universal Service:

Offer a little good service, receive a little blessing.
Offer more good service, receive more blessing.
Offer unconditional service, receive huge blessings.

Why do millions of spiritual beings meditate and chant? Meditating and chanting are good for healing, purification, rejuvenation, prolonging life, for transforming relationships, finances, and intelligence, and for bringing success in every aspect of life. In fact, meditating and chanting are important services. Research has shown the benefits of meditation and chanting for health, reducing crime, bringing love, peace, and harmony to society, and much more.

Why are meditating and chanting good service? To meditate and chant is to bring the love, forgiveness, compassion, and light of Heaven, Mother Earth, and countless planets, stars, galaxies, and universes, as well as countless healing angels, archangels, ascended masters, lamas, gurus, kahunas, saints, buddhas, bodhisattvas, all kinds of spiritual fathers and mothers, the Divine,

---

2. Every soul has a book in the Akashic Records. All of one's actions, behaviors, speech, and thoughts, good and bad, from all lifetimes are recorded in this book.

Tao, and Da Tao to you, your family, society, cities, countries, and Mother Earth. Meditation and chanting will raise the frequency and vibration of all to benefit humanity, Mother Earth, and all souls. Therefore, meditation and chanting are great service.

Soul Language carries soul frequency and vibration with soul love, forgiveness, compassion, and light. To speak Soul Language is to bring these to humanity, Mother Earth, and all universes. Therefore, to chant Soul Language silently or aloud nonstop is service beyond comprehension.

I teach my thousands and thousands of students all over the world to chant Soul Language nonstop, 24/7, because it is one of the greatest services one can offer humanity, Mother Earth, and all souls. Every moment that you chant Soul Language, you are bringing soul frequency and vibration, with soul love, forgiveness, compassion, and light to humanity, Mother Earth, and all universes. This is unconditional service.

To serve is to make others happier and healthier.

The more you chant Soul Language, the more you serve.

The more you serve, the further you purify your soul, heart, mind, and body.

The more you purify your soul, heart, mind, and body, the higher your soul will be uplifted in Heaven.

Therefore, to chant Soul Language has unlimited benefits.

At this time, August 2012, more than two million people on Mother Earth sing and listen to the Divine Soul Song *Love, Peace and Harmony*. Divine Soul Song is the song of the Divine's Soul Language. I received *Love, Peace and Harmony* from the Divine on September 10, 2005. Its lyrics are:

Lu La Lu La Li
Lu La Lu La La Li
Lu La Lu La Li Lu La
Lu La Li Lu La
Lu La Li Lu La

I love my heart and soul
I love all humanity
Join hearts and souls together
Love, peace and harmony
Love, peace and harmony

Divine Soul Songs carry divine frequency and vibration with:

- divine love, which melts all blockages and transforms all life
- divine forgiveness, which brings inner joy and inner peace
- divine compassion, which boosts energy, stamina, vitality, and immunity
- divine light, which heals and prevents sickness, prolongs life, purifies and rejuvenates soul, heart, mind, and body, and transforms all life

You can download *Love, Peace and Harmony* at www.Love PeaceHarmonyMovement.com. There are thousands of heart-touching and moving stories from chanting this Divine Soul Song. To sing this Divine Soul Song is to offer powerful service to all souls. To sing this Divine Soul Song is to self-clear bad karma. Sing this Divine Soul Song as much as possible and receive the benefits.

Now let me offer another set of priceless divine treasures to every reader.

Prepare!

Divine Order: Divine Purple Light Ball and Purple Liquid Spring of Divine Purification Soul Mind Body Transplants

Transmission!

Congratulations! You are blessed. Humanity is blessed.

Now let me show you how to apply these priceless divine treasures together with your Soul Language to purify your soul, heart, mind, and body in order to uplift your soul standing in Heaven.

Apply the Four Power Techniques:

Body Power. Sit up straight. Close your eyes. Place the tip of your tongue gently against the roof of your mouth. Place one palm on your lower abdomen below the navel. Place the other palm over your heart.

Soul Power. Say *hello:*

> *Dear my beloved soul, heart, mind, and body,*
> *I love you.*
> *Dear soul mind body of my Soul Language,*
> *I love you.*
> *You have the power to purify my soul, heart, mind,*
>   *and body.*
> *Do a good job.*
> *Thank you.*

> *Dear Divine Purple Light Ball and Purple Liquid*
> *Spring of Divine Purification Soul Mind Body*
> *Transplants and Divine Soul Language Soul Mind*
> *Body Transplants,*
> *I love you.*
> *Please turn on to purify my soul, heart, mind, and body.*
> *Thank you.*

Mind Power. Visualize purple light radiating in your entire body, from head to toe, skin to bone.

Sound Power. Chant silently or aloud:

> *Divine Purple Light Ball and Purple Liquid Spring of*
> *Divine Purification and Divine Soul Language*
> *Soul Mind Body Transplants purify my soul, heart,*
> *mind, and body. Thank you.*
> *Divine Purple Light Ball and Purple Liquid Spring of*
> *Divine Purification and Divine Soul Language*
> *Soul Mind Body Transplants purify my soul, heart,*
> *mind, and body. Thank you.*
> *Divine Purple Light Ball and Purple Liquid Spring of*
> *Divine Purification and Divine Soul Language*
> *Soul Mind Body Transplants purify my soul, heart,*
> *mind, and body. Thank you.*
> *Divine Purple Light Ball and Purple Liquid Spring of*
> *Divine Purification and Divine Soul Language*
> *Soul Mind Body Transplants purify my soul, heart,*
> *mind, and body. Thank you . . .*

Stop reading now. Chant *Divine Purple Light Ball and Purple Liquid Spring of Divine Purification and Divine Soul Language*

Soul Mind Body Transplants purify my soul, heart, mind, and body. Thank you for five minutes.

Then chant Soul Language for as long as you can. Remember my teaching to chant Soul Language nonstop, silently or aloud. This is one of the most profound secrets that I am releasing to you and humanity now.

If you chant Soul Language silently nonstop:

- You are bringing soul frequency and vibration with soul love, forgiveness, compassion, and light to you, humanity, Mother Earth, and all universes.
- You are serving unconditionally.
- You are receiving healing, rejuvenation, and purification, and prolonging your life.
- Your soul standing will be uplifted gradually.

The more you chant, the more benefits you, humanity, Mother Earth, and all universes will receive.

> *Chant Soul Language. Chant Soul Language. Chant Soul Language.*
> *Serve. Serve. Serve.*
> *Benefit. Benefit. Benefit.*
> *Uplift your soul standing in Heaven. Uplift your soul standing in Heaven. Uplift your soul standing in Heaven.*

The power of Divine Healing Hands blessings cannot be expressed enough. Read this heart-touching story of a woman who awoke from a coma after a twenty-minute Divine Healing Hands blessing.

A woman with whom I had been working called me and told me that her elderly mom was in a coma from liver disease and the doctors said she was never to wake again. The woman said, "Please, please, please, is there anything you can do?" I said, "Yes, I will turn on my Divine Healing Hands and offer a healing." I believe the healing blessing lasted only twenty minutes or so. I got a phone call the next day that the mother had awoken and it was a miracle.

I thank God. I thank Master Sha. I thank every soul who has ever led me to this moment that I can serve, and I can be part of these miracles every day. I want to say from my heart that if you're not experiencing miracles every day, something is wrong. Check your heart. Find this healing. Find these tools. Find Master Sha. Miracles are normal. They're natural. They're here for everyone. There's no separation between you and love and God and the Divine.

And please, please, please, open your heart and receive this gift of Divine Healing Hands. I urge you. It is so profound. We are so blessed.

Marina Hubbard
Vancouver, British Columbia, Canada

APPLY SOUL LANGUAGE TO TRANSFORM RELATIONSHIPS

Why do human beings have relationship challenges? The root cause is bad karma. Think about your life. When you meet someone you could feel a deep connection with him or her. You may have a feeling you have known one another before, even if you are meeting each other for the first time. You could have had a past life relationship. Connecting further with this person could bring a good result or there could be challenges in the relationship.

Let me explain further. When you meet someone and fall in love, you could feel that the person is your life partner or soul mate. The relationship could progress and you could become engaged. Finally you could get married. Then, later you could feel that this is not the right partner for you. You could have this feeling more and more. This could bring more conflicts between the two of you, and you could become separated or divorced.

There is a spiritual reason for everything. I want to share with you that the true spiritual reason for relationship issues is related to past life experiences. Generally speaking, if your relationship has great love and care, you and this person experienced good relationships in past lives. If your relationship has major challenges, you could have experienced unpleasant relationships in past lives. Relationships are a karma issue. Karma is cause and effect.

Relationships are like this. In general, if your partner treats you well, you treated your partner well in a past lifetime or lifetimes. If your partner does not treat you well, you could have treated him or her badly in a previous lifetime or lifetimes. This is not true in every case, but this is a common condition.

I will share a true story in order to further explain relationship karma. In September 2007 I went to Japan and had a private consultation with a woman. Master Peter Hudoba, one of my Worldwide Representatives, was with me. The woman was very upset. She told me, "My husband has six girlfriends. I caught him with some of them. I am so upset."

I told her, "Close your eyes and give me a moment to do a spiritual reading about the reason for this." She closed her eyes. I connected with the Akashic Records leader, Yan Wang Ye. The

Akashic Records is the place in Heaven that records the life of every human being, every animal, and every soul in countless planets, stars, galaxies, and universes. I asked Yan Wang Ye, "Could I know the spiritual reason for this woman's issue with her husband?"

He showed me and said, "Master Sha, in their last lifetime together, this woman was the husband. See how many girlfriends he had." He showed me the girlfriends, one after another. They appeared one by one in my Third Eye. I counted one, two, three, four, five, six, seven, eight, nine, ten, eleven, and then twelve. I asked Yan Wang Ye, "These twelve light beings showed he had twelve girlfriends?" Yan Wang Ye replied, "Yes."

This woman had challenges in her relationship with her husband in this lifetime. The spiritual reason for this was that in a past lifetime she was the husband and her husband was the wife. She (then the husband) had twelve girlfriends in that lifetime. This is a karmic issue between her and her husband.

This story tells us that relationship issues are closely related with karma. In fact, every aspect of life is closely related with karma. Karma is the record of services. Karma is divided into two kinds: good and bad. Good karma means one has offered great service to make others happier and healthier in past lifetimes and in this lifetime, including offering love, forgiveness, care, compassion, sincerity, honesty, generosity, kindness, purity, grace, and more. Bad karma means one has made mistakes in past lifetimes and in this lifetime, including hurting, killing, harming, taking advantage of others, cheating, stealing, lying, and more.

The key to transform relationships is to self-clear bad karma.

Let me lead you to do a practice by applying your Divine Purple Light Ball and Purple Liquid Spring of Divine Forgiveness

Soul Mind Body Transplants and your Soul Language together to self-clear bad karma in order to transform your relationships.

Apply the Four Power Techniques:

Body Power. Sit up straight. Close your eyes. Place the tip of your tongue gently against the roof of your mouth. Put both palms on your lower abdomen below the navel, one on top of the other.

Soul Power. Say *hello:*

> *Dear soul mind body of _____* (name the
>   person[s] with whom your relationship needs
>   healing),
> *I love you.*
> *Dear soul mind body of my Soul Language,*
> *I love you.*
> *Dear Divine Purple Light Ball and Purple Liquid*
>   *Spring of Divine Forgiveness Soul Mind Body*
>   *Transplants,*
> *I love you.*
> *Please turn on to clear the bad karma between*
>   *_____* (name of person[s]) *and me.*
> *Thank you.*

Mind Power. Visualize purple light radiating between the two of you.

Sound Power. Chant silently or aloud:

> *Divine Purple Light Ball and Purple Liquid Spring of*
>   *Divine Forgiveness Soul Mind Body Transplants*

> *clear the bad karma between* _____ (name of
> person[s]) *and me. Thank you.*
> *Divine Purple Light Ball and Purple Liquid Spring of*
> *Divine Forgiveness Soul Mind Body Transplants*
> *clear the bad karma between* _____ (name of
> person[s]) *and me. Thank you.*
> *Divine Purple Light Ball and Purple Liquid Spring of*
> *Divine Forgiveness Soul Mind Body Transplants*
> *clear the bad karma between* _____ (name of
> person[s]) *and me. Thank you.*
> *Divine Purple Light Ball and Purple Liquid Spring of*
> *Divine Forgiveness Soul Mind Body Transplants*
> *clear the bad karma between* _____ (name of
> person[s]) *and me. Thank you . . .*

Stop reading now. Chant *Divine Purple Light Ball and Purple Liquid Spring of Divine Forgiveness Soul Mind Body Transplants clear the bad karma between* _____ *and me. Thank you* for five minutes.

Then chant Soul Language for as long as you can. There is no time limit to chanting Soul Language. The longer and more you chant, the better the results you could receive. Your relationships could be deeply transformed.

To chant Soul Language is one of the most powerful services in Mother Earth, Heaven, and countless planets, stars, galaxies, and universes.

APPLY SOUL LANGUAGE TO TRANSFORM FINANCES

I will share a story. A couple who owns a hotel in Honolulu, Hawaii, played the Divine Soul Song *Love, Peace and Harmony* nonstop in more than twenty places in their hotel. One day a businessman came to the hotel and felt incredible energy. He said, "This hotel is extremely special." He proceeded to book more than one hundred rooms for long-term use. The initial deposit he made was more than $42,000.

The Divine Soul Song *Love, Peace and Harmony* is the song of the Divine's Soul Language. I would like to share it again. The more we share, the more blessings we receive. I teach that everything consists of soul, mind, and body. Every word has a soul, mind, and body. I emphasize again that Divine Soul Songs carry divine frequency and vibration, with divine love, forgiveness, compassion, and light that can transform all life.

Sing this Divine Soul Song as much as you can. Have it playing in your house or place of business 24/7 to create divine feng shui.

Lu La Lu La Li
Lu La Lu La La Li
Lu La Lu La Li Lu La
Lu La Li Lu La
Lu La Li Lu La

I love my heart and soul
I love all humanity
Join hearts and souls together
Love, peace and harmony
Love, peace and harmony

Let me share another story about the power of this Divine Soul Song.

One night in the Netherlands in 2009 I finished my teaching around 9:15 PM. Two students and I went to a small local

Chinese restaurant. A sign on the door of the restaurant read that it closed at 9:30 PM. We went inside the restaurant. The owner said, "Sorry, it is too late. We are closing."

I responded, "We just finished a workshop. There are no other restaurants open around here. The sign outside says that the restaurant closes at 9:30 PM. It is only 9:20 PM now. Could you kindly cook for us?"

The owner said, "Are you Chinese?"

I replied, "Yes, I am."

She said, "We will cook for you."

We were all deeply appreciative. The food was very delicious.

The second day I went back to the same restaurant. I told the woman, "Thank you so much for cooking for us last night. I have a Soul Song CD for you. It could bless your business. Do you have a CD player? Are you willing to play this?"

She said, "Yes, we have a CD player. Do you have the CD? I will play it now."

I gave her a CD of the Divine Soul Song *Love, Peace and Harmony.* She played it right away. I told her if she played the CD nonstop it would bless her business. She said she would do it.

Every day of my retreat we went back to the same restaurant to eat. The last day she said, "Dr. Sha, my husband and I would like to treat all of your volunteers and you to dinner."

I asked "Why?"

She said, "This is our appreciation to you. Since we have been playing the CD of the Divine Soul Song *Love, Peace and Harmony* our small restaurant has been packed for every meal. Our restaurant holds thirty to forty people. Generally speaking, we have about ten people for each meal. The restaurant has been packed for every meal since the second day we played the CD.

We are very grateful. Therefore, we would like to treat all of your volunteers and you to show our appreciation."

They cooked a whole table of food for more than ten volunteers and me. The food was most wonderful and everyone had an unforgettable experience.

This is one of many stories about the power of the Divine Soul Song *Love, Peace and Harmony* to transform finances.

Let me lead you to apply the Divine Soul Song *Love, Peace and Harmony* and the Divine Purple Light Ball and Purple Liquid Spring of Divine Soul Language Soul Mind Body Transplants together to transform your finances.

Apply the Four Power Techniques:

Body Power. Sit up straight. Close your eyes. Place the tip of your tongue gently against the roof of your mouth. Put your hands in the Soul Light Era Prayer Position.

Soul Power. Say *hello:*

> *Dear soul mind body of my finances and business,*
> *I love you.*
> *You have the power to transform yourselves.*
> *Do a good job.*
> *Thank you.*
> *Dear soul mind body of the Divine Soul Song* Love,
>   Peace and Harmony,
> *I love you.*
> *Dear soul mind body of Divine Purple Light Ball and*
>   *Purple Liquid Spring of Divine Soul Language Soul*
>   *Mind Body Transplants,*
> *I love you.*

Please turn on to transform my finances and business.
Thank you.

Mind Power. Visualize purple light radiating in your finances and business.

Sound Power. Chant silently or aloud:

> *Divine Purple Light Ball and Purple Liquid Spring of*
> *Divine Soul Language Soul Mind Body Transplants*
> *transform my finances and business. Thank you.*
> *Divine Purple Light Ball and Purple Liquid Spring of*
> *Divine Soul Language Soul Mind Body Transplants*
> *transform my finances and business. Thank you.*
> *Divine Purple Light Ball and Purple Liquid Spring of*
> *Divine Soul Language Soul Mind Body Transplants*
> *transform my finances and business. Thank you.*
> *Divine Purple Light Ball and Purple Liquid Spring of*
> *Divine Soul Language Soul Mind Body Transplants*
> *transform my finances and business. Thank you . . .*

Stop reading now. Chant *Divine Purple Light Ball and Purple Liquid Spring of Divine Soul Language Soul Mind Body Transplants transform my finances and business. Thank you* for five minutes.

Then sing or chant the Divine Soul Song *Love, Peace and Harmony* for as long as you can.

> *Lu La Lu La Li*
> *Lu La Lu La La Li*
> *Lu La Lu La Li Lu La*
> *Lu La Li Lu La*
> *Lu La Li Lu La*

I love my heart and soul
I love all humanity
Join hearts and souls together
Love, peace and harmony
Love, peace and harmony . . .

There is no time limit to singing or chanting this Divine Soul Song. The more you chant, the better the results you could receive. To chant the Divine Soul Song *Love, Peace and Harmony* is one of the most important practices to transform all life.

Translate Your Soul Language

Soul Language is the language of your soul. Learning how to translate your Soul Language is very important. The major benefits of translating your Soul Language are:

- You can receive guidance from your soul.
- You can receive guidance and teaching from spiritual fathers and mothers in Heaven.
- You can receive guidance and teaching from the Divine.
- You can receive guidance and teaching from Tao.
- You can communicate with any soul.

How do you translate your Soul Language?

Let me lead you in a practice to open or develop your ability to translate your Soul Language. Apply the Four Power Techniques:

Body Power. Sit up straight. Close your eyes. Place the tip of your tongue gently against the roof of your mouth. Put your hands in the Soul Light Era Prayer Position.

Soul Power. Say *hello:*

> *Dear soul mind body of my Soul Language,*
> *I love you.*
> *Dear soul mind body of my Message Center,*
> *I love you.*
> *Dear my beloved soul,*
> *I love you.*
> *When I speak Soul Language, please send the message*
>   *from my Message Center to my brain and translate*
>   *my Soul Language to English* (or whatever lan-
>   guage you wish).
> *I am very grateful.*
> *Thank you.*

The Say Hello Greeting is the secret and key to translating Soul Language.

Mind Power. Visualize purple light radiating in your Message Center and Soul Language Channel.

Sound Power. Chant your Soul Language. Start by repeating the sacred code *San San Jiu Liu Ba Yao Wu* as fast as you can:

> *San San Jiu Liu Ba Yao Wu*
> *San San Jiu Liu Ba Yao Wu*
> *San San Jiu Liu Ba Yao Wu*
> *San San Jiu Liu Ba Yao Wu . . .*

As your Soul Language comes out and you continue to chant your Soul Language, you could suddenly understand the meaning of your Soul Language.

You can also ask a question before you speak Soul Language. For example, if you want to receive guidance from the Divine for your spiritual journey, you would say:

Dear Divine,
I love you.
Could you give me guidance for my spiritual journey
*   through my Soul Language?*
I am very grateful.
Dear my soul,
I love you.
When I speak Soul Language, please send the message
*   from my Message Center to my brain in English*
(or whatever language you wish).
Then I will understand the meaning of my Soul
*   Language.*
Thank you.

Then chant your Soul Language. Suddenly your mouth could flow out the meaning of your Soul Language.

I will give another example. Perhaps you need guidance about which university is the best for your child to attend. Say *hello* as follows:

Dear my beloved Message Center,
Dear my Soul Language,
I would like to receive guidance about the two or three
*   universities that my child would like to attend.*
Could you guide me to know which one is the best for
*   him* (or *her*)?
Thank you.

Relax. Then chant Soul Language. Suddenly you could hear the answer.

You can apply Soul Language to ask any question that you wish. Always remember to ask positive questions. Never ask questions that would cause harm to others in any way or that would invade someone's privacy.

Practice more. The important wisdom is that many beginners may not receive a translation right away. Be patient. Practice again and again. Soul Language translation could come suddenly. You could hear words or you could open your mouth and the translation could flow out.

If you have not received Soul Language translation, do not be disappointed. Continue to practice. Be confident. Relax. You will translate Soul Language one day.

Practice Soul Language and it could transform to Soul Song, the song of your Soul Language. I want to share a beautiful story about applying Divine Healing Hands and Soul Song for healing:

> *The story recounted below occurred as a result of a Divine Healing Hands blessing I offered to a woman who handles marketing for my legal practice. Her name is Kimberly and she lives in Minnesota. She had suffered for more than a year from an ulcerated colon and was still experiencing deep discomfort and passing blood in her stool despite seeking both conventional and alternative medical help. While both had improved her condition, she had not experienced a cure.*
>
> *The healing session occurred via a phone call. I simply*

followed Master Sha's instructions, performed the invoca-
tion, and allowed the Divine to come through me and
through my Soul Song. The results were astounding as you
can see from her words:

> Thank you for the healing. It worked.
>
> Last April I was diagnosed with a nasty case of ulcerative colitis (ulcers in the colon) and was told that most people need to be medicated long term, perhaps for life, and that at least half of them need to have their colon entirely removed to rebound from this nasty condition. Undaunted, I sidestepped that agenda, and proceeded to cure myself to about the 85 percent mark by enjoying a vegan diet, energy work, and other alternative healing remedies.
>
> Since the Divine Healing Hands healing you gave me, for the first time in over a year, I have not passed blood in my stool, and the strange hard, pressured bloating (likened to a 4- or 5-month pregnancy) has mysteriously disappeared.
>
> My stomach is flat and I can bend and move freely. Having always been lean and strong, I finally feel like myself again!
>
> What a beautiful gift you share, and your voice . . . absolutely divine!
>
> Off to do situps now . . . :)
>
> God bless you.
>
> Kimberly

I am extremely blessed and humbled to have been a conduit through which the Divine could offer such a profound and life-changing healing for a colleague who is an independent businessperson and mother of two. What a difference this has made in her life.

I cannot thank Master Sha and the Divine enough.

Humbly,
Erik J. Cecil, Esq.
Superior, Colorado

OPEN YOUR DIRECT SOUL COMMUNICATION CHANNEL

Opening your Direct Soul Communication Channel empowers you to directly communicate with the Divine and all souls. Many people speak to the Divine. Many people cannot hear from the Divine. This means your Direct Soul Communication Channel is not open.

Where is the Direct Soul Communication Channel?

The Direct Soul Communication Channel starts from the Zhong,[3] flows to the Message Center, and ends at the brain.

Why do you need to open your Direct Soul Communication Channel?

Words are not enough to express the significance and power of opening your Direct Soul Communication Channel. Imagine directly communicating with the Divine. When your Direct Soul Communication Channel is open, you can receive guidance anywhere and anytime. The Divine will give you direct guidance

---

3. See page 129 for description of Zhong.

for your physical life and spiritual life. There are truly no words to explain the benefits enough.

How do you open your Direct Soul Communication Channel?

The most important secret is to first learn how to translate Soul Language. This is the shortcut to open your Direct Soul Communication Channel. In one sentence:

**If you can translate your Soul Language,
you will naturally gain the ability to communicate
with the Divine.**

Opening your Message Center is the key to opening your Direct Soul Communication Channel.

I will now offer priceless permanent divine treasures that you can use to open your Direct Soul Communication Channel.

Prepare!

Divine Order: Divine Purple Light Ball and Purple Liquid Spring of Divine Message Center Soul Mind Body Transplants

Transmission!

Congratulations! You are blessed. Humanity is blessed.

Now let me lead you to apply these and other priceless treasures you have received from this book to remove soul mind body blockages in your Direct Soul Communication Channel so that you can communicate directly with the Divine. If you can speak with the Divine, you will be able to speak with any soul.

Apply the Four Power Techniques:

Body Power. Sit up straight. Close your eyes. Place the tip of your tongue gently against the roof of your mouth. Put your hands in the Soul Light Era Prayer Position.

Soul Power. Say *hello:*

> *Dear soul mind body of my Message Center,*
> *I love you.*
> *Dear Divine Purple Light Balls and Purple Liquid*
>   *Springs of Divine Message Center, of Divine Love,*
>   *of Divine Forgiveness, of Divine Compassion for*
>   *Brain, Heart, and Soul, of Divine Light, and of*
>   *Divine Soul Language Soul Mind Body Transplants,*
> *I love you.*
> *Please turn on to remove soul mind body blockages in*
>   *my Direct Soul Communication Channel.*
> *Thank you.*

Mind Power. Visualize purple light radiating in your Message Center.

Sound Power. Chant silently or aloud:

> *Divine Purple Light Balls and Purple Liquid Springs*
>   *of Divine Message Center, of Divine Love, of*
>   *Divine Forgiveness, of Divine Compassion for*
>   *Brain, Heart, and Soul, of Divine Light, and of*
>   *Divine Soul Language Soul Mind Body Transplants*
>   *remove soul mind body blockages in my Direct Soul*
>   *Communication Channel. Thank you.*
> *Divine Purple Light Balls and Purple Liquid Springs*

of Divine Message Center, of Divine Love, of
Divine Forgiveness, of Divine Compassion for
Brain, Heart, and Soul, of Divine Light, and of
Divine Soul Language Soul Mind Body Transplants
remove soul mind body blockages in my Direct Soul
Communication Channel. Thank you.
Divine Purple Light Balls and Purple Liquid Springs
of Divine Message Center, of Divine Love, of
Divine Forgiveness, of Divine Compassion for
Brain, Heart, and Soul, of Divine Light, and of
Divine Soul Language Soul Mind Body Transplants
remove soul mind body blockages in my Direct Soul
Communication Channel. Thank you.
Divine Purple Light Balls and Purple Liquid Springs
of Divine Message Center, of Divine Love, of
Divine Forgiveness, of Divine Compassion for
Brain, Heart, and Soul, of Divine Light, and of
Divine Soul Language Soul Mind Body Transplants
remove soul mind body blockages in my Direct Soul
Communication Channel. Thank you . . .

Stop reading now. Continue to chant for five minutes.

Then chant Soul Language for as long as you can. Practice translating your Soul Language by asking a question of the Divine. You could suddenly hear the answer. You could be very excited. You could be moved to tears.

The very important wisdom to share with you and every reader is to trust the answer you receive from the Divine. Do not doubt. Do not say, "Can I hear the answer again?" That is a major mistake and shows disrespect to the Divine. When you do this you could be blocked from hearing from the Divine for a long time.

When you hear the answer, say *Thank you.* If you cannot hear a clear answer, change the question. You will hear an answer again. Ask a clear, direct question. If you do not clearly hear an answer, do not be upset. Go back and do more practice and chanting. Your Direct Soul Communication Channel could open more and more.

OPEN YOUR THIRD EYE CHANNEL

Millions of spiritual beings in history have opened their Third Eye. To open the Third Eye is to receive guidance from the Divine and the spiritual world in the form of spiritual images. To open any spiritual channel is to receive guidance from the Divine and the Soul World. To receive guidance is to transform every aspect of life according to the guidance received.

Our spiritual fathers and mothers, the Divine, and Tao will guide us to transform our health, relationships, finances, and every aspect of life if we only ask and our spiritual channels are open to receive their guidance and teaching. Therefore, to open the Third Eye and other spiritual channels is very important in one's spiritual journey.

Before opening the Third Eye, one must first develop the kundalini. Then one can open the Third Eye. The kundalini is the key energy center for the kidneys. It provides energy food for the brain and Third Eye. If you do not have a strong kundalini foundation, you should not attempt to open your Third Eye because you will exhaust yourself. An open Third Eye uses a lot of energy.

I have shared the wisdom and practices to develop the kundalini in chapter 3. You may want to go back and re-read that section. Please do a lot of practice to further develop your kundalini power before attempting to open your Third Eye Channel.

Now I am going to boost your kundalini power by applying all of the divine treasures downloaded to you in this book.

Apply the Four Power Techniques:

Body Power. Sit up straight. Close your eyes. Place the tip of your tongue gently against the roof of your mouth. Place one palm over the navel. Place the other palm over the kundalini area.

Soul Power. Say *hello:*

> *Dear soul mind body of my kundalini,*
> *I love you.*
> *You have the power to boost yourself.*
> *Do a good job.*
> *Thank you.*
> *Dear Divine Purple Light Balls and Purple Liquid*
>   *Springs of Divine Love, Divine Forgiveness, Divine*
>   *Compassion for Brain, Heart, and Soul, Divine*
>   *Light, Divine Message Center, Divine Purification,*
>   *Divine Nourishment and Balance, Divine Clarity*
>   *of Mind, Divine Balance of Soul, Heart, Mind,*
>   *and Body, Divine Lower Dan Tian, and Divine*
>   *Soul Language Soul Mind Body Transplants,*
> *I love you all.*
> *Please turn on to boost my kundalini power.*
> *I am very grateful.*
> *Thank you.*

Mind Power. Visualize purple light radiating in your kundalini.

Sound Power. Chant silently or aloud:

> *Divine Purple Light Balls and Purple Liquid Springs*
> *of Divine Love, Divine Forgiveness, Divine*
> *Compassion for Brain, Heart, and Soul, Divine*
> *Light, Divine Message Center, Divine Purification,*
> *Divine Nourishment and Balance, Divine Clarity*
> *of Mind, Divine Balance of Soul, Heart, Mind,*
> *and Body, Divine Lower Dan Tian, and Divine*
> *Soul Language Soul Mind Body Transplants boost*
> *my kundalini power. Thank you.*
>
> *Divine Purple Light Balls and Purple Liquid Springs*
> *of Divine Love, Divine Forgiveness, Divine*
> *Compassion for Brain, Heart, and Soul, Divine*
> *Light, Divine Message Center, Divine Purification,*
> *Divine Nourishment and Balance, Divine Clarity*
> *of Mind, Divine Balance of Soul, Heart, Mind,*
> *and Body, Divine Lower Dan Tian, and Divine*
> *Soul Language Soul Mind Body Transplants boost*
> *my kundalini power. Thank you.*
>
> *Divine Purple Light Balls and Purple Liquid Springs*
> *of Divine Love, Divine Forgiveness, Divine*
> *Compassion for Brain, Heart, and Soul, Divine*
> *Light, Divine Message Center, Divine Purification,*
> *Divine Nourishment and Balance, Divine Clarity*
> *of Mind, Divine Balance of Soul, Heart, Mind,*
> *and Body, Divine Lower Dan Tian, and Divine*
> *Soul Language Soul Mind Body Transplants boost*
> *my kundalini power. Thank you.*
>
> *Divine Purple Light Balls and Purple Liquid Springs*

of Divine Love, Divine Forgiveness, Divine
Compassion for Brain, Heart, and Soul, Divine
Light, Divine Message Center, Divine Purification,
Divine Nourishment and Balance, Divine Clarity
of Mind, Divine Balance of Soul, Heart, Mind,
and Body, Divine Lower Dan Tian, and Divine
Soul Language Soul Mind Body Transplants boost
my kundalini power. Thank you . . .

Stop reading now. Continue to chant *Divine Purple Light Balls and Purple Liquid Springs of Divine Love, Divine Forgiveness, Divine Compassion for Brain, Heart, and Soul, Divine Light, Divine Message Center, Divine Purification, Divine Nourishment and Balance, Divine Clarity of Mind, Divine Balance of Soul, Heart, Mind, and Body, Divine Lower Dan Tian, and Divine Soul Language Soul Mind Body Transplants boost my kundalini power. Thank you* for ten minutes.

Then chant Soul Language for ten minutes. The longer you chant, the better the results you will receive. There is no time limit for chanting Soul Language. I offered the teaching earlier. To turn on all divine treasures and chant Soul Language at the same time is the best way to develop your kundalini, to heal, to rejuvenate, to purify, to transform, and to enlighten all life.

I have shared major secrets with you and every reader. It does not mean that you have a highly developed kundalini. If you want to highly develop your kundalini and develop high-level Third Eye abilities, you must practice a lot. There is no second way. Your progress depends on your personal effort.

In ancient teaching, there is a renowned statement:

只管耕耘，不管收获
Zhi guan geng yun, bu guan shou huo

"Zhi guan" means *just do it regardless*. "Geng yun" means *to plant and cultivate, to properly water and fertilize*. "Bu guan" means *do not bother and expect*. "Shou huo" means *to harvest*.

"Zhi guan geng yun, bu guan shou huo" (pronounced *jr gwahn gung yoon, boo gwahn sho hwaw*) means *just do the proper job of planting the seeds, giving the proper water and fertilizer, and do not expect the harvest*. This phrase is to teach every reader and humanity that as long as you do the proper planting, the harvest will come naturally. It is to teach us not to expect anything.

This phrase is the perfect teaching for opening the Third Eye. Just do your Xiu Lian practice. "Xiu" means *purification*. "Lian" means *practice*. "Xiu Lian" (pronounced *sheo lyen*) is *purification practice*. Xiu Lian is the term that was used for the spiritual journey in ancient times. It means the *totality of one's spiritual journey*. To open the Third Eye and other spiritual channels is an aspect of the Xiu Lian journey.

I am releasing another major spiritual secret to you, every reader, and anyone who desires to open their Third Eye. It can be summarized in one sentence:

To develop the kundalini is to develop the Third Eye.

Let me explain further. There are thousands or tens of thousands of methods to develop the Third Eye. Most methods to open the Third Eye involve concentrating on the Third Eye area. Today I formally share with you and humanity that the divine sacred way to open the Third Eye is to *concentrate on the kundalini area*.

I have explained previously, but I want to emphasize again that the kundalini is the energy food center for the Third Eye. Kundalini energy moves into two invisible holes in the tailbone area. From there it flows up through the spinal cord to the brain to nourish the brain and Third Eye. The sacred wisdom is that kundalini energy will stimulate the Third Eye to open it.

I am asking the Divine a question now. My question to the Divine is:

Dear Divine, could you explain the Third Eye wisdom?

The Divine replied:

Dear my son Zhi Gang,
I am delighted to offer a short teaching about the Third Eye.
The Third Eye is the pineal gland. Generally speaking, the Third Eye is open until a child reaches the age of four. Therefore, a child may tell his or her parents that he or she sees angels. Sometimes a child may see the Dark Side and become afraid. Some parents are not aware of this, and they may tell the child there is no such thing *or* it is just your imagination.
When the child reaches ages four to six, his or her Third Eye goes into a degenerative stage, and about ninety-six percent of humanity's Third Eye closes between the age of four and six. Four percent of humanity's Third Eye does not close. Therefore, there are some people whose Third Eye can see spiritual images since childhood. They have always seen spiritual images because their Third Eye has never closed.

A spiritual being can open the Third Eye when they do spiritual practice. The Third Eye can be stimulated and opened again to see spiritual images. There are many methods to open the Third Eye.

My son Zhi Gang Sha communicates with me all the time. He flows his books from me. He is my servant, vehicle, and channel. I am grateful for Zhi Gang Sha's service. I am grateful for all of his students and their unconditional service. I am also an unconditional universal servant. I love you all. I love humanity. I love wan ling (all souls).

This is my short teaching that Zhi Gang asked me to directly give to you.

Your beloved Divine.

Thank you, Divine. I am honored to serve.

I will now offer priceless permanent divine treasures to you and every reader to develop your kundalini power.

Prepare!

Divine Order: Divine Purple Light Ball and Purple Liquid Spring of Divine Kundalini Soul Mind Body Transplants

Transmission!

Congratulations! You are blessed. Humanity is blessed.

Now I will lead you to apply the Four Power Techniques and your divine treasures to develop your kundalini and Third Eye Channel simultaneously:

Body Power. Sit up straight. Close your eyes. Place the tip of your tongue gently against the roof of your mouth. Place one palm over the navel. Place the other palm over the kundalini area.

Soul Power. Say *hello:*

> *Dear soul mind body of my kundalini and Third Eye Channel,*
> *I love you.*
> *Dear Divine Purple Light Ball and Purple Liquid Spring of Divine Kundalini Soul Mind Body Transplants and all of the Divine Purple Light Ball and Purple Liquid Spring Soul Mind Body Transplants downloaded to me from this book,*
> *I love you.*
> *Please turn on to develop my kundalini and Third Eye Channel simultaneously.*
> *I am very grateful.*
> *Thank you.*

Mind Power. Visualize all of the Divine Purple Light Ball and Purple Liquid Spring treasures rotating and radiating in your kundalini. The important secret to follow is *not to think about the Third Eye Channel. Gently focus your mind on your kundalini area.*

The secret wisdom is that when you build the kundalini area, the Third Eye Channel will open automatically. If one develops a strong foundation, the Third Eye will open by itself. It is just like a bicycle pump or any pump. When you build the power in the kundalini area, the energy becomes more and more dense.

Then it will flow to the spinal cord and move up to the brain, stimulating the Third Eye and opening the Third Eye. This is the natural process.

As you follow the process in this way, you will build a great foundation. When the time is ready, your Third Eye will naturally open. When the Third Eye opens you will already have a good foundation and you will not exhaust yourself. This is the key essence to open the Third Eye Channel and to follow the sacred principles.

As I often teach:

大道至简
Da Tao zhi jian

"Da" means *big*. "Tao" means *The Way*. "Zhi" means *extremely*. "Jian" means *simple*. "Da Tao zhi jian" (pronounced *da dow jr jyen*) means *the Big Way is extremely simple*.

Now let us continue with Sound Power.

Sound Power. Chant silently or aloud:

> *Divine Purple Light Ball and Purple Liquid Spring of*
> *Divine Kundalini Soul Mind Body Transplants and*
> *all Divine Purple Light Ball and Purple Liquid*
> *Spring Soul Mind Body Transplants develop my*
> *kundalini and Third Eye Channel simultaneously.*
> *Thank you.*
> *Divine Purple Light Ball and Purple Liquid Spring of*
> *Divine Kundalini Soul Mind Body Transplants and*
> *all Divine Purple Light Ball and Purple Liquid*
> *Spring Soul Mind Body Transplants develop my*

kundalini and Third Eye Channel simultaneously.
Thank you.
Divine Purple Light Ball and Purple Liquid Spring of
Divine Kundalini Soul Mind Body Transplants and
all Divine Purple Light Ball and Purple Liquid
Spring Soul Mind Body Transplants develop my
kundalini and Third Eye Channel simultaneously.
Thank you.
Divine Purple Light Ball and Purple Liquid Spring of
Divine Kundalini Soul Mind Body Transplants and
all Divine Purple Light Ball and Purple Liquid
Spring Soul Mind Body Transplants develop my
kundalini and Third Eye Channel simultaneously.
Thank you . . .

Stop reading and put the book down now. Continue to chant *Divine Purple Light Ball and Purple Liquid Spring of Divine Kundalini Soul Mind Body Transplants and all Divine Purple Light Ball and Purple Liquid Spring Soul Mind Body Transplants develop my kundalini and Third Eye Channel simultaneously. Thank you* for ten minutes.

Then continue by chanting your Soul Language for thirty minutes.

I am releasing one of the top secrets to you and humanity now.

When you chant Soul Language as fast as you can, suddenly you may not know where you are or what time it is. That is the best condition. You are going into emptiness. This is the best condition that you can achieve. Stay in this condition as long as you can. The benefits for your soul journey cannot be expressed enough. Suddenly you could see light and spiritual images. Do not be excited. Keep calm. This means that your Third Eye is starting to open. Continue to chant Soul Language and focus your mind on your kundalini. Your Third Eye could open further and further.

Remember you must spend enough time to follow this practice. Be patient. You could spend days, weeks, or months to open your Third Eye. Everyone is different. Remember the teaching earlier:

Zhi guan geng yun, bu guan shou hou

Do the proper planning; the harvest will come naturally. Do not expect anything. The more you expect the Third Eye to open, the longer it could take to open.

One wisdom everyone must know is that even if your Third Eye opens, Heaven could close it again. I will share a story with you.

The second daughter of my beloved spiritual father and mentor, Dr. and Master Zhi Chen Guo, opened her Third Eye many years ago. Suddenly it closed. She asked her father, "Could I open my Third Eye again?"

He said, "You will never open your Third Eye again."

She was disappointed, but in her heart she said, "I will open my Third Eye again. I need to seriously practice."

I respect her very much in my heart. When I was in China I saw that she meditates from 10:00 PM to 6:00 AM every day. She sleeps one to two hours a day from 6:00 to 8:00 AM. During the day she works and does Xiu Lian.

It took her a few years to build her foundation enough to get by on one to two hours of sleep per day. I was amazed by her ability to sleep only one or two hours and then work all day and do Xiu Lian.

After her father told her that her Third Eye would never open again she practiced persistently. It took a few years for her Third Eye to re-open. She now has a very advanced Third Eye. Her Third Eye abilities are profound and amazing.

This story is to share with you and humanity that even if your Third Eye is open, it could close again. You must continue to practice. To do practice is a daily job. To do Xiu Lian is a lifetime effort. Highly developed spiritual beings have not practiced for only one lifetime. They have practiced hundreds, thousands, and even more lifetimes to reach their current condition. And they continue to practice.

Practice. Practice. Practice.

Persist. Persist. Persist.

Improve. Improve. Improve.

The potential abilities of the Third Eye Channel and other spiritual channels are unlimited.

Receive unlimited wisdom from Heaven, the Divine, and Tao.

You are the one to decide how much practice you will do.

You are the one to develop your Third Eye Channel and other spiritual channels further and further.

This is your soul journey.

I wish for you to develop your advanced Third Eye Channel and other spiritual channels.

I wish for you to uplift your soul standing in Heaven.

I wish for you to fulfill your spiritual journey.

The soul journey is unlimited.

Continue to grow. Continue to grow. Continue to grow.

OPEN YOUR DIRECT KNOWING CHANNEL

What is the Direct Knowing Channel? Open this channel to have direct knowing through instant soul communication with the Divine and all souls. If you want to know anything, you will know directly and without asking. This is the highest level spiritual channel.

Lao Zi, the author of *Dao De Jing,* said:

坐在家中知天下事

Zuo zai jia zhong zhi tian xia shi

"Zuo" means *sit.* "Zai" means *in.* "Jia zhong" means *home.* "Zhi" means *know.* "Tian xia" means *in the world.* "Shi" means *things.*

"Zuo zai jia zhong zhi tian xia shi" (pronounced *dzwaw dzye jyah jawng jr tyen shya shr*) means *sit at home and know what is happening in the world.* This explains the abilities of those who have direct knowing abilities. You do not need to move one step to know the secrets of the universe.

Where is the Direct Knowing Channel?

The Direct Knowing Channel starts at the heart and ends in the Zhong. I explained the Zhong in chapter 4. Zhong is the most important space in the body. Zhong is Tao inside the body. Tao is the Source of Heaven, Mother Earth, and countless planets, stars, galaxies, and universes. The heart houses the mind and soul. If the heart connects with Zhong, then the heart will receive the messages of everyone and everything in countless universes. Therefore, the Direct Knowing Channel is from the heart to the Zhong.

What is the power and significance of the Direct Knowing Channel?

To have an open Direct Knowing Channel is to connect with the Divine fully. What the Divine knows, you will know. It is vital to remember that having an open Direct Knowing Channel does not mean that you can share what you know with others. The Soul World has a major spiritual law. Many of Heaven's secrets cannot be released.

Think about this. Can you share a country's major government secrets with others? You cannot. In many businesses, employees must sign a nondisclosure agreement. A lawyer cannot share a client's information. A doctor cannot share a patient's information. This also applies to Heaven, only the consequences of releasing information improperly are far more serious than on Mother Earth.

Remember this teaching if you highly develop your Direct Knowing Channel. Many things you may know but cannot share. Do not release Heaven's secrets.

Let me explain further the abilities of a highly developed Direct Knowing Channel.

If you have a highly developed Direct Knowing Channel:

- You could know how long a person will live. You cannot share this knowledge. The person could become very upset.
- You could read a person's past lifetimes and future lifetimes. It is not proper to share this information.
- You could know about a person's relationships: marital status, whether or not they have children, the condition of these relationships, and more. It is not proper to share this information.

- You could know the condition of a person's health. It may not be proper to share this information.
- You could know about a business's success or disaster. It may not be proper to share this information.
- You could know details about Mother Earth's transition for the next ten years. It may not be proper for you to share this information.

There are many other things you could know after you develop your Direct Knowing Channel. Remember that it may not be proper to share many of these things with others. The Divine will guide you about what you can and cannot share.

Now I will lead you to practice to develop your Direct Knowing Channel.

Apply the Four Power Techniques:

Body Power. Sit up straight. Close your eyes. Place the tip of your tongue gently against the roof of your mouth. Place one palm over the heart. Place the other palm on the back, below the Ming Men acupuncture point. The Ming Men acupuncture point is directly behind the navel, on your back.

Soul Power. Say *hello:*

> *Dear soul mind and body of my heart, Zhong, and Direct Knowing Channel,*
> *I love you all.*
> *Dear all of the permanent divine treasures downloaded to me from this book,*

For my advanced students who have read the other books of my Soul Power Series and who have joined many of my workshops, retreats, and teleconferences, please remember to include this sentence:

> *Dear all Divine and Tao permanent treasures in all of the other books in the Soul Power Series and all Divine, Tao, and Da Tao[4] treasures that I have received in all workshops, retreats, and teleconferences,*

All others, continue from here:

> *I love you, honor you, and appreciate you all.*
> *Please turn on together to develop my heart, Zhong, and Direct Knowing Channel.*
> *Please heal and bless me as appropriate.*
> *I cannot thank the Divine, Tao, and Da Tao treasures enough.*
> *Thank you.*

Mind Power. Visualize golden, rainbow, purple, crystal, and beyond crystal light radiating in your Zhong.

Sound Power. Chant silently or aloud:

> *All Divine, Tao, and Da Tao treasures develop my Direct Knowing Channel. Thank you.*

---

4. Divine is the spiritual father and mother for humanity and all souls. Tao is the Source that created Heaven, Mother Earth, and countless planets, stars, galaxies, and universes. Da Tao is the Ultimate Tao Source.

All Divine, Tao, and Da Tao treasures develop my
Direct Knowing Channel. Thank you.
All Divine, Tao, and Da Tao treasures develop my
Direct Knowing Channel. Thank you.
All Divine, Tao, and Da Tao treasures develop my
Direct Knowing Channel. Thank you . . .

Stop reading now. Continue to chant *All Divine, Tao, and Da Tao treasures develop my Direct Knowing Channel. Thank you* for ten minutes.

Then chant Soul Language for thirty minutes. If you cannot chant for thirty minutes now, remember to chant more the next time you practice. You can even chant more than thirty minutes per time. You could chant one to two hours per time or even longer. The more you chant, the more benefits you could receive.

To develop the Direct Knowing Channel takes a long time. It could take you ten years, twenty years, or more. Be patient. The more you practice, the faster you could develop your Direct Knowing Channel.

The most important wisdom to know is that one must reach a high level of purity to develop the Direct Knowing Channel. Not every human being can develop the Direct Knowing Channel or the other spiritual channels. Purity is vital to opening spiritual channels.

How do you purify yourself to reach total purity? I will share the two most important practices:

- Chant or sing the Divine Soul Song *Love, Peace and Harmony*
- Tao Song and Tao Soul Language

Your Soul Song is not a Tao Song. To sing Tao Song you must receive permanent treasures from Tao to your soul, heart, mind, and body. These treasures transform your Soul Song to Tao Song. Your Soul Language will also transform to Tao Soul Language.

I suggest that you read the ninth book of my Soul Power Series, *Tao Song and Tao Dance: Sacred Sound, Movement, and Power from the Source for Healing, Rejuvenation, Longevity, and Transformation of All Life*.[5] You can receive major permanent Tao Song treasures from Tao by reading the appropriate sections of the book. Apply these treasures and receive huge benefits for your soul journey.

If you have not received the Tao Song downloads, continue to chant your Soul Language and sing your Soul Song. They work also. However, after receiving the Tao Song downloads, the frequency, vibration, and power of your Soul Song and Soul Language will increase a lot.

Stop reading now. Let me lead you to do ten minutes of practice.

Body Power. Sit up straight. Close your eyes. Place the tip of your tongue gently against the roof of your mouth. Place one palm over your heart. Place the other palm on your lower back below the Ming Men acupuncture point.

Soul Power. Say *hello:*

> *Dear soul mind body of my Zhong,*
> *I love you.*

---

5. Toronto/New York: Heaven's Library/Atria Books, 2011.

Dear soul mind body of all my Divine, Tao, and
  Da Tao treasures,
I love you.
Please turn on to develop my Direct Knowing
  Channel.
I am very grateful.
Thank you.

Mind Power. Visualize golden, rainbow, purple, crystal, and beyond crystal light radiating in your Zhong area.

Sound Power. Chant silently or aloud:

All of my Divine, Tao, and Da Tao treasures purify my
  soul, heart, mind, and body to reach total purity in
  order to develop my Direct Knowing Channel.
  Thank you.
All of my Divine, Tao, and Da Tao treasures purify my
  soul, heart, mind, and body to reach total purity in
  order to develop my Direct Knowing Channel.
  Thank you.
All of my Divine, Tao, and Da Tao treasures purify my
  soul, heart, mind, and body to reach total purity in
  order to develop my Direct Knowing Channel.
  Thank you.
All of my Divine, Tao, and Da Tao treasures purify my
  soul, heart, mind, and body to reach total purity in
  order to develop my Direct Knowing Channel.
  Thank you . . .

Then chant Soul Language for ten minutes. The most important wisdom is to put your mind on the Zhong and chant Soul Language nonstop.

Stop reading and put the book down. Do ten minutes of practice now.

I remind each of you again: you need great patience and purity to develop this highest spiritual channel. It takes a saint hundreds and thousands of lifetimes to develop these abilities. Therefore, do not expect these abilities to be gained easily.

Total purity.

Total GOLD.

Total unconditional universal servant.

Chant the Divine Soul Song *Love, Peace and Harmony*.

Join the Love Peace Harmony Movement to create love, peace, and harmony for you, your family, humanity, Mother Earth and all universes.

Chant your Soul Language or sing your Soul Song as much as you can.

In ancient spiritual practice there is a major sacred teaching:

咒不离口
Zhou bu li kou

"Zhou" means *mantra*. "Bu li" means *do not leave*. "Kou" means *mouth*.

"Zhou bu li kou" (pronounced *joe boo lee koe*) means *chant the mantra nonstop*.

Soul Language and Soul Song are soul mantras.

The Divine Soul Song *Love, Peace and Harmony* is a divine soul mantra.

Tao Song is a Tao mantra.

Chant nonstop.
To chant is to serve.
To chant is to heal.
To chant is to rejuvenate.
To chant is to purify.
To chant is to transform all life.
To chant is to open your Direct Knowing Channel.
To chant is to enlighten.
To chant is to reach immortality.
To chant is to bring love, peace, and harmony to humanity,
Mother Earth, and all universes.

APPLY DIVINE HEALING HANDS TO OPEN ALL
FOUR OF YOUR SPIRITUAL CHANNELS

I have explained the four spiritual channels. They are:

- Soul Language Channel
- Direct Soul Communication Channel
- Third Eye Channel
- Direct Knowing Channel

I will review the location of the four spiritual channels:

- **Soul Language Channel**—The Soul Language Channel starts at the Hui Yin acupuncture point. It flows straight up through the seven Soul Houses in the center of the body to the top of the head and the Bai Hui acupuncture point. From there it flows down in front of the spinal column back to the Hui Yin acupuncture point.

- **Direct Soul Communication Channel**—The Direct Soul Communication Channel starts in the Zhong, then flows to the Message Center and ends at the brain.
- **Third Eye Channel**—The Third Eye Channel starts in the kundalini. The energy of the kundalini flows to the tailbone area and through two invisible holes in the tailbone area to the spinal cord. From there it flows up through the spinal cord to the brain, where it ends at the Third Eye (pineal gland).
- **Direct Knowing Channel**—The Direct Knowing Channel starts in the heart and ends in the Zhong area.

Now I am going to release one of the most important secrets to open all four spiritual channels together. There is a secret place inside the body that can develop all four spiritual channels together. The secret place is the Zhong area. The secret can be summarized in one sentence:

To develop the Zhong area is to develop the four spiritual channels because every spiritual channel connects with Zhong.

Remember the pump wisdom I explained earlier (see p. 248). If you highly develop your Zhong, the energy and the power will flow through all four of your spiritual channels and develop them. All four spiritual channels connect with Zhong. Zhong is the core to develop all of them.

Now I am going to lead you to apply Divine Healing Hands

and all Divine, Tao, and Da Tao treasures to develop your four spiritual channels together through the Zhong area.

Apply the Four Power Techniques:

Body Power. Sit up straight. Close your eyes. Place the tip of your tongue gently against the roof of your mouth. Place one palm over the navel. Place the other palm on your lower back below the Ming Men acupuncture point.

Soul Power. Say *hello*:

> *Dear soul mind body of my Zhong area,*
> *I love you, honor you, and appreciate you.*
> *Dear soul mind body of my Soul Language Channel,*
>   *Direct Soul Communication Channel, Third Eye*
>   *Channel, and Direct Knowing Channel,*
> *I love you, honor you, and appreciate you.*
> *Dear all of my Divine, Tao, and Da Tao treasures,*
> *I love you, honor you, and appreciate you.*
> *Please turn on to develop my Zhong and my four spiri-*
>   *tual channels.*
>
> *Dear Divine Healing Hands downloaded to this book,*
> *I love you, honor you, and appreciate you.*
> *Please turn on to develop my Zhong and my four spiri-*
>   *tual channels.*
> *I am very grateful.*
> *Thank you.*

I strongly suggest that each time you apply the Divine Healing Hands within this book, spend at least a half-hour practic-

ing because the Divine has guided me clearly that you cannot
continue to use the Divine Healing Hands treasure in this book
more than twenty times. Therefore, apply the Divine Healing
Hands within this book in order to develop your Zhong, and
practice for as long as you can to gain the greatest benefits for
opening all four of your spiritual channels. After that, you will
need to connect with a Divine Healing Hands Soul Healer or
one of my Worldwide Representatives to receive Divine Healing
Hands blessings or to apply to receive Divine Healing Hands
yourself.

Mind Power. Visualize golden, rainbow, purple, crystal, and beyond crystal light radiating in your Zhong area.

Sound Power. Chant silently or aloud:

> *Zhong Zhong Zhong Zhong Zhong Zhong Zhong*
> *Zhong Zhong Zhong Zhong Zhong Zhong Zhong*
> *Zhong Zhong Zhong Zhong Zhong Zhong Zhong*
> *Zhong Zhong Zhong Zhong Zhong Zhong Zhong . . .*

Stop reading now. Continue to chant *Zhong* for thirty minutes.
Chanting *Zhong* is one of the top secrets for developing all
four spiritual channels. There is no time limit. Focus your mind
on the Zhong. Remember, when you focus it does not mean you
should think too much. Generally speaking, to focus is to gently
put your mind on the Zhong area.

The important wisdom to remember is that when you silently chant *Zhong* you could have one or more of the following
experiences:

- an increase in energy, stamina, vitality, and immunity
- sudden ability to translate Soul Language (Soul Language Channel opening)
- sudden ability to hear and have a conversation with the Divine and the Soul World (Direct Soul Communication Channel opening)
- sudden ability to see spiritual images (Third Eye Channel opening)
- sudden direct knowing ability (Direct Knowing Channel opening)

The most important wisdom that I have shared with you—and I emphasize it again—is that when you chant *Zhong* you could suddenly forget where you are and what time it is. You could go into emptiness.

Emptiness is Tao.

Zhong is Tao.

Nothingness is Tao.

When you chant *Zhong*, you are connecting with Tao. Chant *Zhong* to go into the Zhong, which is the Tao condition. You do not know where you are or what time it is. That is the Zhong condition, emptiness condition, nothingness condition, and Tao condition.

This is the most important condition. Stay in this condition for as long as you can. When you become aware of space and time again, chant *Zhong* again. You could go into emptiness again. Keep this condition. When you become aware of the place and time again, chant *Zhong*. Continue this process. Each time you become aware of your surroundings, go back into the Tao condition by chanting *Zhong*.

The divine and Tao sacred wisdom is that when you forget where you are and what time it is, you are in the divine and Tao condition. When you realize where you are and what time it is, you are out of the divine and Tao condition.

Be in the divine and Tao condition for as long as possible. That is *the* top secret for all kinds of spiritual practices, including healing, rejuvenation, and opening your four spiritual channels, as well as for transforming relationships, finances, intelligence, and every aspect of life.

When you are in the divine and Tao condition, you could see spiritual images that you have never seen before. You could have sudden realizations of the secrets, wisdom, and knowledge you have never known before. *In the emptiness condition the wisdom and knowledge are truth.*

Tao is the Source that creates Heaven, Mother Earth, and countless planets, stars, galaxies, and universes. Tao creates all things. What you realize and receive when you are in the emptiness condition is Tao creation.

To study Tao more, see the three Tao books I have written:

- *Tao I: The Way of All Life*
- *Tao II: The Way of Healing, Rejuvenation, Longevity, and Immortality*
- *Tao Song and Tao Dance: Sacred Sound, Movement, and Power from the Source for Healing, Rejuvenation, Longevity, and Transformation of All Life*

In these three books I have shared profound Tao secrets, wisdom, knowledge, and practical techniques to transform all life. Tao has guided me to hold a ten-year series of Tao Retreats (Tao Healing, Rejuvenation, Longevity, and Immortality Retreats—Years 1 through 10). I am honored to serve you on your Tao journey.

Having read this book to this point, you may deeply feel the divine calling to be a chosen servant to receive Divine Healing Hands. You can apply to become a Divine Healing Hands Soul Healer at www.DrSha.com or through one of my Worldwide Representatives. I welcome you to join the thousands of Divine Healing Hands Soul Healers offering divine soul healing service worldwide.

The next major step is to study Tao for healing, rejuvenation, longevity, and immortality. To study Tao is to empower you to become a more powerful Divine Healing Hands Soul Healer and servant. You can then serve humanity better and empower yourself to enlighten your soul, heart, mind, and body in order to move to the Tao journey in order to reach longevity and immortality.

> *Zhong. Zhong. Zhong.*
> *Emptiness. Emptiness. Emptiness.*
> *Nothingness. Nothingness. Nothingness.*
> *Develop all of your spiritual channels at the same time.*
> *Tao. Tao. Tao.*
> *Tao Creation. Tao Creation. Tao Creation.*
> *Tao Manifestation. Tao Manifestation. Tao Manifestation.*
> *Zhong. Zhong. Zhong. Zhong. Zhong. Zhong. Zhong.*
> (This is the top secret practice to open all of your spiritual channels and transform your health, relationships, finances, intelligence, and every aspect of your life forever.)

Conclusion

MILLIONS OF PEOPLE are searching for healing and transformation of their health, relationships, finances, and more. Millions of people want to know their true purpose. Millions of people want to open their spiritual channels and communicate with the Divine, Tao, and all souls. Millions of people want to accomplish their soul journey.

You have learned the wisdom of Divine Healing Hands. You have practiced by applying the Divine Healing Hands downloaded to this book and the permanent divine treasures you have received to heal, transform, and bless all aspects of life, including your energy, your spiritual, mental, emotional, and physical bodies, relationships, finances, and more. You have experienced the power of Divine Healing Hands. You have read many heart-touching stories about Divine Healing Hands.

The purpose of life is to serve. This is the first time that the Divine has given his Divine Healing Hands to the masses.

What are Divine Healing Hands?

Divine Healing Hands are the Divine's soul healing hands that are downloaded to the chosen ones. My Worldwide Representatives and I have been given the authority and honor to download Divine Healing Hands to the chosen ones.

How do Divine Healing Hands work?

- Divine Healing Hands remove soul, mind, and body blockages. Soul blockages are bad karma. Mind blockages are blockages in consciousness, including negative mind-sets, negative attitudes, negative beliefs, ego, and attachments. Body blockages are blockages in energy and matter.
- Divine Healing Hands have the power to boost energy, stamina, vitality, and immunity of all life. All life includes health, relationships, finances, intelligence, and every aspect of life.
- Divine Healing Hands carry divine frequency and vibration that can transform the frequency and vibration of all life.
- Divine Healing Hands carry divine love that melts all blockages and transforms all life.
- Divine Healing Hands carry divine forgiveness that brings inner joy and inner peace to all life.
- Divine Healing Hands carry divine compassion that boosts energy, stamina, vitality, and immunity of all life.
- Divine Healing Hands carry divine light that heals, prevents sickness, purifies and rejuvenates soul, heart, mind, and body, and transforms relationships and finances, as well as every aspect of all life.

In this book you have experienced:

- the power of Divine Healing Hands for healing the spiritual, mental, emotional, and physical bodies; animals; and nature
- the power of Divine Healing Hands for rejuvenation
- the power of Divine Healing Hands for life transformation, including relationships and finances
- the power of Divine Healing Hands for purification
- the power of Divine Healing Hands for increasing mind, heart, and soul intelligence
- the power of Divine Healing Hands for longevity
- the power of Divine Healing Hands for opening spiritual channels

You have also read many heart-touching and moving soul healing miracle stories created by Divine Healing Hands.

Why are Divine Healing Hands being given to the masses?

Mother Earth is in a serious transition period. Humanity has experienced more and more natural disasters and all kinds of challenges in the last nine years. Mother Earth's transition could last eleven more years and could become very heavy.

To receive Divine Healing Hands is to answer the Divine's calling to help humanity pass through this historic period.

To receive Divine Healing Hands is to create love, peace, and harmony for individuals, families, organizations, cities, countries, Mother Earth, Heaven, countless planets, stars, galaxies, and all universes.

I cannot encourage you enough to become a Divine Healing Hands Soul Healer.

This is my heartfelt wish:

> *Divine Healing Hands heal you.*
> *Divine Healing Hands heal your loved ones.*
> *Divine Healing Hands heal humanity.*
> *Divine Healing Hands heal all souls.*
> *Divine Healing Hands heal Mother Earth.*
> *Divine Healing Hands heal countless planets, stars,*
>   *galaxies, and universes.*
> *Divine Healing Hands bring love, peace, and har-*
>   *mony to all souls in all universes.*

The Divine gave me the honor to download Divine Healing Hands to the chosen ones. Now the Divine gave the honor to all of my Worldwide Representatives to download Divine Healing Hands to the chosen ones.

Since 2003 we have created 3,500 Divine Healing Hands Soul Healers. Our task is to create 200,000 Divine Healing Hands Soul Healers on Mother Earth. We are honored beyond words. We cannot serve enough.

> *I love my heart and soul*
> *I love all humanity*
> *Join hearts and souls together*
> *Love, peace and harmony*
> *Love, peace and harmony*

Acknowledgments

$\mathcal{I}$ THANK FROM THE bottom of my heart the beloved thirty-two saints, and the Divine, Tao, and Da Tao Committees who flowed this book through me. All of my books are their books. They are above my head and I flow the entire book from them. I am so honored to be a servant of all of them, of humanity, and of all souls. I am eternally grateful.

I thank from the bottom of my heart my beloved spiritual fathers and mothers, including Dr. and Master Zhi Chen Guo. Dr. and Master Zhi Chen Guo is the founder of Body Space Medicine and Zhi Neng Medicine. He was one of the most powerful spiritual leaders, teachers, and healers in the world. He taught me the sacred wisdom, knowledge, and practical techniques of soul, mind, and body. I cannot honor and thank him enough.

I thank from the bottom of my heart Professor Liu Dajun, the top *I Ching* and feng shui authority in China at Shandong University. He taught me profound secrets of *I Ching* and feng shui. I cannot thank him enough.

I thank from the bottom of my heart Dr. and Professor Liu Dehua. He is a medical doctor and was a university professor in China. The 372nd-generation lineage holder of the Chinese "Long Life Star," Peng Zu, the teacher of Lao Zi (the author of *Dao De Jing*), he has taught me great secrets, wisdom, knowledge, and practical techniques of longevity. I cannot thank him enough.

I thank from the bottom of my heart my beloved sacred masters and teachers who wish to remain anonymous. They have taught me sacred wisdom of Xiu Lian. They are extremely humble and powerful. They have taught me priceless secrets, wisdom, knowledge, and practical techniques but they do not want any recognition. I cannot thank them enough.

I thank from the bottom of my heart my physical father and mother and all of my ancestors. I cannot honor my physical father and mother enough. Their love, care, compassion, purity, generosity, kindness, integrity, confidence, and much more have influenced and touched my heart and soul forever. I cannot thank them enough.

I thank from the bottom of my heart my co-publisher, Judith Curr of Atria Books. She chose me to be one of Atria's authors in 2008. This is my tenth book with Atria. Her incredible support and care have deeply touched my heart. I cannot thank her enough.

I thank from the bottom of my heart my editor at Atria Books, Johanna Castillo. Her great support of all of my books has touched my heart deeply. I cannot thank her enough.

I thank from the bottom of my heart Chris Lloreda, Amy Tannenbaum, Lisa Keim, Isolde Sauer, Tom Spain, Dan Vidra, Natalie Gutierrez, Kitt Reckord, Mike Noble, Desiree

Vecchio, Lourdes Lopez, Laywan Kwan, and others at Atria and Simon & Schuster whose names I may have omitted or whose names I do not know, for their great support. I cannot thank them enough.

I thank from the bottom of my heart Sylvia Chen, CEO of Universal Soul Service Corporation. She has given me unconditional support since 1992. She has contributed enormously to the mission. I cannot thank her enough.

I thank from the bottom of my heart Johannes Ziebarth, business manager of Universal Soul Service Corporation. He has made an invaluable contribution to the mission. He is an unconditional universal servant. I cannot thank him enough.

I thank from the bottom of my heart D. R. Kaarthikeyan for his unconditional support of the mission. I am honored and privileged to have him as the Patron of the worldwide Love Peace Harmony Movement. He is a leader to unite all. I honor and appreciate him deeply from my heart. I cannot thank him enough.

I thank from the bottom of my heart my chief editor, Master Allan Chuck, for his excellent editing of this book and all of my other books. He is one of my Worldwide Representatives. He has contributed greatly to the mission, and his unconditional universal service is one of the greatest examples for all. I cannot thank him enough.

I thank from the bottom of my heart my senior editor, Master Elaine Ward, for her excellent editing of this book and many of my other books. She is also one of my Worldwide Representatives. I thank her deeply for her great contribution to the mission. I cannot thank her enough.

I thank from the bottom of my heart my assistant, Master Cynthia Marie Deveraux, one of my Worldwide Representatives.

She has typed the whole book and many of my other books. She also offered great insight during the flowing of this book. She has made a great contribution to the mission. I cannot thank her enough.

I thank from the bottom of my heart Master Lynda Chaplin, one of my Worldwide Representatives. She has designed the figures for this book and many of my other books. I am extremely grateful. I cannot thank her enough.

I thank from the bottom of my heart my devoted students Min Lei and Shi Gao for assisting with the Chinese characters and pinyin in this book and many of my other books. I am very grateful. I cannot thank them enough.

I thank from the bottom of my heart my devoted students Henderson Ong and Lenore Cairncross for the photographs within and on the cover of this book. I am very grateful. I cannot thank them enough.

I thank from the bottom of my heart all of my Worldwide Representatives. They are servants of humanity and servants, vehicles, and channels of the Divine. They have made incredible contributions to the mission. I thank them all deeply. I cannot thank them enough.

I thank from the bottom of my heart all of my business team leaders and members for their great contribution and unconditional service to the mission. I am deeply grateful. I cannot thank them enough.

I thank from the bottom of my heart the 3,500 Divine Healing Hands Soul Healers worldwide for their great healing service to humanity and all souls. I am deeply touched and moved. They have received and responded to the divine calling to serve. I deeply thank them all.

I thank from the bottom of my heart the Divine Soul Heal-

ing Teachers and Healers and the Divine Master Teachers and Soul Operation Master Healers worldwide for their great contribution to the mission. I am deeply touched and moved. I cannot thank them enough.

I thank from the bottom of my heart all of my students and friends worldwide for their unconditional service to humanity. I cannot thank them enough.

I thank from the bottom of my heart my family, including my wife, her parents, our children, and our brothers and sisters. They have all loved and supported me unconditionally. I cannot thank them enough.

May this book serve humanity and Mother Earth to help them pass through this difficult time in this historic period.

May this book serve humanity to heal, rejuvenate, purify, and transform all life.

May this book bring love, peace, and harmony to humanity, Mother Earth, and all souls in countless planets, stars, galaxies, and universes.

May this book serve your soul journey and the soul journey of humanity.

I am extremely honored to be a servant of you, humanity, and all souls.

I love my heart and soul
I love all humanity
Join hearts and souls together
Love, peace and harmony
Love, peace and harmony

A Special Gift

PRACTICE IS NECESSARY in order to heal and transform. Practice by applying the Divine Healing Hands downloaded to this book twenty times. Practice as much as possible using the permanent divine treasures you have received as you read this book. Experience their power and receive the benefits. Practice dedicatedly and consistently to experience healing, blessing, rejuvenation, purification, and life transformation.

Watch the inspiring video included with this book. Witness the heart-touching stories of healing and transformation. This is a special gift to you, dear reader. Scan the code at the bottom of the following page or on the back cover using your smartphone or other device to access the video. Or, go to http://www.you tube.com/watch?v=NyFTMSrHnf8.

The Divine has guided me to create 200,000 Divine Healing Hands Soul Healers on Mother Earth. Mother Earth's transition could be very severe. To receive Divine Healing Hands is to help humanity pass this difficult time in history. To receive is to serve.

You are extremely blessed. Humanity is extremely blessed. We are all extremely blessed that the Divine is offering his soul healing hands to the chosen ones.

Practice. Practice. Practice.

Heal. Heal. Heal.

Rejuvenate. Rejuvenate. Rejuvenate.

Purify. Purify. Purify.

Serve. Serve. Serve.

Spread love, peace, and harmony.

Spread love, peace, and harmony.

Spread love, peace, and harmony.

Spread Divine Healing Hands.

Spread Divine Healing Hands.

Spread Divine Healing Hands.

Serve more. Serve more. Serve more.

Thank you. Thank you. Thank you.

Experience the power of soul to heal your
soul, mind, and body with Dr. and Master Sha.

Index

A

Acupuncture, 70, 130. *See also specific acupuncture point*
Adults'/seniors' intelligence, 175–77, 178–79
Akashic Records, 36, 217, 217*n*, 224–25
Anger, 105, 107–8, 120–21, 124, 125
Animals/pets, 99, 181–88, 196, 214, 215, 271
Anxiety. *See* depression and anxiety
As appropriate, requests for blessings, 18, 20, 21, 22, 23, 40–41, 43, 46
Asking questions of Divine, 234, 235, 240–41, 246–47

B

Bad karma
blockages and, 6
chanting and, 211–13
definition of, 225
Divine Healing Hands blessings and removing, 5–6, 20–21, 23
Divine Karma Cleansing and, 5
Divine Protection Package and, 20–21
examples of, 87
forgiveness and, 210–13
Four Power Techniques for self-clearing, 211–13, 226–27
lessons learned from, 5, 6
mistakes and, 87
proper use of Divine Healing Hands blessings and, 20–21, 23
relationships and, 223, 225–27
self-clearing of, 210–13, 225–27
as sickness of spiritual body, 125
soul and, 87
Soul Language and, 210–13
Soul Songs and, 219
spiritual channels and, 210–13, 219, 223, 225–27
as spiritual debt, 6
types of, 20
unconditional service and, 5–6
why of Divine Healing Hands and, 4–5
Bai Hui acupuncture point, 201, 201*n*, 261
Belief system, 213

Bing lai ru shan dao, bing qu ru chou si
    (sickness comes like a mountain
    falling; sickness leaves like spinning
    silk), 42–43
Blockages
    forgiveness and, 145, 211
    intelligence and, 159
    karma and, 210
    love as melting, 56, 119, 168, 202,
        219, 270
    negativity and, 101
    power of Divine Healing Hands and, 7,
        41–43, 49, 52, 141, 217, 270
    removal of, 41–43, 49, 52, 87, 88, 101,
        145, 167
    sickness and, 86–87, 125
    spiritual channels and, 202, 206, 210,
        211, 219, 238, 270
    3396815 code and, 167, 206
    See also type of blockage
Body
    bad karma and, 6
    blockages in, 6, 7, 20, 21, 42, 73, 125,
        167, 206, 238, 270
    energy and matter in, 7, 189
    everything as having a, 100, 188, 189
    Five Elements and, 124
    foundation of Soul Mind Body
        Medicine and, 87
    frequency and vibration and, 168, 202
    light and, 56, 152
    Mind Power and, 31
    power of Divine Healing Hands and, 8,
        26, 31, 37, 42, 44, 46, 49, 270
    proper use of Divine Healing Hands
        and, 19, 20, 21
    purification of, 3, 56, 152, 167, 205,
        213–18, 219, 220–22, 270
    rejuvenation of, 56, 84, 152, 167, 206,
        219, 270

response to soul healing blessing and,
    44, 45, 46
seven Soul Houses and, 71*n*
Soul Language and, 202, 205
soul light and, 169
spiritual channels and, 202, 205, 206,
    213–18, 219, 220–22, 238, 258,
    270
Tao and, 258
3396815 code and, 167, 206
uplifting of soul standing in Heaven
    and, 213–18, 220–22
why of Divine Healing Hands and, 7
See also Body Power; emotional body;
    mental body; spiritual body
Body Power
    animals/pets and, 182, 185
    applying Divine Healing Hands for
        healing and, 15, 39
    bad karma and, 211, 227
    chanting and, 32
    Divine Inner Yin Yang Circle and, 73,
        75
    downloading of Divine Healing Hands
        to this book and, 30–31, 32, 39
    emotional body and, 107, 109, 112,
        113–14, 115, 117, 120, 122
    finances and, 152–53, 154, 230
    intelligence and, 158, 160, 161–62,
        163–64, 167, 170, 172, 174, 176
    kundalini and, 59, 62, 248
    for longevity, 77, 79
    Lower Dan Tian and, 64, 68
    mental body and, 102, 103
    nature and, 189, 194–95
    opening of all spiritual channels
        together and, 263
    physical body and, 128, 132
    power of Divine Healing Hands and,
        30–31, 32, 39

power of, 15, 30–31
for rejuvenation, 77, 79
relationships and, 143, 147, 149,
   150–51, 226
Sacred Circle and, 73, 75, 77, 79
Soul Language and, 203, 204, 208,
   232, 258
spiritual body and, 94, 96
spiritual channels and, 203, 204, 208,
   211, 220, 226, 230, 232, 239, 242,
   248, 255, 258, 263
uplifting of soul standing in Heaven
   and, 220
Yin Yang Palm Hand Position and,
   64
Brain
   Adults'/seniors' intelligence and,
      175–77
   kundalini and, 58, 60, 241, 246, 249
   number codes and, 157–59
   spiritual channels and, 237, 241, 246,
      249, 262
Business, 5, 6, 7, 40, 87, 90, 210, 255.
   See also finances; workplace

C

Cancer, 89, 125, 133–34
   ulcerated colon healing story of, 235–37
Chakras, 71*n*. *See also* Message Center
   (heart chakra); seven Soul Houses
Chant
   *All Divine, Tao, and Da Tao treasures
      develop my Direct Knowing Channel.
      Thank you.,* 256–57
   *All of my Divine, Tao, and Da Tao
      treasures purify my soul, heart, mind,
      and body to reach total purity in order
      to develop my Direct Knowing
      Channel. Thank You.,* 259

Develop my kundalini. Thank you., 60
*Divine Healing Hands bring clarity to
   my mind and transform my negative
   mind-sets, negative attitudes, negative
   beliefs, ego, attachments, and more.
   Thank you.,* 104–5
*Divine Healing Hands clear soul mind
   body blockages in my seven Soul
   Houses, Wai Jiao, and Divine Inner
   Yin Yang Circle in order to heal all my
   sicknesses. Thank you.,* 76–77
*Divine Healing Hands develop my
   Divine Sacred Circle for Rejuvenation
   and Longevity. I am so grateful. Thank
   you.,* 80
*Divine Healing Hands develop my
   kundalini. Thank you.,* 62–63
*Divine Healing Hands develop my Lower
   Dan Tian. Thank you.,* 68–69
*Divine Healing Hands heal and bless me.
   Thank you.,* 43
*Divine Healing Hands heal my spiritual
   body. Thank you.,* 97
*Divine Healing Hands heal (name of pet
   and unhealthy condition). Thank
   you.,* 185–86
*Divine Healing Hands heal and
   transform my emotional body. Thank
   you.,* 122–23
*Divine Healing Hands heal and
   transform my physical body. Thank
   you.,* 132–33
*Divine Healing Hands heal and
   transform the relationship between
   (name) and me. Thank you.,*
   151–52
*Divine Healing Hands heal and
   transform the relationship between
   (name) and (name). Thank you.,*
   150

Chant (*cont.*)

Divine Healing Hands increase the brain
function and intelligence of my (or
name of person[s]) *mind, heart, and
soul. Thank you.*, 177

Divine Healing Hands increase my child's
mind, heart, and soul intelligence.
Thank you.*, 173

Divine Healing Hands increase my heart
intelligence. Thank you.*, 164

Divine Healing Hands increase my mind
intelligence. Thank you.*, 161

Divine Healing Hands increase my soul
intelligence. Thank You.*, 170–71

Divine Healing Hands increase the
student's mind, heart, and soul
intelligence. Thank you.*, 174–75

Divine Healing Hands, please heal,
rejuvenate, and transform. Thank
you.*, 17

Divine Healing Hands transform my
finances. Thank you.*, 155

Divine Love Peace Harmony Rainbow
Light Ball boosts my kundalini power.
Thank you.*, 60

Divine Purple Light Ball and Purple
Liquid Spring of Divine Balance of
Soul, Heart, Mind, and Body Soul
Mind Body Transplants heal and
rejuvenate my pet. Thank you.*,
183–84

Divine Purple Light Ball and Purple
Liquid Spring of Divine Forgiveness
heal and transform our relationship.
Thank you.*, 144

Divine Purple Light Ball and Purple
Liquid Spring of Divine Forgiveness
heal and transform the relationship
between the organizations. Thank
you.*, 148

Divine Purple Light Ball and Purple
Liquid Spring of Divine Forgiveness
Soul Mind Body Transplants clear the
bad karma between (name of
person[s]) *and me. Thank you.*,
226–27

Divine Purple Light Ball and Purple
Liquid Spring of Divine Kundalini
Soul Mind Body Transplants and
all Divine Purple Light Ball and
Purple Liquid Spring Soul Mind
Body Transplants develop my
kundalini and Third Eye Channel
simultaneously. Thank you.*,
249–50

Divine Purple Light Ball and Purple
Liquid Spring of Divine Light
transform my finances. Thank you.*,
153–54

Divine Purple Light Ball and Purple
Liquid Spring of Divine Love heal
and transform my emotional body.
Thank you.*, 120–21

Divine Purple Light Ball and Purple
Liquid Spring of Divine Love
increase my heart intelligence.
Thank You.*, 162–63

Divine Purple Light Ball and Purple
Liquid Spring of Divine Lower Dan
Tian Soul Mind body Transplants
boost my Lower Dan Tian power.
Thank you.*, 66

Divine Purple Light Ball and Purple
Liquid Spring of Divine
Nourishment and Balance Soul
Mind Body Transplants nourish
and balance (name the part of
nature for which you are requesting
a healing blessing). *Thank you.*,
190–91

Divine Purple Light Ball and Purple
  Liquid Spring of Divine Purification
  and Divine Soul Language Soul Mind
  Body Transplants purify my soul,
  heart, mind, and body. Thank you.,
  221–22
Divine Purple Light Ball and Purple
  Liquid Spring of Divine Soul
  Language Soul Mind Body Transplants
  heal my spiritual, mental, emotional,
  and physical bodies. Thank you.,
  209–10
Divine Purple Light Ball and Purple
  Liquid Spring of Divine Soul
  Language Soul Mind Body Transplants
  transform my finances and business.
  Thank you., 231
Divine Purple Light Ball and Purple
  Liquid Spring of Divine Soul
  Language Soul Mind Body Transplants
  heal my spiritual, mental, emotional,
  and physical bodies. Thank you.,
  209–10
Divine Purple Light Ball and Purple
  Liquid Spring of Divine Forgiveness
  Soul Mind Body Transplants and
  Divine Soul Language Soul Mind
  Body Transplants clear soul mind
  body blockages to heal (repeat your
  request). Thank you., 212–13
Divine Purple Light Balls and Purple
  Liquid Springs of Divine Love,
  Divine Forgiveness, Divine
  Compassion for Brain, Heart, and
  Soul, Divine Light, Divine Message
  Center, Divine Purification, Divine
  Nourishment and Balance, Divine
  Clarity of Mind, Divine Balance of
  Soul, Heart, Mind, and Body, Divine
  Lower Dan Tian, and Divine Soul
Language Soul Mind Body Transplants
  boost my kundalini power. Thank
  you., 243–44
Divine Purple Light Balls and Purple
  Liquid Springs of Divine Message
  Center, of Divine Love, of Divine
  Forgiveness, of Divine Compassion for
  Brain, Heart, and Soul, of Divine
  Light, and of Divine Soul Language
  Soul Mind Body Transplants, remove
  soul mind body blockages in my Direct
  Soul Communication Channel. Thank
  you., 239–40
Divine treasures heal and transform my
  mental body. Thank you., 102–3
Divine treasures heal and transform my
  spiritual body. Thank you., 95
Gong Ya Jian Pi (Tao Song strengthens
  the spleen), 113
Hei Heng Hong Ah Xi Yi Weng You,
  74–75, 81, 82–83
I forgive you. You forgive me. Bring love,
  peace, and harmony. Bring love, peace,
  and harmony, 145–46
Jiao Ya Shu Gan (Tao Song smoothes
  the liver), 108
Jiao Zhi Gong Shang Yu, 118–19
Shang Ya Xuan Fei (Tao Song
  promotes the function of the
  lungs), 114–15
3396815 (San San Jiu Liu Ba Yao
  Wu), 168, 169, 207, 210, 213, 233
You Weng Yi Xi Ah Hong Heng Hei,
  78–79, 81, 82–83
Yu Ya Zhuang Shen (Tao Song makes
  the kidneys strong), 116
01777-908-01777-92244, 159
Zhi Ya Yang Xin (Tao Song nourishes
  the heart), 109–10
Zhong, 131, 264–65, 267

Chanting
  benefits of, 217
  Divine Inner Yin Yang Circle and,
    74–77
  Divine Sacred Circle for Rejuvenation
    and Longevity and, 77–84
  divine treasures and, 244
  going into the Tao condition and, 265
  how to apply Divine Healing Hands,
    16, 17
  Na Mo A Mi Tuo Fo and, xxxvii
  nonstop (Zhou bu li kou), 260–61
  opening of all four spiritual channels
    together and, 263, 264–65
  power of Divine Healing Hands and,
    32, 33, 43, 52
  power of, 217–18
  proper use of Divine Healing Hands
    blessings and, 19, 20, 21
  saying hello and, 20
  soul journey and, 250–51
  speed of, 250–51
  uplifting of your soul standing in
    Heaven and, 217–18, 220–22
  what you chant is what you become,
    xxxvi
  when to do, 81–82
  See also chants; specific topic
Children
  bad karma and, 5
  blockages and, 7
  intelligence of, 171–73
  jing qi shen and, 7
  power of Divine Healing Hands and, 7
  Third Eye of, 246, 251–52
  3396815 code and, 167
Chosen one
  definition of, 3
  downloading of Divine Healing Hands
    to, 272

  power of Divine Healing Hands and,
    27, 30
  purpose of, 27
Chronic conditions
  animal healing and, 184
Divine Sacred Circle for Rejuvenation and
    Longevity and, 75
  emotional body and, 108, 110, 113,
    116, 119, 121
  kundalini and, 60, 61
  length of time for blessing/chanting
    and, 18, 61, 67, 75
  Lower Dan Tian and, 67
  mental body and, 103
  physical body and, 131
  possible responses to soul healing
    blessings and, 42, 43
  power of Divine Healing Hands and,
    41, 42, 43
  proper use of Divine Healing Hands
    and, 20
  removal of blockages for, 42, 87
  requests for Divine Healing Hands
    concerning, 41
  Soul Language and, 213
  spiritual body and, 95
Coma, woman in, story about, 222–23
Compassion
  benefits of, 169
  Divine Healing Hands as carrying,
    56
  downloading of Divine Healing
    Hands to this book and, 36, 38
  energy and, 202, 219
  immunity and, 202, 219
  intelligence and, 176
  karma and, 5, 225
  meditation and chanting and, 217
  Message Center and, 205
  need for, 3

power of Divine Healing Hands and, 7, 36, 38, 47, 270

response to soul healing blessing and, 47

Soul Language and, 202

Soul Songs and, 219, 228

spiritual channels and, 202, 205, 215, 217, 219, 225, 228, 270

stamina and, 202, 219

uplifting of soul standing in Heaven and, 215, 222

vitality and, 202, 219

D

Da Tao, definition of, 256*n*

Da Tao zhi jian (the Big Way is extremely simple), 2, 249

Depression and anxiety, 90, 105, 109–10, 120–21, 124, 125

Direct Knowing Channel

chanting and, 255–57, 258–59, 265

Divine and, 253, 254

Four Power Techniques and, 255–57, 258–61

frequency and vibration and, 258

heart and, 253, 255, 262

Heaven and, 254

location of, 253, 262

Message Center as key to, 205

Mother Earth and, 255

opening of all four spiritual channels together and, 262–65

opening of, 253–61

power and significance of, 10, 253, 254–55

purity and, 257

sharing of knowledge and, 254–55

Soul Language and, 205, 206, 257, 259

Soul Songs and, 257–58

as spiritual channel, 10, 52, 199

3396815 code and, 167, 206

Zhong and, 253, 258, 259, 262, 265

Direct Soul Communication Channel

chanting and, 239–40, 265

downloading of Divine Healing Hands to this book and, 33, 34–39

Four Power Techniques and, 238–41

location of, 237, 262

Message Center and, 205, 237, 238, 262

opening of all four spiritual channels together and, 262–65

opening of, 237–41, 261

power of Divine Healing Hands and, 33, 34–39

power of, 10, 237–38

Soul Language and, 205, 206, 238

as spiritual channel, 10, 52, 199

3396815 code and, 167, 206

Zhong and, 262, 265

Divine

asking questions of, 234, 235, 240–41, 246–47

definition of, 256*n*

Divine Healing Hands as direct connection to, 179

gratitude to, 137, 197

layers in Heaven and, 214

Master Sha's communications with, 9–12

as serving others, 216

Soul Language translation and, 232, 234

soul of, 31

spiritual channels and, 10, 200, 237–38, 241, 252, 253, 254

as spiritual mother and father of all souls, 200

trusting answers received from, 240–41

Zhong chant and, 265

Divine Channels
  application for Divine Healing Hands
    and, 13
  authority for downloading and
    transmitting of, 4
  as chosen ones, 3–4
  as honor, 13
  power and authority of, 21, 26–27
  power of Divine Healing Hands and,
    26–27, 44
  proper use of Divine Healing Hands
    blessings and, 21
  reasons for Divine's release of soul
    hands and, 13
  receiving of Divine Healing Hands
    blessings by, 44
  as trainers, 4
  See also Worldwide Representatives
Divine Healing Hands
  application for, 13
  close for blessings of, 42
  as direct connection to Divine, 179
  Divine involvement in all blessings
    of, 14
  Divine's first time release of, 9–12
  downloading to this book of, 29–54
  downloading of, 3–4
  and first time for giving Divine
    Healing Hands to the masses,
    11–12, 37, 271
  forcing of blessings of, 22, 41
  gratitude for receiving, 179
  honor and respect for, 19, 20, 85
  how to apply for, 15–17
  and how do Divine Healing Hands
    work, 270–71
  and how many times can blessings be
    offered, 18–19
  how of, 2, 3
  light line for, 14, 41

  names of people receiving, 11
  number of people who have received,
    10–11
  and offering blessings as appropriate,
    18, 20, 21, 22, 23, 40–41, 43, 46
  and plans for creation of Divine
    Healing Hands Soul Healers, 85–86
  possible responses to receiving, 41–43
  power and significance of, 7–9, 13,
    25–54, 88, 97–100, 126–28, 133–34,
    177–79, 197, 222–23, 270–72
  proper use of, 19–23, 186, 191, 196
  reasons for Divine's release of, 12–15,
    271
  as sacred treasures, 27, 56
  size of, 4
  as unconditional blessings, 43
  what are, 1, 2, 3–4, 269–70
  why of, 1–2, 3, 4–9
  See also specific topic
Divine Healing Hands Blessings
    teleconferences, 92, 99, 141, 142,
    178, 192
Divine Healing Hands Certification
    Training, lviii, 4, 13, 15, 19, 30
Divine Healing Hands (Master Sha),
    downloading of Divine Healing
    Hands for, 29–54
Divine Healing Hands Movement, 92
Divine Healing Hands Soul Healers
  animals/pets and, 185
  apply for, 13, 15–17, 29, 267
  approval/selection of, 13, 30
  authority of, 21
  as divine calling, 29–30
  Divine Protection Package for, 21–22,
    21n
  finances and, 154
  healing blessings of, 14
  as honor and blessing, 8, 19

intelligence and, 160, 161–62, 163, 164, 170, 172, 174, 176

kundalini and, 62

length of time for blessings by, 18–19

light line of, 14, 41

limitations of, 21

Lower Dan Tian and, 67

nature healing and, 195

need for, 271

number of, 272

opening all four spiritual channels and, 264

physical body and, 131–32

plans for creation of more, 85–86

possible responses to receiving a soul healing from, 41–43

proper use of Divine Healing Hands blessings and, 19–23

relationships and, 149, 150–51

as serving others, 136, 267, 272

soul healing blessings of, 4

spiritual journey to become, 88–93

story about opportunity to become a, 97–100

Tao studies of, 267

training and certification of, lviii, 4, 13, 15, 19, 30

Divine Healing Hands Soul Mind Body Transplants

downloaded to this book, 29

Master Sha's gratitude for receiving, 197

serving others and, 136

See also specific chant

Divine Inner Yin Yang Circle, 70–77, 81–84. *See also* Sacred Circle

Divine Karma Cleansing, 5, 6, 21

Divine Light Wall Soul Mind Body Transplants, as part of Divine Protection Package, 21*n*

Divine Love Peace Harmony Rainbow Light Ball, 59, 59*n*, 60

Divine Order

Divine Golden Light Ball and Golden Liquid Spring of Divine Forgiveness Soul Mind Body Transplants, liv

Divine Healing Hands Soul Mind Body Transplants to this book, 33

Divine Purple Light Ball and Purple Liquid Spring of Divine Balance of Soul, Heart, Mind, and Body Soul Mind Body Transplants, 182

Divine Purple Light Ball and Purple Liquid Spring of Divine Clarity of Mind Soul Mind Body Transplants, 101

Divine Purple Light Ball and Purple Liquid Spring of Divine Compassion for Brain, Heart, and Soul Soul Mind Body Transplants, 175

Divine Purple Light Ball and Purple Liquid Spring of Divine Forgiveness Soul Mind Body Transplants, 94

Divine Purple Light Ball and Purple Liquid Spring of Divine Kundalini Soul Mind Body Transplants, 247

Divine Purple Light Ball and Purple Liquid Spring of Divine Light Soul Mind Body Transplants, 152

Divine Purple Light Ball and Purple Liquid Spring of Divine Love Soul Mind Body Transplants, 119

Divine Purple Light Ball and Purple Liquid Spring of Divine Lower Dan Tian Soul Mind Body Transplants, 65

Divine Order (*cont.*)
  Divine Purple Light Ball and Purple
    Liquid Spring of Divine Message
    Center Soul Mind Body Transplants,
    238
  Divine Purple Light Ball and Purple
    Liquid Spring of Divine
    Nourishment and Balance Soul
    Mind Body Transplants, 189
  Divine Purple Light Ball and
    Purple Liquid Spring of Divine
    Purification Soul Mind Body
    Transplants, 220
  Divine Purple Light Ball and Purple
    Liquid Spring of Divine Soul
    Language Soul Mind Body
    Transplants, 208
Divine Power Series (Master Sha), 42
Divine Prevention and Healing of
    Communicable Diseases Soul Mind
    Body Transplants, 21*n*
Divine Protection Package, 21–22, 21*n*
Divine Protection Soul Mind Body
    Transplants, 21*n*
Divine Purple Light Ball
  as divine treasure, 137
  uplifting of soul standing in Heaven
    and, 222
  *See also specific chant, Divine Order, or
    topic*
Divine Sacred Inner Circle
  chanting and, 74–75, 76–80
  Four Power Techniques and, 73–74,
    75–83
  for healing all sickness, 69–83
  location of, 70–71
  for longevity, 77–84
  Master Sha receives, 70
  practice and applying of, 73–75,
    81–84
  for rejuvenation, 77–84
  yin and yang, 69–70
*Divine Soul Mind Body Healing and
    Transmission System* (Master Sha),
    286
Divine Soul Mind Body Transplants,
    Master Sha's authority to offer, 5
Divine Soul Songs
  as Soul Power, xlvii, 32
  significance of, 219, 228
Divine Soul Songs (Master Sha), 74, 78,
    90, 285
Divine Transformation (Master Sha), 91,
    288
Divine transformation
  Divine Healing Hands and, 26
Divine treasures
  authority for downloading and
    transmitting of, 3–4
  chanting and, 244
  characteristics of, 2
  how of, 2
  power of Divine Healing Hands
    and, 25
  return of, 18
  size of, 4
  Soul Language and, 244
  subdividing, 18–19
  See also specific treasure
Dolphins, healing of, 187
Du meridian, 69, 70, 71, 72

E

Ear acupuncture, 130
Ear reflection, 130
Earth element, 105, 124
Elements. *See* Five Elements
Emergency situations, length of time
    of blessing for, 18–19

Emotional body
    chanting and, 107–8, 109–10,
        112–13, 114–16, 117–19, 120–21,
        122–23
    connection between physical body and,
        105
    examples of sicknesses of, 125
    Five Elements and, 117–23, 124, 125
    Four Power Techniques and, 39,
        107–8, 109–10, 112–16, 117–23
    healing of, 26, 39, 105–24, 136
    power of Divine Healing Hands and,
        26, 39, 46, 271
    responses to soul healing blessings and,
        46
    Soul Language and, 204, 208, 209–10
    spiritual channels and, 204, 206, 208,
        209–10
    3396815 code and, 206
    See also specific emotion
Empowerments, xi-xii
Emptiness, 250–51, 265–66, 267
Energy
    blockages in, 7, 21, 270
    in body, 7, 21, 189
    compassion and, 56, 169, 176, 202,
        219
    jing qi shen and, 7
    kundalini and, 58, 59–63
    Lower Dan Tian and, 63
    need for more, 81
    power of Divine Healing Hands and,
        7, 26, 270
    Snow Mountain Area and, 34
    soul intelligence and, 165
    spiritual channels and, 202, 219, 241,
        265, 270
    Third Eye and, 241
    3396815 code and, 166
    workplace relationships and, 146

Zhong chant and, 265
    See also kundalini

F

Facebook, Master Sha's page on, 91
Failure, karma and, 87, 210
Fear, 105, 115–16, 120–21, 125
Feet reflection, 130
Feng shui, 228
Finances
    applying Divine Healing Hands to
        transform, 154–55
    bad karma and, 5, 6, 87
    blockages concerning, 7, 42, 210
    cause of problems with, 6
    chanting and, 153–55, 217, 230–32,
        267
    Four Power Techniques and, 16,
        30–31, 40, 152–55, 230–32
    frequency and vibration of, 55
    how to apply Divine Healing Hands
        and, 16
    jing qi shen and, 7
    light and, 56, 152, 202
    love and, 168, 202
    meditation and, 217
    power of Divine Healing Hands and, 7,
        8, 26, 27, 30–31, 40, 42, 48, 270,
        271
    proper use of Divine Healing Hands
        and, 23
    Soul Language and, 227–32
    Soul Power Series and, 2
    Soul Songs and, 227–32
    spiritual channels and, 200, 202, 210,
        217, 227–32, 241, 267, 270, 271
    3396815 code and, 167
    transformation of, 2, 26, 30–31,
        152–55

Fire element, 105, 124

Five Elements
emotional body and, 105, 117–23, 124, 125
every sickness is due to soul mind body blockages in, 125
physical body and, 124–33

Five Elements Hand Position, 117, 120

Foot reflexology, 130

Forcing of soul healings and blessings, 41

Forgiveness
blockages and, 145, 211
by both sides, 210–11
Divine Healing Hands as carrying, 56
forgiveness practice as technique of, 2
inner joy and peace and, 168, 202, 210, 219, 270
karma and, 5, 145, 210–13, 225
meditation and chanting and, 217
Message Center and, 205
mistakes and, 210, 211
need for application of, 3
power of Divine Healing Hands and, 7, 50, 52, 270
power of, 168, 211
relationships and, 145
of self, 89
soul, 168
Soul Language and, 202, 210–13
Soul Songs and, 219, 228
spiritual channels and, 202, 210–13, 215, 217, 219, 222, 225, 228, 270
unconditional, 210–11
uplifting of soul standing in Heaven and, 215, 222

Four Power Techniques
applying Divine Healing Hands and, 15–17
chanting and, 32–33
definition of, xxxv–xxxvi, 30–33
downloading of Divine Healing Hands to book and, 30–33, 39–43
opening of all four spiritual channels together and, 263–65
power of Divine Healing Hands and, 32–33, 39–43
pregnancy story and, 9
Sacred Circle and, 73–74, 75–84
for self-healing, 39–43
uplifting of soul standing in Heaven and, 220–22
See also specific power technique or topic

Frequency
Divine Healing Hands as carrying, 85, 177–79
downloading of Divine Healing Hands to book and, 36
meditation and chanting and, 218
power of Divine Healing Hands and, 7, 32, 36, 46, 270
responses to soul healing blessings and, 46
Soul Songs and, 219, 228, 258
Sound Power and, 32
Tao Songs and, 258
See also specific topic

G

Generosity, 6, 48, 225

God Gives His Heart to Me (Divine Soul Song), 90, 91

GOLD (gratitude, obedience, loyalty, and devotion), 35, 92, 93, 259

Good karma, 4–5, 225. *See also* karma

Gratitude to Divine, 137, 197
importance of showing, 43
power of Divine Healing Hands and, 43, 49, 50, 51, 53

for receiving Divine Healing Hands,
179
See also GOLD and Total GOLD
Grief and sadness, 105, 113–15, 120–21,
125
Guan Yin, xiii, xiv, 11

H
Harmony, 26, 56, 210–11, 217, 271
Hawaiian hotel, Master Sha's story about,
227–28
Healing
applying Divine Healing Hands for,
39–54
being in divine and Tao condition and,
266
demanding/forcing, 21, 41
downloading of Divine Healing Hands
to book and, 38
how to apply Divine Healing Hands
for, 15–17
light and, 56, 270
meditation and chanting and, 217
Message Center as key to, 205
need for, 2
power of Divine Healing Hands and, 7,
26, 30–31, 38, 39–54, 270
proper use of Divine Healing Hands
and, 22, 23
remote, 26
self-, 9, 26, 39, 43
Soul Power Series and, 2
Tao and, 267
unconditional, 43
See also specific topic
Health
animals/pets and, 181–82
bad karma and, 5, 6, 87
blockages and, 210

frequency and vibration of, 55
light as transforming, 56
love and, 168, 202
power of Divine Healing Hands and, 7,
8, 178–79, 270
Soul Language and, 203, 213
spiritual channels and, 200, 202, 203,
210, 213, 241, 267, 270
3396815 code and, 167
Zhong chant and, 267
Heart
downloading of Divine Healing Hands
to this book and, 38
Five Elements and, 105, 124
Four Power Technique and, 40
as house for mind and soul, 253
light and, 56, 152, 169
love and, 161
Mind Power and, 31
opening of, 3, 40, 47
power of Divine Healing Hands and,
8, 26, 31, 37, 38, 40, 47, 50,
270
proper use of Divine Healing Hands
blessings and, 19–20
purification of, 3, 56, 152, 167, 169,
205, 213–18, 219, 220–22, 270
rejuvenation of, 26, 56, 84, 152, 167,
169, 206, 219, 270
relationships and, 143
response to soul healing blessing and,
47
Soul Language and, 205
spiritual channels and, 202, 205, 206,
213–18, 219, 220–22, 253, 255,
258, 262, 270
Tao and, 258
3396815 code and, 167
traditional Chinese medicine teachings
about, 156

Heart (*cont.*)
  uplifting of soul standing in Heaven
    and, 213–18
  as yin organ, 69
  Zhong and, 253
Heart intelligence, 155, 156, 161–64,
    167, 171, 173, 174–75, 205, 271
Heart valve replacement story, 135–36
Heaven
  Divine Healing Hands as bringing
    love, peace, and harmony to, 56
  downloading of Divine Healing
    Hands to this book and, 35, 36,
    38
  healing all animals in, 186
  layers in, 213–16
  meditation and chanting and, 217
  as most fair, 5
  secrets of, 254
  Soul Language translation and, 232
  spiritual channels and, 200, 232, 251,
    252, 253, 254, 256*n*
  Tao as source of, 200, 253, 256*n*
  uplifting of soul standing in, 213–18,
    220–22, 252
Hello, saying. *See* Soul Power
Hui Yin acupuncture point, 73, 75, 77,
    78, 79, 129, 130, 201, 261
  location of, 70, 129

I

*If you want to know if a pear is sweet, taste
    it,* xxi
I love my heart and soul (Divine Soul
    Song), 228
Immortality, 205, 206, 267
Immunity
  compassion and, 56, 83, 169, 176,
    202, 219

Lower Dan Tian and, 63
  need for more, 81
  power of Divine Healing Hands and,
    26, 270
  spiritual channels and, 202, 219, 265,
    270
  Zhong chant and, 265
Inner joy and peace
  forgiveness and, 168, 202, 210–11,
    219, 270
  meditation and chanting and, 217
  power of Divine Healing Hands and,
    26, 56, 270
  and reasons for giving Divine Healing
    Hands to the masses, 271
  spiritual channels and, 202, 210–11,
    217, 219
Intelligence
  blockages of, 7, 159
  chanting and, 156–57, 158, 159, 160,
    161–63, 164, 167, 168, 169, 170–
    71, 172–73, 174–75, 176–77, 217,
    267
  compassion and, 176
  downloading of Divine Healing Hands
    to book and, 38
  Four Power Techniques and, 40,
    158–59, 160–64, 165–77
  frequency and vibration of, 55
  heart and, 155, 156
  jing qi shen and, 7
  life transformation and, 171
  light and, 56, 152
  love and, 168, 202
  meditation and, 217
  mind and, 155
  number codes and, 156–59
  power of Divine Healing Hands and,
    8, 26, 38, 40, 270
  soul and, 155

spiritual channels and, 200, 202, 217, 267, 270
3396815 code and, 167
transformation of, 3, 26, 56, 152, 155–77
types of, 156
Zhong chant and, 267
See also type of intelligence

J
Japan, Master Sha's visit to, 224–25
Jesus, xiii-iv, 11
Jing qi shen, 7
Jiu Er Er Si Si. *See* 92244
Jiu Ling Ba. *See* 908
Jiu Tian (Nine layers of Heaven), 213–16
Jobs/careers. *See* workplace

K
Karma
    blockages and, 210
    forgiveness and, 5, 145, 210–13, 225
    Message Center as key to, 205
    relationships and, 224–27
    as root cause of success and failure, 87, 210
    service and, 5–6, 225
    Soul Language and, 226
    spiritual channels and, 205, 210–13
    why do Divine Healing Hands work and, 4–5
    See also bad karma; good karma
    workplace story of, 146–47
Kidneys, 58, 60, 69, 105, 125, 241
Kundalini
    boosting power of, 56–63, 242–46, 247–50

brain and, 241, 246, 249
chanting and, 59–61, 62–63
development of, 56–63, 244–46
fear and, 115
Four Power Techniques and, 59–61, 62–63, 247–50
importance of, 58, 63
intelligence and, 158
life transformation and, 244
location of, 57, 58
purification and, 244
rejuvenation and, 208, 244
soul healing and, 208
Soul Language/Soul Language Channel and, 208, 250
spiritual channels and, 241, 242–46, 247–50, 251, 262
Third Eye and, 241, 242–46, 247–50, 251, 262
Kun Gong, 129, 130

L
Lao Zi, 253
Life
    purpose of, 215, 269
    soul life and physical, 215
    spiritual channels and, 200, 215
    See also life-threatening conditions; life transformation
Life-threatening conditions
    animal healing and, 184
    emotional body and, 108, 110, 113, 116, 119, 121
    kundalini and, 60
    length of time for blessing/chanting for, 18, 61, 67, 75
    Lower Dan Tian and, 67
    mental body and, 103
    physical body and, 126–28, 131

Life-threatening conditions (*cont.*)
  possible responses to soul healing/
    blessings and, 42, 43
  power of Divine Healing Hands and,
    41, 42, 43
  proper use of Divine Healing Hands
    and, 20
  removal of blockages for, 42, 87
  requests for Divine Healing Hands
    concerning, 41
  Sacred Circle and, 75
  Soul Language and, 213
  spiritual body and, 95
Life transformation
  compassion and, 176
  divine treasures and, 137
  Four Power Techniques and, 15–17,
    30–31
  frequency and vibration and, 177–79
  how to apply Divine Healing Hands
    for, 15–17
  intelligence and, 171
  kundalini and, 244
  light and, 152, 169, 202, 219
  love and, 56, 119, 168, 202, 219
  Message Center and, 205
  power of Divine Healing Hands and,
    26, 30–31, 177–79, 197, 270, 271
  proper use of Divine Healing Hands
    blessings and, 23
  soul healing and transformation and,
    211
  Soul Songs and, 228, 232
  spiritual channels and, 202, 205, 211,
    213, 219, 228, 232, 241, 244, 267,
    270, 271
  3396815 code and, 167
  Zhong chant and, 267
  See also finances; intelligence;
    relationships

Life transformation story, 178–79
Light
  benefits of Divine, 152, 169
  Divine Healing Hands as carrying, 56
  downloading of Divine Healing
    Hands to this book and, 36, 38
  line of, 14, 41
  Message Center and, 205
  power of Divine Healing Hands and,
    7–8, 36, 38, 44, 45–46, 47, 48,
    49, 50, 51, 56, 270
  response to soul healing blessing and,
    44, 45–46, 47
  soul and, 56, 168, 169
  Soul Songs and, 219, 228
  spiritual channels and, 202, 205, 219,
    222, 228, 270
  story about, 134, 135
  and transformation of physical body
    to light body, 206
  uplifting of soul standing in Heaven
    and, 222
Ling Yao Chi Chi Chi. *See* 01777
Liver, 69, 105, 124
Liver cirrhosis, story about healing of,
    106–7
Longevity
  chanting for, 77–84, 217
  desire for, 81
  Four Power Techniques and, 30–31,
    77–79
  kundalini and, 58
  light and, 219
  Lower Dan Tian and, 63
  meditation and, 217
  Ming Men area and, 57
  power of Divine Healing Hands and,
    26, 30–31, 271
  Sacred Circle for, 77–84
  Soul Language and, 205

spiritual channels and, 205, 206, 217, 219, 222, 254, 267, 271

Tao and, 267

3396815 code and, 167, 206

uplifting of soul standing in Heaven and, 222

Lotus flower, 215

Love

benefits of, 168

Divine Healing Hands as bringing, 56

downloading of Divine Healing Hands to this book and, 36, 38

finances and, 168, 202

forgiveness and, 210–11

health and, 168, 202

heart and, 161

intelligence and, 168, 202

karma and, 5, 225

life transformation and, 56, 119, 168, 202, 219

meditation and chanting and, 217

as melting blockages, 56, 119, 168, 202, 219, 270

Message Center and, 205

power of Divine Healing Hands and, 7, 26, 36, 38, 49, 50, 51, 270

and reasons for giving Divine Healing Hands to the masses, 271

relationships and, 168, 202

soul and, 168

Soul Language and, 202, 205, 210–11, 224

Soul Songs and, 228

spiritual channels and, 202, 205, 210–11, 213–18, 219, 222, 224, 225, 228, 270, 271

success and, 202

uplifting of soul standing in Heaven and, 213–18, 222

Love Peace Harmony Movement, 92, 259

Love, Peace and Harmony (Divine Soul Song), 90, 91, 218–19, 227–32, 257–58, 260

Lower Dan Tian ("light ball field"), 56, 63–69

Loyalty. *See* GOLD

Lu La Lu La Li (Divine Soul Song), 228, 231–32

See also *Love, Peace and Harmony*

Lungs, 69, 105, 124–25, 165

M

Matter, 7, 21, 189, 270

Meditation, 217–18

Mental body

blockages in, 101

chanting and, 102–3, 104–5

examples of sickness of, 125

Four Power Techniques for, 40, 101–5

healing of, 26, 40, 100–105, 136

power of Divine Healing Hands and, 26, 40, 46, 271

responses to soul healing blessings and, 46

Soul Language and, 204, 208, 209–10

spiritual channels and, 204, 206, 208, 209–10

3396815 code and, 206

Message Center (heart chakra)

applying Divine Healing Hands and, 15

finances and, 153

location of, 205

Lower Dan Tian and, 65

mental body and, 101

power and significance of, 205

proper use of Divine Healing Hands and, 20

Message Center (heart chakra) (*cont.*)
  Soul Language and, 204, 205, 206–7,
    233, 234
  spiritual body and, 94
  spiritual channels and, 204–5, 206–7,
    233, 237, 238, 262
Metal element, 105, 124
Mind
  blockages in, 6, 7, 20, 21, 42, 73, 125,
    167, 206, 238, 270
  as consciousness, 189
  everything as having a, 100, 188, 189
  Five Elements and, 124
  foundation of Soul Mind Body
    Medicine and, 87
  frequency and vibration and, 168,
    202
  heart as house for, 253
  intelligence and, 155
  light and, 56, 152, 169
  Mind Power and, 31
  number codes for, 156–57
  power of Divine Healing Hands and,
    8, 26, 31, 37, 42, 48, 270
  proper use of Divine Healing Hands
    and, 19–20, 21
  purification of, 3, 56, 152, 167, 205,
    213–18, 219, 220–22, 270
  rejuvenation of, 26, 56, 84, 152, 167,
    206, 219, 270
  Soul Language and, 202, 205
  spiritual channels and, 202, 205, 206,
    213–18, 219, 220–22, 238, 253,
    258, 270
  Tao and, 258
  3396815 code and, 167, 206
  traditional Chinese medicine teachings
    about, 156
  uplifting of soul standing in Heaven
    and, 213–18
  why of Divine Healing Hands and, 7
  See also mind intelligence; Mind Power
Mind intelligence, 156–61, 167, 171,
    173, 174–75, 205, 271
Mind Power
  animals/pets and, 183, 185
  applying Divine Healing Hands for,
    43
  bad karma and, 212, 227
  chanting and, 32
  as creative visualization, 31
  Divine Inner Yin Yang Circle and, 74,
    76
  downloading of Divine Healing Hands
    to this book and, 32, 43
  emotional body and, 108, 109, 113,
    114, 116, 118, 120, 122
  finances and, 153, 155, 231
  Four Power Techniques and, 43, 95,
    96, 102, 104, 108
  how to apply Divine Healing Hands
    and, 16
  intelligence and, 159, 161, 162, 164,
    168, 170, 172, 174, 177
  kundalini and, 60, 62, 248–49
  longevity and, 78, 80
  Lower Dan Tian and, 66–67, 68
  mental body and, 102, 104
  nature healing and, 190, 195
  opening all four spiritual channels
    together and, 264
  physical body and, 129–31, 132
  power of Divine Healing Hands and,
    31, 32, 43, 45, 50, 51
  power of, 16, 31
  rejuvenation and, 78, 80, 209
  relationships and, 144, 148, 150, 151,
    226
  response to receiving soul healing
    blessing and, 45

Sacred Circle and, 74, 76, 78, 80

Soul Language and, 206–7, 209, 233, 259

spiritual body and, 95, 96

spiritual channels and, 206–7, 209, 212, 221, 226, 231, 233, 239, 242, 248–49, 256, 259, 264

uplifting of soul standing in Heaven and, 220, 222

Ming Men acupuncture point, 129, 130, 255, 258, 263

Ming Men area ("life gate"), 56–57, 58

Ming Men fire, 57, 58, 63, 130

Ming Men water, 57, 58, 63

Miracles, soul healing, 41, 43, 61, 87, 88, 203, 204

Mistakes, 5, 87, 210, 211, 225

Mother Earth

Divine Channels as serving, 4

Divine Healing Hands as bringing love, peace, and harmony to, 56

Divine Love Peace Harmony Rainbow Light Ball and, 59

downloading of Divine Healing Hands to this book and, 35, 36, 37

healing all animals on, 186

healing all nature on, 191, 196

Love Peace Harmony Movement and, 259

meditation and chanting and, 217, 218

need for transformation of, 3

pollution on, 215

power of Divine Healing Hands and, 25, 26, 27, 31, 35, 36, 37

proper use of Divine Healing Hands blessings and, 22

purification of souls and, 215

reasons for Divine's release of Soul Hands and, 12–13

reasons for giving Divine Healing Hands to masses and, 271

spiritual channels and, 200, 215, 217, 218, 222, 253, 255, 256, 256*n*, 259, 271

Tao as source for creation of, 200, 253, 256*n*, 266

transition period of, 12–13, 14, 22, 25, 27, 35, 37, 152, 196, 255, 271

uplifting of soul standing in Heaven and, 222

Mother Mary, xxiii-iv, 11

Movie star with blood clot, story of power of pets and, 181–82

N

Natural disasters, 12, 13, 22, 27, 191, 196, 271

Nature, 188–97, 214, 215, 271

Neck and shoulder healing, story of, 186–87

Negativity, 101, 110–12, 125, 270

Netherlands, Master Sha's story about power of Love, Peace and Harmony in, 228–30

908 (Jiu Ling Ba), 156–57, 158, 159

92244 (Jiu Er Er Si Si), 156–57, 158, 159

Nine layers of Heaven (Jiu Tian), 214

Nosebleed, story about healing of serious, 125–28

Number codes, 156–59

O

Obedience. *See* GOLD

Opening Spiritual Channels Workshop (Vancouver, British Columbia), 30, 32–33, 34, 37–39, 44–47, 49–54

Organizational relationships, 140, 147–48, 149–50

Outer Yin Yang Circle, 71–2

P

Pain, 52, 98–99, 100, 125

Peace. *See* inner joy and peace

Pear analogy, 8–9, 25

Physical body
  chanting and, 128–29, 131, 132–33
  connection between emotional body and, 105
  examples of sickness of, 125
  Ferlan story and, 135
  Five Elements and, 124–33
  Four Power Techniques and, 39, 128–33
  healing of, 26, 39, 124–33, 136
  power of Divine Healing Hands and, 26, 39, 46, 51, 131–33, 271
  responses to soul healing blessings and, 46
  Soul Language and, 204, 208, 209–10
  spiritual channels and, 204, 206, 208, 209–10
  3396815 code and, 206
  transformation to light body of, 206
  Zhong and, 129–31, 132

Pineal gland, Third Eye as, 246, 262

Police investigations, proper use of Divine Healing Hands blessings and, 23

Politics, proper use of Divine Healing Hands blessings and, 23

Postnatal energy center, Lower Dan Tian and, 63

Power of Soul (Master Sha), xlv, 91, 284

Pregnancy, story about, 8–9

Prenatal energy center, kundalini and, 58

Promises, Divine Healing Hands blessings and, 22

Pump wisdom, 248, 262

Purity/purification
  chanting and, 217, 257–58
  importance of, 3, 215
  karma and, 225
  kundalini and, 244
  light and, 152, 169, 202, 219, 270
  meditation and, 217
  power of Divine Healing Hands and, 7–8, 26, 52, 270, 271
  purifying yourself to reach total, 257–58
  Soul Language and, 205, 213–18, 220–22
  spiritual channels and, 202, 205, 213–18, 219, 220–22, 225, 244, 257–58, 259, 270, 271
  3396815 code and, 167
  uplifting of soul standing in Heaven and, 222
  See also Xiu Lian practice

Purple Light Ball and Purple Liquid Spring of Soul Mind Body Transplants
  as divine treasure, 137
  See also specific chant or topic

Q

Qi, 69, 70
  chanting while lying down and, 81*n*

R

Reflection, 130

Reincarnation, 165, 215, 216

Rejuvenation
  being in divine and Tao condition and, 266

chanting for, 77–84, 217
Four Power Techniques and, 30–31,
    77–79, 208–10
kundalini and, 58, 244
light and, 152, 169, 202, 219, 270
Lower Dan Tian and, 63
meditation and, 217
Ming Men area and, 57
power of Divine Healing Hands and,
    26, 30–31, 197, 270, 271
Sacred Circle for, 77–84
search for, 2, 81
Soul Language and, 205, 208–10
Soul Power Series and, 2
spiritual channels and, 202, 205, 206,
    208–10, 217, 219, 222, 244, 266,
    267, 270, 271
Tao and, 267
3396815 code and, 167, 206
uplifting of soul standing in Heaven
    and, 222
Relationships
blockages and, 7, 42, 210
cause of broken, 6
chanting and, 143–44, 145–46,
    147–48, 149–50, 151–52, 217,
    226–27
forgiveness and, 145
Four Power Techniques and, 16,
    30–31, 40, 143–44, 147–48,
    149–52, 226–27
frequency and vibration of, 55
how to apply Divine Healing Hands
    and, 16
of Japanese woman with husband,
    224–25
jing qi shen and, 7
karma and, 5, 6, 87, 223, 224–27
light and, 56, 152, 202
love and, 168, 202

meditation and, 217
organizational, 140, 147–48, 149–50
past experiences as basis of, 224
power of Divine Healing Hands and,
    7, 8, 26, 30–31, 40, 42, 51–52,
    140–43, 270, 271
Soul Language and, 223–27
soul of, 140
Soul Power Series and, 2
soul transformation of, 145
spiritual channels and, 200, 202, 210,
    217, 223–27, 241, 254, 267
story about, 123–24
3396815 code and, 167
transformation of, 2, 26, 30–31, 40,
    139–52
types of, 139
in workplace, 139, 141–42, 146–47
Zhong chant and, 267
Ren meridian, 69, 70, 71, 72

S

Sacred Circle. *See* Divine Sacred Circle.
Safety, power of Divine Healing Hands
    and, 50, 51
San Jiao (Triple Energizer), 69–70, 72–73
San San Jiu Liu Ba Yao Wu (*sahn sahn jeo
    leo bah yow woo*). *See* 3396815
Self-healing, Four Power Techniques for,
    39–43
Serving others
chosen ones as, 27
Divine as, 216
Divine Healing Hands orientation
    toward, 1–2
Divine Healing Hands Soul Healers as,
    136, 267, 272
Divine Healing Hands Soul Mind
    Body Transplants and, 136

Serving others (*cont.*)
  happiness and, 218
  karma and, 5–6, 225
  and lessons from bad service, 5
  power of Divine Healing Hands and,
    27, 48, 50, 53
  as purpose of life, 269
  and reasons for giving Divine Healing
    Hands to the masses, 271
  rewards for, 5
  simplicity as key to, 3
  Soul Power and, 214
  spiritual channels and, 53, 214,
    216–17, 218, 222, 225, 259, 267,
    269, 271, 272
  unconditional, 5–6, 48, 53, 216–17,
    218, 222, 259
  uplifting of soul standing in Heaven
    and, 214, 216–17
Seven Soul Houses (seven energy chakras),
    71, 71*n*, 72, 74, 75–83, 201, 261
Sha, Dr. Zhi Gang
  authority of, 2, 3–4, 5
  as chosen one, 2, 3–4, 5, 9
  as Divine Channel, 3–4
  Divine means of communication with,
    9–10
  Divine's communications/conversations
    with, 9–14, 29, 36–37, 246–47
  downloading of Divine Healing Hands
    to, 12
  receives Divine Soul Song *Love, Peace
    and Harmony*, 218
Shakyamuni, 11
Shi Jia Mo Ni Fo, 11
Shoulder pain, story about, 27, 28–29
Sickness
  blockages and, 86–87, 125
  causes of, 4, 6–7, 42, 69, 86–87, 125
  chanting for healing all, 69–77, 81–84
    divine treasures as healing, 137
    light and, 56, 152, 169, 202, 219, 270
    possible responses to soul healing/
      blessings concerning, 41–43
    power of Divine Healing Hands and, 7,
      41–43, 270
    Sacred Circle for healing all, 69–77,
      81–84
    spiritual channels and, 202, 219, 270
    why of Divine Healing Hands and, 4
    See also specific sickness
Siddhartha Gautama, 11
Simplicity, 2–3
Soul body. *See* spiritual body
Soul chart, 86
Soul communication
  as Divine's way of communicating, 9–12
  See also specific channel
Soul Communication (Master Sha), 10, 90,
    91, 283
soul enlightenment center, Message
    Center and, 205
Soul Hands. *See* Divine Healing Hands
Soul Healing and Enlightenment Retreat
    (Toronto, Ontario, Canada), 203
Soul intelligence, 155, 156, 165–71, 173,
    174–75, 205, 271
Soul is the boss., xxiii
Soul journey, 200, 213–14, 250–51, 252,
    258
Soul Language
  chanting and, 17, 169, 204–5, 208–10,
    213, 218, 222, 227, 233, 234, 235,
    240, 244, 250, 251, 257, 258, 259
  compassion and, 202
  definition of, 17*n*
  development of, 204–7
  divine treasures and, 244
  finances and, 227–32
  forgiveness and, 202, 210–13

Four Power Techniques and, 204–7,
  208–10, 232–35, 258–60
frequency and vibration and, 168, 202,
  218, 222
for healing and rejuvenation, 208–10
health and, 203
how to apply Divine Healing Hands
  and, 17
how do you know when you are
  speaking, 168, 207
karma and, 210–13, 226
as language of soul, 203–4, 232
love and, 202, 224
Message Center and, 205, 233, 234
power and significance of, 201–4, 205,
  218
purification and, 213–18, 220–22
relationships and, 223–27
soul intelligence and, 168–69
Soul Language Channel and, 201, 205,
  206, 233, 234
soul light and, 202
Soul Light Era Prayer Position and,
  204, 232
as soul mantra, 259
Soul Song as language of, 235
sound of, 207
spiritual channels and, 205, 206,
  223–37, 238, 240, 244, 250, 251,
  257, 258, 259, 265
3396815 code and, 169
translation of, 232–37, 238, 240, 265
understanding meaning of, 233, 234
uplifting of soul standing in Heaven
  and, 213–18, 220–22
Zhong chant and, 265
Soul Language Channel
  kundalini and, 250
  location of, 202, 261
  Message Center as key to, 205

Mind Power and, 206–7
opening of all four spiritual channels
  together and, 262–65
opening of, 201–7, 261
path of, 201
power of, 10, 201–3
seven Soul Houses and, 261
soul healing and rejuvenation and,
  210
Soul Language development and, 205,
  206
Soul Language translation and, 233,
  234
as spiritual channel, 10, 52, 199
3396815 code and, 167, 206
what is the, 201
Zhong chant and, 265
Soul Light Era
  commitment to serve in, 20
  definition of, xii–xiii
  "soul mind body" as term for, 7
  See also body; mind; soul(s)
Soul Light Era Prayer Position
  animals/pets and, 182, 185
  applying Divine Healing Hands and,
    15, 16
  bad karma and, 211
  finances and, 154, 230
  intelligence and, 160, 161–62, 164,
    167, 170, 172, 174, 176
  Lower Dan Tian and, 65
  mental body and, 102
  nature and, 189, 195
  physical body and, 132
  proper use of Divine Healing Hands
    and, 20
  relationships and, 149, 150–51
  Soul Language and, 204, 232
  spiritual body and, 94
  spiritual channels and, 230, 232, 239

Soul Mind Body Medicine, xxxiii, 42, 86, 87
Soul Mind Body Medicine (Master Sha), xx*n*
Soul Operation, 98
Soul Power (Say *Hello*)
    animals/pets and, 182–83, 185
    applying Divine Healing Hands for healing and, 39
    bad karma and, 211–12, 227
    chanting and, 32
    Divine Inner Yin Yang Circle and, 74, 75–76
    downloading of Divine Healing Hands to this book and, 31, 32, 35, 39
    emotional body and, 107–8, 109, 112–13, 114, 115–16, 117–18, 120, 122
    finances and, 153, 154–55, 230–31
    how to apply Divine Healing Hands and, 16
    inner and outer souls and, 31
    intelligence and, 158, 160, 162, 164, 167, 170, 172, 174, 176–77
    kundalini and, 59–60, 62, 248
    for longevity, 77–78, 79–80
    Lower Dan Tian and, 64–66, 68
    mental body and, 102, 104
    nature and, 189–90, 195
    opening of all four spiritual channels together and, 263
    physical body and, 128–29, 132
    power of Divine Healing Hands and, 31, 35, 39
    power of, 16, 31
    for rejuvenation, 77–78, 79–80, 208–9
    relationships and, 143–44, 147–48, 149–50, 151, 226
    Sacred Circle and, 74, 75–76, 77–78, 79–80

as Say Hello Healing and Blessing, 31
    serving others and, 214
    Soul Language and, 203, 204–6, 208–9, 233, 234, 258–59
    specialness of, 31
    spiritual body and, 94–95, 96
    spiritual channels and, 203, 204–5, 208–9, 211–12, 214, 220–21, 226, 230–31, 233, 234, 239, 242, 248, 255–56, 258–59, 263–64
    uplifting of soul standing in Heaven and, 220–21
Soul Power Series (Master Sha), 2, 30, 42, 55, 91–92, 256, 258, 281–90
Soul reading, 99
Soul Song(s)
    animals/pets and, 187
    bad karma and, 219
    compassion and, 228
story and, 134
    finances and, 227–32
    forgiveness and, 228
    frequency and vibration of, 219, 228, 258
    life transformation and, 228
    light and, 228
    love and, 228
    physical body and, 127
    power of, 227–30
    as song of Soul Language, 235
    as soul mantra, 259
    Sound Power and, 32
    spiritual channels and, 53, 227–32, 235–37, 258, 259
    transforming to Tao Song of, 258
    ulcerated colon story and, 235–37
    See also specific song
Soul teacher story, desire to become, 92
Soul Wisdom (Master Sha), 90–1, 169*n*, 281

Soul wisdom story, spiritual journey and, 90, 91

Soul World, 10, 200, 254, 265

Soul(s)
  of animals/pets, 188
  bad karma and, 20, 87
  blockages in, 4, 6, 7, 20, 42, 73, 86–87, 88, 125, 167, 206, 238, 270
  body and, 86, 169
  compassion and, 168, 169
  and Direct Soul Communication Channel to other souls, 237
  Divine Channels as serving, 4
  Divine Karma Cleansing and, 6
  Divine as spiritual mother and father of all, 200
  energy and, 169
  as eternal, 215
  everything as having a, 100, 140, 188–89, 197, 213
  Five Elements and, 124
  forgiveness and, 168
  foundation of Soul Mind Body Medicine and, 87
  Four Power Techniques and, 31, 39–40, 208–10
  healing of, 3, 6, 39–40, 41–43, 61, 203, 204, 208–10, 211
  heart and, 169, 253
  immunity and, 169
  importance of healing and transforming of, 211
  inner, 95
  jing qi shen and, 7
  kundalini and, 208
  life of, 215
  life transformation and, 169
  light and, 56, 152, 168, 169
  love and, 168
  mind and, 169
  Mind Power and, 209
  in nature, 188
  number of, 86
  opening of, 3, 40
  power of Divine Healing Hands and, 8, 26, 31, 37, 39–40, 42, 44, 47, 270
  proper use of Divine Healing Hands blessings and, 19, 20
  purification of, 3, 56, 152, 167, 169, 205, 213–18, 219, 220–22, 270
  reincarnation of, 165, 215
  rejuvenation of, 26, 56, 84, 152, 167, 169, 206, 208–10, 219, 270
  relationships and, 140, 145
  response to soul healing blessing and, 41–43, 44, 47
  seven Soul Houses and, 71n
  Soul Language as means of communicating with, 10
  spiritual channels and, 200, 202, 203–4, 205, 206, 211, 213–18, 219, 220–22, 232, 237, 238, 252, 253, 258, 270
  stamina and, 169
  Tao and, 258
  3396815 code and, 167, 206
  traditional Chinese medicine teachings about, 156
  uplifting of soul standing in Heaven and, 213–18, 220–22, 252
  vitality and, 169
  why Divine Healing Hands work and, 4, 7
  and wisdom and knowledge of soul as hidden, 165

Sound Power
  animals/pets and, 183–84, 185–86
  applying Divine Healing Hands and, 17, 43
  bad karma and, 212–13, 226–27

Sound Power (*cont.*)
  chanting and, 32, 33, 43
  Divine Inner Yin Yang Circle and,
    74–75, 76–77
  downloading of Divine Healing Hands
    to book and, 32, 33, 43
  emotional body and, 108, 109–10, 113,
    114–15, 118–19, 120–21, 122–23
  finances and, 153–54, 155, 231–32
  how to apply Divine Healing Hands
    and, 17
  intelligence and, 159, 161, 162–63,
    164, 168, 170–71, 172–73, 174–75,
    177
  kundalini and, 60–61, 62–63, 249–50
  for longevity, 78–79, 80–81
  Lower Dan Tian and, 66, 68–69
  mental body and, 102–3, 104–5
  nature and, 190–91, 195–96
  opening all four spiritual channels
    together and, 264
  physical body and, 131, 132–33
  power of Divine Healing Hands and,
    32, 33, 43
  power of, 17, 32
  rejuvenation and, 78–79, 80–81,
    209–10
  relationships and, 144, 148, 150,
    151–52, 226–27
  Sacred Circle and, 74–75, 76–77,
    78–79, 80
  soul healing and, 209–10
  soul intelligence and, 168–69, 170–71
  Soul Language and, 207, 209–10,
    233–35, 259–60
  spiritual body and, 95, 96–97
  spiritual channels and, 207, 209–10,
    212–13, 221, 226–27, 231, 233,
    239–41, 243–44, 249–50, 256–57,
    259–60, 264–65

uplifting of soul standing in Heaven
    and, 221–22
Spinal cord/column, 60, 201, 249, 261, 262
Spiritual body
  chanting and, 94–95, 96–97
  examples of sicknesses of, 125
  Four Power Techniques and, 94–97
  healing of, 26, 86–100, 136
  power of Divine Healing Hands and,
    26, 46, 271
  responses to soul healing blessings and,
    46
  as soul body, 86
  Soul Language and, 204, 208, 209–10
  spiritual channels and, 204, 206, 208,
    209–10
  3396815 code and, 206
Spiritual channels
  chanting and, 203, 204–5, 207, 208–10,
    211–13, 217–18, 220–22, 267
  Divine Soul Songs and, 227–30
  Four Power Techniques and, 204–7,
    208–10, 211–13, 220–22, 226–27,
    230–31, 232–34, 238–41, 242–44,
    247–50, 255–57, 258–61, 263–65
  frequency and, 202, 218, 219, 222,
    228, 258, 270
  opening of, 52–54, 200, 241, 257–58,
    262–67, 271
  potential abilities of, 252
  power of Divine Healing Hands and,
    49, 52–54, 271
  power of, 10, 200, 241
  purity and, 257–58
  3396815 code and, 165, 167
  what are, 52
  Zhong chant and, 267
  See also specific channel
Spiritual images. *See* Third Eye; Third Eye
    Channel

Spiritual journey
    story of, 88–93
    purpose of, 215–16
    Third Eye Channel and, 241, 252
    uplifting of soul standing in Heaven
        and, 213–18
    Xiu Lian practice and, 245
Stamina
    boosting, 56, 83, 169
    compassion and, 56, 169, 176, 202,
        219
    Lower Dan Tian and, 63
    need for more, 81
    power of Divine Healing Hands and,
        26, 270
    spiritual channels and, 202, 219
    Zhong chant and, 265
Student's intelligence, 173–75
    relationship story of, 123–24
Success
    karma and, 87, 210
    love and, 202
    meditation and chanting and, 217
    spiritual channels and, 200, 202, 210,
        217

T

Tao, xxxvii, 31, 92, 200, 232, 241, 252,
    253, 256*n*, 259, 265–67
Tao I (Master Sha), 23, 23*n*, 91, 92, 266,
    287
Tao II (Master Sha), 23, 23*n*, 91, 92, 266,
    289
Tao Retreats, 50–51, 91, 266–67
Tao Song and Tao Dance (Master Sha), 91,
    258, 266, 290
Tao Songs, 32, 52, 53, 90, 91, 108, 110,
    257–58, 259. *See also specific song*
Tao Soul Downloads, xxiii-iv, xxiii*n*

Tao Soul Language, 257–58
Third Eye
    age and, 246
    of children, 246, 251–52
    daughter of Zhi Chen Guo and story
        of, 251–52
    Divine explanation of wisdom of,
        246–47
    downloading of Divine Healing Hands
        for book and, 32, 33, 34–39
    energy and, 241
    kundalini and, 58, 60, 245–46
    as pineal gland, 246, 262
    power of Divine Healing Hands and,
        32, 33, 34–39, 49–50, 52
    relationships and, 225
    soul journey and, 252
    spiritual channels and, 225, 241,
        245–47, 251–52, 262
    Time is kung fu. Kung fu is time., xxxvi
    uplifting of soul standing in Heaven
        and, 215, 252
    See also Third Eye Channel
Third Eye Channel
    chanting and, 243–44, 248, 249–50,
        265
    Four Power Techniques and, 241–44,
        247–50
    Heaven and, 251
    kundalini and, 241, 242–46, 247–50,
        251, 252, 262
    location of, 262
    Message Center as key to, 205
    opening of all four spiritual channels
        together and, 262–65
    opening of, 241–52, 261
    power of, 10, 241, 252
    Soul Language and, 205, 206, 244,
        250, 251
    as spiritual channel, 10, 52, 199

Third Eye Channel (*cont.*)
   spiritual journey and, 241, 252
   3396815 code and, 167, 206
   Xiu Lian practice and, 245, 251, 252
   Zhong chant and, 265
   3396815 (sacred code) (San San Jiu Liu
     Ba Yao Wu), 165–71, 204–5, 206,
     207, 210, 213
Tian Wai Tian (*Heaven beyond Heaven*),
   214, 216
Total GOLD (gratitude, obedience,
   loyalty, and devotion), 35, 92, 93,
   259
Touching, when offering Divine Healing
   Hands blessings, 22
Traditional Chinese medicine (TCM), 70,
   86, 105, 124, 156
Tui na (Chinese massage), 70

U

Ulcerated colon, story about, 235–37
Universal Law of Universal Service, xv–xvi,
   217

V

Vancouver, British Columbia, Opening
   Spiritual Workshop in, 30, 32–33,
   34, 37–39, 44–47, 49–54
Vibrations
   of body, 168, 202
   Divine Healing Hands as carrying, 85,
     177–79
   downloading of Divine Healing Hands
     to book and, 36
   of finances, 55
   of health, 55
   of intelligence, 55
   life transformation and, 177–79

   meditation and chanting and, 218
   of mind, 168, 202
   number codes and, 156–57
   power of Divine Healing Hands and, 7,
     32, 36, 45, 46, 270
   of relationships, 55
   response to receiving soul healing
     blessing and, 45, 46
   soul intelligence and, 165
   Soul Language and, 168, 202, 218, 222
   Soul Songs and, 219, 228, 258
   Sound Power and, 32
   spiritual channels and, 202, 218, 219,
     222, 228, 258, 270
   story and, 134
   Tao Songs and, 258
Virtue, 6, 53, 217
Visualization. *See* Mind Power
Vitality
   boosting, 56, 83
   compassion and, 56, 169, 176, 202, 219
   Lower Dan Tian and, 63
   need for more, 81
   power of Divine Healing Hands and,
     26, 270
   spiritual channels and, 202, 219
   Zhong chant and, 265

W

Wai Jiao, 72–73, 74, 75–77
Wan ling rong he (all souls join as one), 35
Wan wu jie you ling (everything has a
   soul), 188–89
War, proper use of Divine Healing Hands
   blessings and, 22
Wei Lü, 129, 130
"What you think is what happens"
   abilities, 48
Wood element, 105, 124

Workplace
   power of Divine Healing Hands and,
      40, 48
   relationships in, 139, 141–42, 146–47
World Health Organization (WHO), 69
Worldwide Representatives
   authority of, 3–4, 270
   becoming a Divine Healing Hands
      Soul Healer and, 267
   Divine Karma Cleansings offered by, 6
   downloading of Divine Healing Hands
      and, 272
   finances and, 154
   intelligence and, 160, 163, 170
   kundalini and, 62
   Lower Dan Tian and, 67
   opening all four spiritual channels and,
      264
   physical body and, 132
   power of Divine Healing Hands and,
      26–27
   relationships and, 149
   story about desire to become, 92
   as trainers of Divine Healing Hands
      Soul Healers, 30
   transmission of Divine Healing Hands
      by, 12
   See also Divine Channels
Worry, 105, 112–13, 120–21, 124, 125

X

Xiu Lian practice (purification practice),
   92, 245, 251, 252

Y

Yan Wang Ye, 224–25
Yin shui si yuan ("Drink water, remember
   the source"), 50

Yin and yang, 2, 58, 69, 70. *See also*
   Sacred Circle
Yin Yang Palm Hand Position, 64, 64*n*,
   68
YouTube, soul healing stories and miracles
   posted on, 6

Z

01777 (Ling Yao Chi Chi Chi), 156–57,
   158, 159
Zhi Chen Guo (Master), 72, 156, 165,
   251–52
Zhi guan geng yun, bu guan shou huo (just
   do the proper job of planting the
   seeds, giving the proper water and
   fertilizer, and do not expect the
   harvest), 245, 251
Zhong
   development of, 262, 264
   emptiness and, 265
   Five Elements and, 131
   heart and, 253
   location of, 129, 130
   Mind Power and, 129–31
   opening of all four spiritual channels
      together and, 262–65
   physical body and, 129–31, 132
   power of, 130–31
   space reflection and, 130
   spiritual channels and, 237, 253, 256,
      258, 259, 262–65
   Tao and, 253, 265
Zhong (chant), 131, 264–65, 267
Zhou bu li kou (chant the mantra
   nonstop), 260
Zhu Lu, story of, 140–43
Zuo zai jia zhong zhi tian xia shi (sit at
   home and know what is happening
   in the world), 253

Other Books of the Soul Power Series

Soul Wisdom: Practical Soul Treasures to Transform Your Life (revised trade paperback edition). Heaven's Library/Atria Books, 2008. Also available as an audiobook.

The first book of the Soul Power Series is an important foundation for the entire series. It teaches five of the most important practical soul treasures: Soul Language, Soul Song, Soul Tapping, Soul Movement, and Soul Dance.

Soul Language empowers you to communicate with the Soul World, including your own soul, all spiritual fathers and mothers, souls of nature, and more, to access direct guidance.

Soul Song empowers you to sing your own Soul Song, the song of your Soul Language. Soul Song carries soul frequency and vibration for soul healing, soul rejuvenation, soul prolongation of life, and soul transformation of every aspect of life.

Soul Tapping empowers you to do advanced soul healing for yourself and others effectively and quickly.

Soul Movement empowers you to learn ancient secret wisdom and practices to rejuvenate your soul, mind, and body and prolong life.

Soul Dance empowers you to balance your soul, mind, and body for healing, rejuvenation, and prolonging life.

This book offers two permanent Divine Soul Transplants as gifts to every reader. Includes bonus Soul Song for Healing and Rejuvenation of Brain and Spinal Column MP3 download.

Soul Communication: Opening Your Spiritual Channels for Success and Fulfillment (revised trade paperback edition). Heaven's Library/Atria Books, 2008. Also available as an audiobook.

The second book in the Soul Power Series empowers you to open four major spiritual channels: Soul Language Channel, Direct Soul Communication Channel, Third Eye Channel, and Direct Knowing Channel.

The Soul Language Channel empowers you to apply Soul Language to communicate with the Soul World, including your own soul, all kinds of spiritual fathers and mothers, nature, and the Divine. Then, receive teaching, healing, rejuvenation, and prolongation of life from the Soul World.

The Direct Soul Communication Channel empowers you to converse directly with the Divine and the entire Soul World. Receive guidance for every aspect of life directly from the Divine.

The Third Eye Channel empowers you to receive guidance and teaching through spiritual images. It teaches you how to develop the Third Eye and key principles for interpreting Third Eye images.

The Direct Knowing Channel empowers you to gain the highest spiritual abilities. If your heart melds with the Divine's heart or your soul melds with the Divine's soul completely, you do not need to ask for spiritual guidance. You know the truth because your heart and soul are in complete alignment with the Divine.

This book also offers two permanent Divine Soul Transplants as gifts to every reader. Includes bonus Soul Song for Weight Loss MP3 download.

The Power of Soul: The Way to Heal, Rejuvenate, Transform, and Enlighten All Life. Heaven's Library/Atria Books, 2009. Also available as an audiobook and a trade paperback.

The third book of the Soul Power Series is the flagship of the entire series. *The Power of Soul* empowers you to understand, develop, and apply the power of soul for healing, prevention of sickness, rejuvenation, transformation of every aspect of life (including relationships and finances), and soul enlightenment. It also empowers you to develop soul wisdom and soul intelligence, and to apply Soul Orders for healing and transformation of every aspect of life.

This book teaches Divine Soul Downloads (specifically, Divine Soul Transplants) for the first time in history. A Divine Soul

Transplant is the divine way to heal, rejuvenate, and transform every aspect of a human being's life and the life of all universes.

This book offers eleven permanent Divine Soul Transplants as a gift to every reader. Includes bonus Soul Song for Rejuvenation MP3 download.

Divine Soul Songs: Sacred Practical Treasures to Heal, Rejuvenate, and Transform You, Humanity, Mother Earth, and All Universes. Heaven's Library/Atria Books, 2009. Also available as an audiobook and a trade paperback.

The fourth book in the Soul Power Series empowers you to apply Divine Soul Songs for healing, rejuvenation, and transformation of every aspect of life, including relationships and finances.

Divine Soul Songs carry divine frequency and vibration, with divine love, forgiveness, compassion, and light, that can transform the frequency and vibration of all aspects of life.

This book offers nineteen Divine Soul Transplants as gifts to every reader. Includes bonus Soul Songs CD with seven samples of the Divine Soul Songs that are the main subjects of this book.

Divine Soul Mind Body Healing and Transmission System: The Divine Way to Heal You, Humanity, Mother Earth, and All Universes. Heaven's Library/Atria Books, 2009. Also available as an audiobook.

The fifth book in the Soul Power Series empowers you to receive Divine Soul Mind Body Transplants and to apply Divine Soul Mind Body Transplants to heal and transform soul, mind, and body. Divine Soul Mind Body Transplants carry divine love, forgiveness, compassion, and light. Divine love melts all blockages and transforms all life. Divine forgiveness brings inner peace and inner joy. Divine compassion boosts energy, stamina, vitality, and immunity. Divine light heals, rejuvenates, and transforms every aspect of life, including relationships and finances.

This book offers forty-six permanent divine treasures, including Divine Soul Transplants, Divine Mind Transplants, and Divine Body Transplants, as a gift to every reader. Includes bonus Soul Symphony of Yin Yang excerpt (MP3 download).

Tao I: The Way of All Life. Heaven's Library/Atria Books, 2010. Also available as an audiobook.

The sixth book of the Soul Power Series shares the essence of ancient Tao teaching and reveals the Tao Jing, a new "Tao Classic" for the twenty-first century. These new divine teachings reveal how Tao is in every aspect of life, from waking to sleeping to eating and more. This book shares advanced soul wisdom and practical approaches for *reaching* Tao. The new sacred teaching in this book is extremely simple, practical, and profound.

Studying and practicing Tao has great benefits, including the ability to heal yourself and others, as well as humanity, Mother Earth, and all universes; return from old age to the health and purity of a baby; prolong life; and more.

This book offers thirty permanent Divine Soul Mind Body Transplants as gifts to every reader and a fifteen-track CD with Master Sha singing the entire Tao Jing and many other major practice mantras.

Divine Transformation: The Divine Way to Self-clear Karma to Transform Your Health, Relationships, Finances, and More. Heaven's Library/Atria Books, 2010. Also available as an audiobook.

The teachings and practical techniques of this seventh book of the Soul Power Series focus on karma and forgiveness. Bad karma is the root cause of any and every major blockage or challenge that you, humanity, and Mother Earth face. True healing is to clear your bad karma, which is to repay or be forgiven your spiritual debts to the souls you or your ancestors have hurt or harmed in all your lifetimes. Forgiveness is a golden key to true healing. Divine self-clearing of bad karma applies divine forgiveness to heal and transform every aspect of your life.

Clear your karma to transform your soul first; then transformation of every aspect of your life will follow.

This book offers thirty rainbow frequency Divine Soul Mind Body Transplants as gifts to every reader and includes four audio tracks of major Divine Soul Songs and practice chants.

Tao II: The Way of Healing, Rejuvenation, Longevity, and Immortality. Heaven's Library/Atria Books, 2010. Also available as an audiobook.

The eighth book of the Soul Power Series is the successor to *Tao I: The Way of All Life*. *Tao II* reveals the highest secrets and most powerful practical techniques for the Tao journey, which includes one's physical journey and one's spiritual journey.

Tao II gives you the sacred keys for your whole life's practice and shares the Immortal Tao, two hundred and twenty sacred phrases that include not only profound sacred wisdom but also additional simple and practical techniques. *Tao II* explains how to reach *fan lao huan tong*, which means to *transform old age to the health and purity of the baby state;* to prolong life; and to reach immortality to be a better servant for humanity, Mother Earth, and all universes.

This book offers twenty-one Tao Soul Mind Body Transplants as gifts to every reader and includes two audio tracks of major Tao chants for healing, rejuvenation, longevity, and immortality.

Tao Song and Tao Dance: Sacred Sound, Movement, and Power from the Source for Healing, Rejuvenation, Longevity, and Transformation of All Life. Heaven's Library/ Atria Books, 2011. Also available as an audiobook.

The ninth book in the Soul Power Series and the third of the Tao series, *Tao Song and Tao Dance* introduces you to the highest and most profound Soul Song. Sacred Tao Song mantras and Tao Dance carry Tao love, which melts all blockages; Tao forgiveness, which brings inner joy and inner peace; Tao compassion, which boosts energy, stamina, vitality, and immunity; and Tao light, which heals, prevents sickness, purifies and rejuvenates soul, heart, mind, and body, and transforms relationships, finances, and every aspect of life. Includes access to video recording of Master Sha practicing Tao Song mantras for healing, rejuvenation, longevity, and purification.

"This inspiring documentary has masterfully captured the vital healing work and global mission of Dr. Guo and Dr. Sha."

– Dr. Michael Bernard Beckwith – Founder, Agape International Spiritual Center

This film reveals profound soul secrets and shares the wisdom, knowledge, and practices of Dr. Guo's Body Space Medicine and Dr. Sha's Soul Mind Body Medicine. Millions of people in China have studied with Dr. Guo, who is Dr. Sha's most beloved spiritual father. Dr. Guo is "the master who can cure the incurable." After Dr. Sha heals her ailing father, American filmmaker Sande Zeig accompanies Dr. Sha to China to visit his mentor. At Dr. Guo's clinic, she captures first-ever footage of breakthrough healing practices involving special herbs, unique fire massage, and revolutionary self-healing techniques. These two Soul Masters have a special bond. They are united in their commitment to serve others. As you see them heal and teach, your heart and soul will be touched. Experience the delight, inspiration, wonder, and gratitude that *Soul Masters* brings.

In English and Mandarin with English subtitles. Also in French, German, Japanese, Mandarin and Spanish.

© 2008 926363 ONTARIO LIMITED   ALL RIGHTS RESERVED   3396815

PPV Video Streaming and DVD at
www.soulmastersmovie.com